ISLAMIC PHILOSOPHY AND THEOLOGY

ISLAMIC PHILOSOPHY AND THEOLOGY

An Extended Survey

W. MONTGOMERY WATT

AT THE UNIVERSITY PRESS
EDINBURGH

Edinburgh University Press
22 George Square, Edinburgh

First published 1962
Second edition 1985

Set in Linoterm Trump Medieval by
Speedspools, Edinburgh, and
printed in Great Britain by
Redwood Burn Ltd, Trowbridge

British Library Cataloguing
in Publication Data
Watt, W. Montgomery
Islamic philosophy and theology:
an extended survey—2nd ed.
1. Islam—Doctrines
I. Title
297.'2 BP166

ISBN 0 85224 487 8

CONTENTS

ABBREVIATIONS

*EI*¹, *EI*² = *Encyclopaedia of Islam*, first, second edition

EIS = *Shorter Encyclopaedia of Islam* or *Handwörterbuch*

GAL = Brockelmann, *Geschichte der arabischen Literatur*, second edition

GALS = Supplementbände of *GAL*, first edition

GAS = Sezgin, *Geschichte des arabischen Schrifttums* (details of these works will be found in the General Bibliography, section A, p.164)

N.B. n.14/6 means chapter 14, note 6; and similarly B/D means section D of the General Bibliography.

NOTE ON THE SOURCES

For theologians and philosophers who died after about 900 the primary source is their own works, and these are now relatively easy of access. Many of the most important works are now in printed editions, and these are continually being added to. There are also much wider facilities for obtaining photographic reproductions of manuscripts. Carl Brockelmann's *Geschichte der arabischen Literatur* (see Bibliography) aimed at providing a complete list of manuscripts and printed editions; but of course it has nothing after its date of publication (1943, 1949). It is in process of being supplemented and brought up to date by Fuat Sezgin's *Geschichte des arabischen Schrifttums*, but that is progressing only slowly. Details of printed books and of important articles, sometimes with brief descriptions, are contained in the *Abstracta* which constitute the second half of each annual volume of the *Revue des études islamiques.*

For the earlier period only a few complete works exist, and these mostly short, though further discoveries are made from time to time. Much reliance has thus to be placed on the secondary information derived from historians and other writers, and notably from the heresiographers (writers of accounts of the sects). The secondary sources have to be handled cautiously and critically, especially since the names of the sects were originally nicknames and could be used differently by different people. It has also to be realized that the material in the best-known works of heresiography comes from Muʿtazilite and Ashʿarite sources, and that in other strands of Islamic theology many points were viewed differently. In my book *The Formative Period of Islamic Thought* I attempted a radical critique of the sources for the early period, and I will here assume that this is accepted. I will also omit detailed references to matters dealt with in the *Formative Period.* The German translation of this work has some small additions which take account of material published after the English version went to print, notably some works of Professor Josef van Ess of Tübingen dealing with the Murji'ites and the Qadarites. The same volume also contains a section on 'Islamische Theologie, 950–1850', which is parallel to the second half of the present book.

Part One

THE UMAYYAD PERIOD AND ITS PRELUDE

Chapter One

THE BEGINNINGS OF SECTARIANISM

Between Muḥammad's migration to Medina in 622 and his death in 632 he was able to build up a state of considerable power. A measure of the size of the state is that on an expedition towards Syria at the end of 630 Muḥammad had 30,000 men behind him. Many, perhaps most, of the nomadic tribes of Arabia were in alliance with him, the chief exceptions being those in the Byzantine sphere of influence. The immediately following period, from 632 to 661, is known as that of the 'rightly-guided caliphs'. Abū-Bakr (632–4) was mostly occupied in quelling the revolt of certain tribes against the Medinan political system. Under ʿUmar I (634–44) a phenomenal expansion took place; Syria and Egypt were wrested from the Byzantine empire and Iraq from the Persian. For the first half of the reign of ʿUthmān (644–56) expansion continued into North Africa and Persia; but about 650 it slowed down, discontent appeared among the troops (who were identical with the citizen body), and in 656 ʿUthmān was killed by mutineers. ʿAlī, the cousin and son-in-law of Muḥammad, was then acclaimed as caliph in Medina, but Muʿāwiya, governor of Damascus, among others, refused to recognize him. In the struggle between ʿAlī and Muʿāwiya the latter was slowly gaining the upper hand when in 661 ʿAlī was murdered for a private grievance. Muʿāwiya's caliphate was then generally recognized, and the Umayyad dynasty thereby established.

This recital of historical events is not irrelevant to our theological concern. Exponents of the sociology of knowledge would hold that all theological and philosophical ideas have a political or social reference; and the standpoint of this survey is in accordance with such an outlook. The connection between theology and politics is particularly close and obvious in the Middle East. The Old Testament is full of it. In the early seventh century the disaffection of the native Christians of Syria and Egypt to the Byzantine emperor found a focus in the Monophysite and Nestorian heresies. It is therefore not surprising that in the discussions in chapters 1–3 it will be difficult to say what is politics and what theology. Nevertheless, apart from the 'false prophets' who inspired the revolts, known as the Ridda or 'apostasy', from about 632 to 634, no theological element is discernible in the political conflicts within the Islamic state until just before the beginning of the Umayyad period. This was not due, either, to the absence of strife and tension. The rivalry between the two main tribes of Medina continued almost to the time of Muḥammad's death; in the appointment of a successor the jealousy of the Medinans towards the Meccans came to light; in the wars of 'apostasy' certain nomadic tribes were opposing the Medinans, Meccans and certain other nomadic tribes; and the accession of ʿAlī brought into the open a clash of interests between at least three different groups of Meccans.

A theological factor first comes into contact with politics in certain disputes which took place among the followers of ʿAlī. These were mostly men from nomadic tribes, now settled in military camp-towns in Iraq; and the disputes occurred when ʿAlī, after defeating one group of Meccan opponents in a battle near Basra, was trying to collect a sufficient army to meet his more serious rival, Muʿāwiya, who had at his disposal the army occupying Syria. Among the troops under ʿAlī's command were some who were deeply attached to him; they are said to have sworn that they would be 'friends of those whom he befriended and enemies of those to whom he was hostile'. In other words, these men believed that a leader or imam such as ʿAlī could make no mistakes and do no wrong. The opposing group not merely thought that ʿAlī was capable of making mistakes, but regarded him as actually in error because he was not sufficiently definite in his support of those responsible for the murder of ʿUthmān. This second group considered themselves in a sense the spiritual descendants of the men who had killed ʿUthmān (though there does not appear to have been much personal continuity). ʿUthmān, they held, had sinned in that he had not punished the crime of a prominent member of his administration; and by this sin he had forfeited the privileges that went with membership of the community, thereby rendering it not merely no sin but even a duty for Muslims to kill him.

There were probably many men in ʿAlī's army whose views came somewhere between these extremes; but it is the extremes that are important for the later theological developments. The two groups described are in fact the beginnings of the two great sects of the Shīʿites and the Khārijites. The Shīʿites derive their name from the fact that they are *par excellence* the 'party' (*shīʿa*), that is, of ʿAlī. The Khārijites (in Arabic usually Khawārij, singular Khārijī) were so called because they 'went out' or 'seceded' (*kharajū*), first from ʿAlī and then from Muʿāwiya and the Umayyads. The best-known instances of such 'secessions' are two which occurred while ʿAlī was getting ready to march against the army of Syria. The first party, who went to a place called Ḥarūrā', returned when 'Alī met some of their grievances; but some of the second party refused to be reconciled and were eventually massacred.[1] The frequency with which the story of these events is repeated should not be allowed to obscure the fact that there were five other small risings against 'Alī and about twenty during the reign of Mu'āwiya (661–80). There were also, of course, several more serious Khārijite risings at various times during the Umayyad period, and some historians have suggested that 'Khārijite' simply means 'rebel'; but a study of the theological side of the movement will show that this is not so.

The occurrence of risings under both 'Alī and Mu'āwiya proves that they were not due to personal dislike of the rule of either man, but must have resulted from some general features of the situation. Reflection suggests what these features were. The men concerned in the Khārijite risings were not of Meccan or Medinan origin, but men from nomadic tribes. Thirty years earlier these men and their fathers had been living the free life of the desert. Now they were caught up into the vast organization of the Muslim army. When the campaigns were over, they went back not to the familiar desert but to camp-cities in Iraq or Egypt. At this early period all Muslims were expected to take part in military service, and in return they received a stipend from the state. The amount of the stipend varied according to the priority of the family in adhesion to Islam. Though there is scope here for many economic grievances, there do not appear from the records to have been any such. It therefore seems probable that the underlying reason for the risings was the general sense of *malaise* and insecurity consequent on the rapid and abrupt changes. It is further probable that the incipient Shī'ite movement is a different response to the same sense of *malaise* and insecurity.

This hypothesis makes possible an explanation both of the different responses to the situation of the Shī'ites and the Khārijites, and also of the intense hostility between them. In a time of change, insecurity and crisis men tend to look for salvation to the thing in their past experience that has proved most fundamental and satisfying (whether they are fully conscious of what they are doing or not). It appears to be a fact that some men believe that salvation (or the attainment of the supreme end of human life) is to be found in the following of a leader who is endowed with more than human qualities. Such qualities are usually believed to be the gift of a god, though occasionally they may be thought of rather as a natural endowment. It is convenient to use the sociological term 'charismata' and to speak of a 'charismatic leader'. It also appears to be a fact that other men look for salvation not to a leader but to a community possessing certain charismata. By being a member of such a community (and by doing nothing to forfeit one's membership) a man attains salvation.

The negative form of this belief occurs in the tag: *extra ecclesiam nulla salus.* The positive aspect was prominent in the thought of many Muslims, for they spoke of the Islamic community as 'the people of Paradise', implying that all the members would eventually attain to Paradise.

The existence of deep-seated beliefs of this kind explains the appearance of the Khārijite and Shīʿite movements during the caliphate of ʿAlī. In the stresses and strains of the completely new life into which they had been plunged, men were in need of something firm and secure. Deep, probably unconscious, impulses made them seek this security, some by following a leader with the charisma of infallibility, others by trying to ensure that the community of which they were members was a charismatic one. For the first group the old Arab belief that special qualities of character were handed down in certain families justified them in taking ʿAlī as a leader of infallible wisdom, even when his actual political decisions were hardly in accordance with this belief. The second group had a certain advantage in that the community of Muslims had undoubtedly been founded by a divinely inspired prophet and possessed a way of life supernaturally revealed to it; to ensure that this community remained the people of Paradise, however, it was necessary, some of them felt, that those who broke the rules should be excluded from it. In this way there arose the distinctive Khārijite tenet that those who have committed a grave sin are thereby excluded from the community. Positively the Khārijites were seeking security in the knowledge that the community to which they belonged was a supernatural or charismatic one.

Further reflection along these lines shows why there was such bitterness between Khārijites and Shīʿites. For both groups the question was one of whether they were going to attain salvation or realize their supreme end; one might say roughly that it was a matter of life and death. In this situation the beliefs of each group contradicted those of the other; and so each group was in the position of preventing the other from attaining salvation. The Khārijites, not convinced of the infallibility of the leader, saw rather that he might make a mistake and thereby lead the whole community into a course of action which would cause them to forfeit their status as people of Paradise. The Shīʿites, on the other hand, were horrified at the prospect that ordinary uninspired members of the community might, by their interpretation of its scriptures (which the Shīʿites did not regard as infallible), cause the inspired leader to adopt a course of action which he knew to be wrong. In this way each group's chance of salvation, as they saw it, was endangered by the other group. It is not surprising that there was bitter hostility between them.

What has been said so far is fairly well established. When it comes, however, to the question why some men should turn to the charismatic leader and others to the charismatic community, there is an explanation that can be given, but for the moment it must be regarded as a hypothesis needing further examination (chiefly by comparing parallel instances in other cultures). It is conceivable that the two reactions to the same situation are due to ultimate and fundamental differences in the human constitution; but this is a dubious theory with serious consequences, and so it is preferable, if it can be done, to explain the differences by hereditary or environmental factors. There are two points which help towards an explanation.

The first point is that there are resemblances between the little groups of Khārijite rebels and the effective units of nomadic society. In the risings during the reigns of ʿAlī and Muʿāwiya we are usually told the number of men involved, and it varies between thirty and five hundred, with an average of about two hundred. They did not retire to the desert, so far as we can judge, but merely withdrew to a safe distance from the towns of Iraq, and presumbly kept themselves alive by raiding or by levying food from the countryside, until a government force suppressed them. Each little band presumably regarded itself as the core of the community of genuine Muslims, though not denying that there were genuine Muslims apart from the band. Most other men, however, were not genuine Muslims and therefore could be killed with impunity. Thus in various ways the little revolting bands were creating a form of life not unlike that of the divisions of a nomadic tribe. It was not exactly regression to desert conditions, for the basis of the Khārijite group was religion and not kinship. Yet it is significant that the Khārijites, like the nomads in earlier days, became noted for their skill as poets and orators; and, despite their Islamic faith, the sentiments expressed in their poems are close to those of the pagan nomads.

The second point to be noted is that, when one asks to which tribes the early Shīʿites and Khārijites belonged, a definite difference is found. The difference is not absolute, for a great many tribes are mentioned on both sides; but what can be asserted is that (1) a significant proportion of the early Shīʿites came from the tribes of South Arabia, and (2) the doctrinally important individuals and sects among the Khārijites (during the Umayyad period as a whole) were mainly from three northern tribes. Moreover, there does not seem to be anything in the history of the period from 622 to 656 to explain this difference of reaction. The northern tribes as a whole had been earlier in joining the Muslim raids into Iraq; but at least one tribe prominent among the Shīʿites had shared in the early raids. ʿAlī had been sent by Muḥammad to perform special duties in South Arabia, but there is no mention of his gaining the special affection of the people. Whether the environments from which the members of these tribes came had been deeply influenced by Judaism or Monophysite or Nestorian

Christianity is a point that could be further investigated; but, even if some such influence can be proved, it does not look like giving the whole explanation.

The hypothesis to be put forward is that the difference in reaction is due to century-old traditions. The South Arabian tribes stood somehow within the tradition of the ancient civilization of that region, more than a thousand years old. In this civilization there had been divine or semi-divine kings. Even if the Arab tribesmen of the seventh century had not themselves lived under kings, they must unconsciously have been affected by the tradition, within which it had been usual in times of danger to rely on the superhuman leadership of the king. Because of this they in their time of crisis looked about for a leader of this type, and thought they had found one in ʿAlī. The members of the northern tribes had not been within the sphere of influence of the belief in divine kingship. On the contrary, the normal practice in the desert tribes was for all the adult males to be regarded as in certain respects equal; and there are traces of 'democratic communities' of this kind far back in the pre-history of Iraq. Along with this practice of equality went a belief that outstanding excellence belonged to the tribe and the tribal stock, so that merely to have the blood of the tribe in one's veins gave one a place of honour in the world. The Arabs of the time just before Muḥammad gave this belief a this-worldly interpretation; but in the crisis round about 656 it would not be surprising if the idea of a small community of genuine Muslims evoked a deep unconscious response from those who had lived in this 'democratic' tradition. This at least is the view that is here propounded as a hypothesis.[2]

NOTES

1. See the sources given in notes 2/1, 2/6.
2. The views expressed in this chapter are formulated with greater detail in my previous writings: 'Shīʿism under the Umayyads', *Journal of the Royal Asiatic Society,* 1960, 158-72; 'Khārijite Thought in the Umayyad Period', *Der Islam,* xxxvi (1961), 215-31; 'The Conception of the Charismatic Community in Islam', *Numen,* vii (1960), 77-90; *Islam and the Integration of Society,* London 1961, 94-114. These works are summarized and supplemented in my *Formative Period,* 9-59.

Chapter Two

THE KHĀRIJITES

Muʿāwiya reigned as universally recognized caliph from 661 to 680. His power rested chiefly on the army composed of the Arabs settled in Syria, and he made Damascus his capital. In the practice of the nomadic Arabs a chief was usually succeeded by the best qualified member of his family; primogeniture and even sonship gave no special rights. This gave little guidance in arranging for the succession to the caliphate. Muʿāwiya tried to have his son Yazīd acknowledged as successor before his own death, but even so there were some who did not accept Yazīd. The opposition led to a catastrophic civil war when Yazīd died in 683, leaving only a minor son. ʿAbd-Allāh ibn-az-Zubayr (or, more simply, Ibn-az-Zubayr), who had defied Yazīd from Mecca, now gained control of much of Iraq as well as of the region of Mecca and Medina. There was widespread confusion, and vast tracts of the caliphate were under the effective control of neither the Umayyads nor Ibn-az-Zubayr. Under the leadership of a member of another branch of the family the Umayyads fought back; in 691 they completed the recovery of Iraq, and before the end of 692 extinguished the last flames of revolt in Mecca.

The expansion of the caliphate, which had continued under Muʿāwiya but had been stopped by the civil war, was now resumed. In the east the Muslims extended their sway to Central Asia and north-west India; while in north Africa they pressed westwards into Morocco, and in 711 crossed the straits into Spain. To the north there were frequent expeditions against the Byzantines, but no permanent occupation of territory proved possible. The vastness of the territories ruled led to ever-increasing internal tensions, and the clumsy administrative machine lumbered along with creaks and groans. From about 730 or 735 it must have been clear to acute observers that the empire was slowly breaking up, and some of these observers attempted, by staging a revolt, to create an alternative government. None was successful, however, though they played a part in weakening the Umayyads, until eventually in 750 the armies of the ʿAbbāsid movement from the east swept into Iraq, liquidated the Umayyad regime, and established the new dynasty of the ʿAbbāsids.

Two Khārijite movements which greatly stimulated theological development sprang up and grew to a considerable size during the civil war of Ibn-az-Zubayr.[1] The first of these is the sub-sect of the Azraqites (Azāriqa), so named from their original leader, Nāfiʿ ibn-al-Azraq.[2] Some of the Khārijites from Basra had sympathized with Ibn-az-Zubayr (as an opponent of the Umayyads) and had given him active help. In time, however, they seem to have realized that, even if successful, he would not rule according to their ideas. When Basra went over to him in 684, the Azraqites took to the mountains eastwards. Though their leader was killed in the following year, they were able to increase and maintain their strength, so that for a time (about 691) they were a threat to Basra. After the end of the civil war the Umayyad armies were able to exterminate them (but there are some mysterious references to isolated Azraqites in the eastern parts of the caliphate at later dates).

The Azraqites stimulated theological thinking because, with a fair measure of logic, they worked out the Khārijite position to an extreme conclusion. The basic principle, which had been formulated in Qur'ānic words by some of ʿAlī's followers who disagreed with him, was: 'no decision but God's' (*lā ḥukma illā li-llāh*), that is, 'the decision is God's alone'; by this was meant that judgement was to be given in accordance with the Qur'ān. This further implied that all who had committed a grave sin were destined for Hell and belonged to the 'people of Hell', since in the Khārijite view this was clearly stated in the Qur'ān. In addition it was held that ʿUthmān had sinned in not inflicting a punishment prescribed in the Qur'ān.

The Azraqites now went still further, on the ground that the existing authorities had also sinned, and asserted that those who did not join their band in fighting the existing authorities were sinners. The members of their band were the true Muslims; their camp alone was the 'house of Islam' (*dār al-Islām*) where Islam was truly observed. Those who 'sat still' at home and did not make the *hijra* or 'migration' to their camp were sinners and unbelievers, outside the community of Islam. This migration, of course, was parallel to the *hijra* of Muḥammad from Mecca to Medina in 622. By thus excluding from the Islamic community even those Muslims who did not agree with them in every detail, they made it lawful to kill such persons, and also their wives and children; for according to old Arab usage there was no wrong in killing someone not a member of one's tribe or an allied tribe, though it would be unwise to do so if the victim's tribe was strong. This puritanical theology became a justification for sheer terrorism, and the Azraqites became noted and feared for their widespread massacres. It is said that when a man went to them and said he wanted to join their band he was given a prisoner to kill; if, as is likely, it was a prisoner from the man's tribe, the killing would break his ties with his tribe and attach him irrevocably to the Azraqites. Doubtless this happened sometimes, but whether it was a regular practice we cannot be certain.

The second sub-sect that became prominent about the same time was the Najdites (Najadāt or Najdiyya).[3] The nucleus consisted of Khārijites from central Arabia (from a district called the Yamāma) who helped Ibn-az-Zubayr in Mecca, but later returned to their native region and established a form of autonomous rule. From 686 to 692 their leader was Najda; hence their name. For a time they ruled vast tracts of Arabia—more even than Ibn-az-Zubayr—including Bahrein and Oman ('Umān) on the east coast, and parts of the Yemen and Ḥaḍramawt in the south and south-west. There were many quarrels about the leadership, and after the death of Najda in 692 the sect split up, and the parts either disappeared or were suppressed by the Umayyad generals.

The Najdites originally held views similar to those of the Azraqites, but their responsibility for governing a large territory made them less rigorous in their interpretation. Those who 'sat still' and did not actively support them were not regarded as unbelievers (and so outside the community) but only as 'hypocrites' (*munāfiqūn*). It is also reported that they authorized members of their sub-sect who lived under non-Khārijite rule to conceal their true opinions—a practice known as *taqiyya* or 'prudent fear'. Such points show that the Najdites did not have the same clear line of demarcation between themselves and other Muslims as did the Azraqites. Much of the accounts of Najdite views is taken up with legal points of the kind that would naturally arise in the administration of a large state; for example, there were questions about the treatment of captured women by the leaders of an expedition, and about the punishment of isolated cases of theft and adultery.

In what is recorded of Najdite views on such matters we see the beginnings of a reconsideration of the Khārijite conception of the true Islamic community so as to make allowances for human imperfections. The strict Khārijite view, from which the Najdites presumably started, was that a man who commits a grave sin belongs to the 'people of Hell'. For the Azraqites living in a camp the man guilty of theft or adultery could easily be excluded from the camp; but it was not easy for the Najdites to banish every thief and adulterer from the entire region which they ruled. They may have thought that it was not even desirable. This was not due to any moral laxity, for they are said to have been strict about wine-drinking, but presumably to the realization that any normal community is bound to contain both good and bad.

It was necessary, however, to find a theoretical justification for the course of action that was practically desirable. This the Najdites did by making a distinction between fundamentals in religion and non-fundamentals. Among the latter they included novel legal points where no official decision had been given. Persistence in theft or adultery was regarded as 'idolatry' (*shirk*), presumably on the ground that it implied a false view of the nature of the community and its law or way-of-life. This would be one of the fundamentals, and like errors in the other fundamentals would involve exclusion from the community and inclusion in the 'people of Hell'. Isolated lapses into theft or adultery, however, were not regarded as affecting fundamentals. The common view that thieves and adulterers went to Hell had therefore to be modified. The Najdites allowed that God might punish them, but insisted that, if he did so, it would not be in Hell, and that he would eventually admit them to Paradise. Thus membership of the community and soundness on fundamentals led to salvation, to Paradise.

While the Azraqites and Najdites were facing the problems of autonomous Khārijite rule, there was a body of moderate Khārijites in Basra who were concerned rather with the problems of living under non-Khārijite Muslim rule. This body of pious men, with little direct interest in politics, seems to have been in existence throughout the reign of Muʿāwiya. Some of them helped Ibn-az-Zubayr in Mecca for a time; after 684 they accepted, perhaps actively supported, his lieutenant in Basra, and in due course also accepted the Umayyad governor. Unfortunately our information about these people is slight. There appears to have been intense theological activity in Basra about this time, during which the foundations of most later Islamic theology were laid, but we have only tantalizing glimpses of it. It is possible, however, to say something about the chief questions discussed.

The main problem was how to justify the acceptance by Khārijites of a non-Khārijite government. It had been customary for Muslims to distinguish between the 'sphere of Islam' (*dār al-islām*) and the 'sphere of war' (*dār al-ḥarb*); the former was where the sovereign ruled according to Islamic principles, the latter was where there was no such sovereign and where it was the duty of Muslims to fight if success seemed possible. Neither of these descriptions fitted the position of the moderate Khārijites in Basra. Some therefore spoke of themselves as being in the 'sphere of prudent fear', in which they had to conceal their true opinions. This was associated with the view that non-Khārijites were 'unbelievers' and 'idolaters' (*kāfirūn, mushrikūn*). As time went on, however, it began to seem paradoxical to apply the term 'idolaters' to upright God-fearing Muslims who differed from them on a few points. Some therefore allowed that these were at least 'monotheists' and that they themselves were living in the 'sphere of monotheism'. Yet others spoke of their sphere as that of 'mixing', and apparently held that, because the government is neither pagan nor strictly Islamic, some things cannot be precisely stated, and a measure of compromise, or rather of indefiniteness and indecision, is necessary.

One of the questions to which much attention was given was that of the marriage of believing women (that is, Khārijites) to 'unbelievers' (that is, non-Khārijites), or—what really amounted to the same thing—the sale of believing slave-girls to unbelievers. This raised in a serious form the problem of the relation of the small community of true believers (as they considered it) to the wider community of ordinary 'unbelieving' Muslims. According to the Qur'ān a Muslim woman might not marry any but a Muslim man; in other words, her marriage had to be within the community. Since the purchaser of a slave-girl was entitled to have marital relations with her, the sale of a slave-girl to an 'unbeliever' made a breach of the Qur'ānic rule likely. The story is told of a man called Ibrāhīm who was kept waiting by a slave-girl and vowed he would sell her to the bedouin. Another member of his sect challenged him, but the majority seems to have gone with Ibrāhīm. That is to say, they decided that they were in some sense members of the wider community. In making this decision they were coming near to abandoning the original Khārijite conception of a 'community of saints', which committed no grave sins and held all the right views.

Among the politically quiescent Khārijites of Basra is a small group called the Wāqifites (Wāqifiyya, Wāqifa). Their name means 'those who suspend judgement'. They were not important in themselves, but they merit attention because they mark a transitional stage between the Khārijites and the Murji'ites (Murji'a), who will be described in chapter 4. It has been noticed above how some even of the morally stricter Khārijites, because they felt that a single lapse into theft or adultery did not deserve to be punished by exclusion from the community, were forced to say that the persons guilty of these crimes would not be punished in Hell. In a sense, then, they were playing down the importance of immoral or anti-social conduct. This was inevitable because of their rigid distinction between the 'people of Paradise' and the 'people of Hell'; and that distinction was part of the communalistic way of thinking natural to the Arabs. For the pre-Islamic Arab the courage of an individual man had not been simply his own, but also in a sense his tribe's; it was only possible for him to be courageous because he came of courageous stock. The morality of the nomadic Arabs was dominated by loyalty to kin, that is, to one's tribe or clan or family; on behalf of a kinsman almost anything was permitted. This communalistic way of thinking is finding expression in those Khārijites who emphasized the corporate unity of the 'people of Paradise' at the expense of certain points of individual morality. In so doing they were going against the more individualistic outlook of the Qur'ān, according to which each man as an individual has to answer for his own sins on the Day of Judgement.

The distinctive position of the Wāqifites was that they suspended judgement on such questions as whether slave-girls should be sold to 'unbelievers'. In effect they were saying that it is impossible for men to draw a clear dividing-line between the 'people of Paradise' and the 'people of Hell'. This further enabled them to insist that wrongdoers should be punished but not excluded from the community, on the ground that a human being was unable to know their ultimate fate and so had to suspend judgement on it. In this way they countered the tendency to minimize the seriousness of crime and wrongdoing. Thus the Wāqifites and other Khārijites thinking along similar lines were preparing the way for the later Sunnite conception of the Islamic community. They managed to retain something of the old Arab communal outlook and communal feeling, and to attach to the Islamic community as a whole the values formerly attached by the nomad to his tribe. At the same time they made provision for the maintenance of law and order that was essential for the survival of a large civilized community. It is hardly possible to over-estimate the importance of the theological discussions in Basra in the period from about 690 to 730. It was here that the foundations of all later Islamic theology were laid. Why theology should have developed in Iraq, especially Basra, rather than in Syria, Egypt or even Medina, is not clear; but it is a fact, and it is worthy of being further pondered.

Perhaps the most important contribution of the Khārijites to the development of Islamic thought and Islamic civilization was their insistence that the life of the community and the decisions of its rulers must be based on the Qur'ān. Presumably many Muslims agreed with this in theory, but the Khārijites were prepared to stand up to the governmental authorities in defence of their view. Had they not felt so strongly about this, the empire might well have gone back to pre-Islamic principles and developed into a secular Arab state. The point was eventually accepted by the whole community in the form of the doctrine that all social and political life must be based on the Sharī'a or revealed divine law. To the Qur'ān, however, as a source of our knowledge of the Sharī'a, the main body added another, namely, Muḥammad's *sunna* or standard practice as recorded in sound Ḥadīth, taking his acts and words to be based on the divine 'wisdom' (*ḥikma*) given to him according to several verses of the Qur'ān.[4]

There continued to be manifestations of Khārijism of various kinds after 700. In the closing decades of Umayyad rule there were several risings involving larger numbers of men than the risings against Muʿāwiya, but, though these were nominally attached to one or other of the more moderate sub-sects, none contributed appreciably to the development of theology. Khārijite doctrines also came to be held by various groups in the Arabian peninsula, North Africa and elsewhere.[5] As a result more or less durable states were constituted in two regions, both based on the Ibāḍite form of Khārijism.[6] From 777 to 909 the Rustamid dynasty united all the Ibāḍites of North Africa from a centre in western Algeria, while in 793 the Ibāḍites of Oman established a polity which has continued to exist to the present day, though not without some periods of eclipse. The existence of these states led to modifications of Ibāḍite doctrine, to make it a suitable basis for a permanent community, and not just for a rebel band; but their arguments had ceased to be of interest to the main body of Muslims. The small Ibāḍite states were thus able to preserve their form of life in almost complete isolation from the world around them, thanks to their professing a distinctive doctrine; and the doctrine, instead of being the basis for the life of the whole Islamic community, became the instrument of cohesion and distinctive identity for various small groups. Meanwhile the important doctrines which had characterized the earliest Khārijites—their conception of the true Islamic community and their insistence that its life should be based on the Qur'ān—had, after being purged of unsatisfactory aspects, been taken up by other Muslims, while the main theological discussions had moved away from the topics to which other special Khārijite doctrines were relevant.

NOTES

1. Julius Wellhausen, *The Religio-political Factions in Early Islam,* Amsterdam 1975; translation (with additional notes) by R. C. Ostle of the German original, Göttingen 1901; thoroughly studies the Sunnite historical sources for the Khārijites and Shīʿites under the Umayyads. The main risings are also described in Wellhausen's *The Arab Kingdom and its Fall,* Calcutta 1927.
2. *EI*², art. Azāriḳa (R. Rubinacci); *Formative Period,* 20-3.
3. *Formative Period,* 23-5.
4. See below, ch.9.
5. L. Veccia Vaglieri, 'Le vicende del Harigismo in epoca abbaside', *Rivista degli Studi Orientali,* xxiv (1944), 31-44; Watt, 'The Significance of Khārijism under the ʿAbbāsids', *Recherches d'Islamologie* (Anawati-Gardet Festschrift), Louvain 1978, 381-7.
6. *EI*², art. Ibāḍiyya (T. Lewicki). Khārijite (Ibāḍite) sources have been studied with interesting results by Italian scholars in Naples; see references in *EI*², art. ʿAlī b. Abī Ṭālib (Veccia Vaglieri).

Chapter Three

THE EARLY SHĪʿITES

Although the Shīʿites and the Khārijites were at opposite poles theologically for most of the Umayyad period, and were in this way complementary, their history was altogether different. Among the Shīʿites there were none of the intellectual debates that took place in Khārijite circles in Basra. For much of the time Shīʿism was quiescent, and anything that was happening was happening under the surface. Then suddenly, when a leader appeared, there would be an explosion. This is perhaps inevitable in a movement which places the emphasis on the leader.[1]

On the death of ʿAlī in 661 some of his followers were inclined to support the claims of al-Ḥasan, the son of ʿAlī and Muḥammad's daughter Fāṭima; but al-Ḥasan had no political ability or ambition, and readily gave up his claims in return for the payment of a substantial sum of money by Muʿāwiya. In the troubled period following the death of the latter in 680 al-Ḥasan's full brother al-Ḥusayn was encouraged to lead a revolt in Iraq. The promised support was not forthcoming, but al-Ḥusayn and his small band could not be prevailed on to surrender and were eventually massacred by a vastly superior army at Kerbela (Karbalāʾ) in October 680. These tragic events are still annually commemorated by Shīʿites with a kind of Passion Play during the month of Muḥarram—the Arabic month in which the original disaster occurred. In 684 in the confusion of the civil war a group of men from Kufa calling themselves the Penitents raised an army of 4,000 men, not only to show their penitence but also to avenge al-Ḥusayn. When they marched against an Umayyad force, however, they were utterly defeated. Thus the beginning of the Shīʿite movement was a series of political failures.

The next event in Shīʿite history is slightly more successful and, apart from that, of great significance. This is the rising of al-Mukhtār in Kufa from 685 to 687. Up to this time all the Shīʿites, or at least all the prominent Shīʿites, had been Arabs. In Kufa, however, al-Mukhtār was also joined by *mawālī* or 'clients' and, because of tension between the Arabs and the clients, was more and more forced to rely on the latter. Though the rising was crushed by Ibn-az-Zubayr's general, it had sufficient success to give the clients the idea that they had a certain amount of political power if they wielded it aright. A man could become a client in various ways, but the clients intended in this context are probably all non-Arab Muslims. A member of one of the protected communities of Christians, Jews, etc., on becoming a Muslim left his own community and was attached as client to an Arab tribe (presumably because the Islamic community was regarded as a federation of Arab tribes). This was an inferior status, however, in some respects, and as more non-Arabs became Muslims there was a growing volume of dissatisfaction with it and a demand for equality. The clients attracted to Shīʿism appear to have included both persons from the older strata of the population of Iraq (who may be called Aramaeans) and persons of Persian stock. In the Persian empire under the Sasanian dynasty Iraq had been persianized somewhat, while Aramaean culture had spread in Persia proper. In Iraq there was a long tradition of divine kingship, and it would therefore be natural for the Aramaeans in particular to adhere to an Islamic sect which emphasized charismatic leadership. There were many Persians among the Shīʿites during the Umayyad period, but it must be borne in mind that the close identification of Shīʿism with Persia only dates from the sixteenth century. Nevertheless the rising of al-Mukhtār is an important stage in the development of Islam as a religion, because from this time onwards Shīʿism was linked with the political grievances and aspirations of non-Arab Muslims.

For fifty years after the death of al-Mukhtār in 687 there was no overt political activity among the Shīʿites, though Shīʿite religious ideas were doubtless spreading quietly beneath the surface. There are frequent references to the sub-sect which supported al-Mukhtār, though they are called not Mukhtārites but Kaysānites.[2] This is doubtless a nickname intended to emphasize their non-Arab character, since Kaysān was a prominent client. As signs of collapse became evident in the Umayyad regime, the Shīʿites appear once more on the political stage. Two leaders were executed in Kufa in 737 and another in 742, all suspected of organizing an underground resistance. In 740 there was a serious insurrection under a great-great-grandson of Muḥammad called Zayd, but it was quickly suppressed. Still more serious for the Umayyads was the revolt of ʿAbd-Allāh ibn-Muʿāwiya, a great-grandson of Muḥammad's cousin Jaʿfar; this lasted from 744 to 747. Finally, the movement which replaced the Umayyads by the ʿAbbāsids had much Shīʿite support, and on the religious side might be regarded as primarily a manifestation of Shīʿism. It remains to look at the theological developments accompanying these external events.[3]

The first point to be made is that although, as the sources suggest, there may have been widespread sympathy for the Shī'ite position, this position itself was still extremely vague. In particular there was no general recognition that the imams later acknowledged by the Imāmite and Ismā'īlite branches of Shī'ism, the descendants of al-Ḥusayn, son of 'Alī, had any special status or special gifts. The tendency was rather to consider that the charismata requisite for the position of imam belonged potentially to all members of Muḥammad's clan of Hāshim, whether descended from Muḥammad through Fāṭima or not. (Descent from Muḥammad never in fact was prominent in Shī'ite claims, but at most secondary, since the position of 'Alī was independent of this.) Thus al-Mukhtār claimed that he was acting on behalf of the imam Muḥammad ibn-al- Ḥanafiyya ('the son of the Ḥanafite woman'), a son of 'Alī but not by Fāṭima. Some held that the imam after him was his son, Abū-Hāshim. A small group for a time took as imam a great-grandson of al-Ḥasan, known as Muḥammad the Pure Soul (an-Nafs az-Zakiyya). The rising under the great-grandson of Ja'far (Muḥammad's cousin and 'Alī's brother) has already been mentioned. Finally, the 'Abbāsids at first claimed to have inherited the imamate from Muḥammad ibn-al-Ḥanafiyya and Abū-Hāshim, but at a later date (officially from about 780) asserted instead that the true imam after the Prophet was his uncle al-'Abbās, who was of course their ancestor.

Complementary to this acceptance of a variety of men as having the divinely given qualities needed for leadership of the Islamic community there is the fact that no group of importance recognized the descendants of al-Ḥusayn as having any special position. For later Shī'ite theory the first three rightful imams of the community after Muḥammad are 'Alī, al-Ḥasan and al-Ḥusayn; the fourth is the latter's son 'Alī Zayn-al-'Ābidīn, who died about 714; the fifth is his son Muḥammad al-Bāqir (d.733); and the sixth his son Ja'far aṣ-Ṣādiq (d.765). Even Imāmite sources, however, make it clear that these men, the fourth, fifth and sixth imams, were not active politically; and it would have been difficult for Muslims of this period to conceive of a religious claim that was not also a political one. Nothing at all is recorded of the fourth imam. Of the fifth imam it is reported that the men executed at Kufa in 737 and 742 claimed to be his emissaries; but there is confusion in the stories and it is doubtful if he gave them any support. The sixth imam, Ja'far aṣ-Ṣādiq, seems to have realized the possibilities of a Shī'ite movement and to have set about, doubtless with much caution and circumspection, organizing a body of supporters; but this would mostly take place before the end of the Umayyad period.

The Shī'ism of the Umayyad period was thus vaguer and more indefinite than later Shī'ism, and lacked any semblance of a coherent theory. It was the manifestation of a deep unconscious need—a feeling in men's hearts that they would be happier and more satisfied spiritually if they had a charismatic leader to follow. The imam of whom the Shīʿites dreamed is precisely what is meant by a charismatic leader. The history of early Shīʿism, and indeed of much later Shīʿism also, is that of a pathetic quest for individuals to whom the dignity of imam may be attached. Most of those accepted as imam belied the hopes set on them; and yet the quest went on. The persistence of the quest shows the depth of the feeling involved. Men with political ambitions and qualities of leadership, but no shadow of a claim to the charismata of the Hāshimites, found a way of using this widespread desire for an imam. Al-Mukhtār, for example, asserted that he was acting as the emissary of a genuine imam, Muḥammad ibn-al-Ḥanafiyya; he may have had the consent of the latter in making this assertion, but it is certain that he received no active help from him. There are several later instances of a similar proceeding, and in some of them the imam invoked repudiated the self-styled emissary. Others seem to have resigned themselves to political inactivity in the foreseeable future; and they found a theological justification for this attitude in the theory that the imam was not dead but in concealment and that at an appropriate time he would return as the Mahdī or Guided One (a kind of Messiah) to right all wrongs and establish justice on earth.

Thus Umayyad Shīʿism is a veritable chaos of ideas and attitudes. A beginning of order was introduced by the idea of designation (*naṣṣ*) —this involves the view that there is only one imam at a time and that the imam designates his successor. In the Umayyad period, however, this was not wholly effective, since different groups recognized different imams. A different line was taken by the Zaydites, the followers of the Zayd who revolted in 740. They would have nothing to do with the idea of a hidden imam; one of the conditions of being imam was that the claim to be such was made publicly (and, of course, was made effective by military success). Zayd's revolt was a realistic attempt to provide an alternative government to that of the Umayyads. He therefore tried to gain the support not merely of the Shīʿites but also of the main body of Muslims, and to do this he made the assertion that, though ʿAlī was the rightful imam after the Prophet and superior to Abū-Bakr and ʿUmar, the 'imamate of the inferior' (*imāmat al-mafḍūl*) was permissible. This concession, however, seems to have alienated the more thorough-going Shīʿites and may have contributed to Zayd's failure.

The ʿAbbāsid movement shows a mixture of genuine religious feeling (though perhaps not in the top leadership) and shrewd political calculation. Realizing how widespread Shīʿite sympathies were, they claimed to be the rightful imams through inheritance by designation from Muḥammad ibn-al-Ḥanafiyya. Because they saw the weakness of this claim, however, in much of their propaganda they simply called for support for 'him of the family of the Prophet who shall be chosen'; and by the time it was made public who this was they were already in power. To gain the Zaydites they maintained that they were seeking vengeance for the blood of Zayd. Another of their aims was the defence of 'the weak', which in fact meant the clients or non-Arab Muslims; and actually much of the support for the ʿAbbāsids came from the clients, and their leading general, Abū-Muslim, was himself a client. The volume of support for the ʿAbbāsids from the clients meant that, when they achieved control of the caliphate, clients, especially Persians and persianized Aramaeans, received a due share of power, and the inferior status of the non-Arab Muslims gradually disappears. The success of this at least partly Shīʿite movement in 750 is another stage in the development of Shīʿism, but, as will be seen, its immediate effects are difficult to assess.

NOTES

1. J. Wellhausen, works mentioned in n.2/1. Dwight M. Donaldson, *The Shīʿite Religion*, London 1933, gives the material from the Imāmite sources but without full discussion; S. Husain M. Jafri, *Origins and Early Development of Shiʿa Islam*, London 1979, a critical account by a Shīʿite of the period to 765.
2. *EI*², art. Kaysāniyya (W. Madelung), follows the heresiographers. The name Saba'iyya was also used in the period round about 700, but there is some obscurity about it and about ʿAbd-Allāh b. Saba'; see *Formative Period*, 59-61.
3. *Formative Period*, ch.2. I. Friedlaender, 'The Heterodoxies of the Shiites in the presentation of Ibn Ḥazm', *Journal of the American Oriental Society*, xxviii (1907), 1-80; xxix (1909), 1-183.

Chapter Four

THE GENERAL RELIGIOUS MOVEMENT

Up to this point the discussion has been of 'heretical' sects, and the question naturally arises whether there was at this time a body of 'orthodox' opinion and, if so, whether anything more can be said about it. The form of this question, however, is not altogether satisfactory. The term 'orthodox' applies in the first place to Eastern Christendom, where there was an authority to say what was 'orthodoxy' or 'right belief' and what was 'heresy'. In Islam, however, there was no such authority. There was only the main or central body of opinion in the various schools or sections of the community. In these, too, there was not always the emphasis on the intellectual aspect of religion that there was in Eastern Christendom (though such an emphasis is sometimes found). Thus it is best in Islamic studies to avoid the term 'orthodox' and to ask instead whether there was a central body of moderate opinion.

There is not the same objection to the term 'heresy'. The Arabic term *bid'a* roughly corresponds to the English in effect, though it has a different connotation. *Bid'a* properly means 'innovation', and the implication of this term is that the true belief and practice is the original belief and practice—'innovation' is not confined to intellectual matters. This serves to explain why the central body of opinion in Umayyad Islam has not been much studied and why it is difficult to investigate. Muslims of the centre were quite happy to write about the divergent views of the sects; but when it came to the views of their own party they considered that these were in essence identical with those of Muḥammad and his Companions, and therefore they tended to hide any changes and developments or pass them over in silence. There is thus no material for the direct study of this central body, but only large masses of semi-relevant material in biographical dictionaries and similar works—and so far only a beginning has been made with the investigation of all this.[1]

There is evidence to show that there always was a central body of moderate opinion, but some greater precision is desirable. Early in the caliphate of ʿAlī there was a body of men in Medina who adopted an attitude of political neutrality; their leader was ʿAbd-Allāh ibn-ʿUmar, a son of the caliph ʿUmar. At a later date there was in Medina and elsewhere what modern Western scholars have called a 'pious opposition', though its outlines are somewhat hazy. It appears that in the main centres, and notably in Medina, Damascus, Basra and Kufa, there were numbers of men who met in the mosques to discuss religious questions. These included legal matters, ascetic and mystical practices, the interpretation of the Qur'ān and occasionally theological doctrine. Those most competent in these disciplines gave what amounted to lectures to their disciples.

After about 750 another discipline became of great importance, the study of Ḥadīth or Traditions. The common view among Muslim scholars has been that the Companions—those Muslims who had seen and talked to Muḥammad—handed on anecdotes about him during their lifetime, and that the anecdotes were then handed on from generation to generation. It is these anecdotes which are technically known as Ḥadīth (or *akhbār*), which has commonly been rendered as 'traditions' in English, though because of the ambiguity of this word scholars are now preferring to retain Ḥadīth. In handing on an anecdote a man was expected to give an *isnād,* that is, to name the chain of transmitters through whom the anecdote had reached him, and this chain was expected to go back without a break to the Companion who had been present when Muḥammad uttered the saying or performed the action. Modern European scholarship, however, has criticized this idyllic picture, and has suggested that for much of the Umayyad period the anecdotes were handed on without any *isnād,* or with an incomplete one, and that at a later date *isnāds* could be forged or conjecturally restored and anecdotes invented. This may be called the Goldziher-Schacht view. At a fairly early date Muslim scholars had indeed recognized the possibility of invention, and had worked out an elaborate critique of the soundness of Ḥadīth; but this was far from satisfying the sceptical Europeans. More recently, however, largely thanks to the work of Fuat Sezgin, the Goldziher-Schacht view has been felt to be too radical.[2] Even so, however, it would appear that a complete *isnād* was not *de rigueur* until about the year 800.

While the idealized picture of groups of men meticulously handing on Ḥadīth with their *isnāds* has thus to be abandoned, at least in part, there certainly were groups of pious men regularly meeting in the mosques and talking or lecturing. They were intelligent serious Muslims, concerned with the application of their religious principles to social and political life, for in an Islamic environment politics was closely linked with piety. Presumably all these men had adopted some political stance or other. We know that among them, not counting active or moderate Khārijites and active or quiescent Shī'ites, there were supporters of Ibn-az-Zubayr, who claimed the caliphate in Mecca from 680 to 692 (though most of these were later reconciled with the Umayyads), also whole-hearted supporters of the Umayyads, and again others who accepted their rule but severely criticized it. Since most of these men seem to have taken part in the discussions in the mosques, it seems better not to separate off the opponents and critics of the regime, but to refer to them all as the 'general religious movement'.

Apart from those belonging to clearly heretical sects like the Khārijites, the Shī'ites and the Qadarites (to be described in the next chapter), most of the members of this general religious movement would be regarded by later Sunnites as their own predecessors. Yet it has to be firmly emphasized that at this time there were no 'Sunnites' in the strict sense, though there were individuals and groups whose practice and beliefs were Sunnite, at least to the extent that Sunnism had been defined and standardized during the Umayyad period.

There was no Sunnite self-awareness as such, however, since it had not occurred to anyone to think of himself as a *sunnī* or as belonging to the 'people of the Sunna' (Ahl as-Sunna). The latter phrase (with some variants) begins to be used in the later ninth century, but was not in common use until the tenth century, and the adjective *sunnī* seems to be first recorded towards the end of the tenth century.[3]

The period of twelve years following the death of the caliph Mu'āwiya in 680 was a time in which the Islamic empire was rent by civil strife, with al-Mukhtār leading a Shī'ite rising in Kufa from 685 to 687, Ibn-az-Zubayr claiming the caliphate in Mecca till 692, and groups of Khārijites maintaining independence in various regions. It was probably in response to these circumstances that a new idea was introduced into the thinking of Muslims, the idea of *irjā'* or 'postponement'. It seems to have been first used about 695 by a grandson of 'Alī, al-Ḥasan ibn-Muḥammad ibn-al-Ḥanafiyya, in a short epistle which is extant and appears to be authentic.[4] In this the author expresses his political attitude by saying that 'we' approve of Abū-Bakr and 'Umar, and 'postpone' the decision about those involved in the first civil conflict, meaning 'Uthmān, 'Alī and az-Zubayr (father of the Meccan rebel). By this formulation he tried to heal the rifts in the community. He refused to side with the revolutionary Shī'ites who were asserting the superior claims of 'Alī and his descendants, and he distanced himself from the Khārijites who denied the legitimacy of the Umayyad caliphs since their claim was based on their being heirs of the 'sinner' 'Uthmān. In general this political attitude seems to arise mainly from a concern for the unity of the community of Muslims, and this leads not to unwavering support for the Umayyads but to acceptance or toleration of their rule combined with criticism of it. Several of those who believed in 'postponement' joined in risings against the Umayyads, though others thought it wrong to revolt against even a bad ruler. Statements are found to the effect that *irjā'* is 'the religion of the kings', but this cannot mean that it was the religion followed by the Umayyads themselves, only that it discouraged rebellion.[5]

Though 'postponement' meant in the first place postponing a decision about 'Uthmān and 'Alī (with or without az-Zubayr), the term was sometimes given other meanings in the course of debate. Some opponents said that it implied asserting that the grave sinner *is* a believer, not merely that he is to be regarded as one; and in a sense this is indeed an implication of leaving the decision about him to God, and was accepted by the upholders of 'postponement'. Again, there were later writers who said it meant postponing 'Alī to fourth place, a view which became the standard Sunnite view. It was also noted that *irjā'* could come from a different root and mean 'the giving of hope'; and it would then apply to the grave sinner. It has also been noted that 'postponement' together with some associated ideas resembles certain teachings of Hellenistic Sceptics and Empiricists, though there is no evidence of a channel by which such ideas could have reached the Muslims. Even if the idea of 'postponement' was first suggested by some such source, however, it was only adopted because it was appropriate to the internal political situation in the caliphate. Another possible source is the Qur'ānic phrase (9.106) 'some are postponed for the command of God', and this verse was certainly used to justify the doctrine of 'postponement'.

While the original reason for taking up the idea of 'postponement' was probably concern for the unity of all Muslims and the avoidance of sectarianism, a further set of ideas came to be associated with it, namely, ideas about the definition of *īmān*. This word is commonly translated 'faith' but it often refers rather to whatever makes a man a *mu'min* or 'believer'. When grave sin does not exclude a man from the community, it is desirable to have some positive account of what is needed for membership. The terms commonly used by the upholders of 'postponement' are that *īmañ* consists of the knowledge (*ma'rifa*) of God and of his Messenger, the counting true (*taṣdīq*) of this knowledge, and the confession (*iqrār*) of it with the tongue. There were also minor additions and variants; but it is significant that in keeping with the view that the grave sinner is a believer there is no mention of the performance of religious duties, either ethical or liturgical. In this way something like the Christian conception of 'orthodoxy' is brought into Islam, though the intellectual content is much less complex than that of the ecumenical Christian creeds, and there were always many Muslims who insisted that an element of performance must also be included.

Opponents used the collective term Murji'a for those who held the doctrine of *irjā'* or 'postponement', and Murji'ites is employed in English. Though the heresiographers spoke of the Murji'a as a sect, careful examination of the sources shows that there was no such 'sect' in any important sense. Those who believed in 'postponement' differed on other matters, and are often described as belonging to other sects with greater cohesion. The extent of the problem is made clear by the difficulties experienced by the heresiographer ash-Shahrastānī. He subdivided the Murji'a into Murji'a of the Khārijites, those of the Qadarites, those of the Jabrites and pure Murji'a; but then he had to deal with Abū-Ḥanīfa, whom he could not regard as heretical, and so he suggested that he was a Murji'ite of the Sunna. Apart from Abū-Ḥanīfa, however, and those definitely belonging to other sects, the only Murji'ites described by the heresiographers are people of minor importance. All these facts point to the conclusion that the doctrine of 'postponement' by itself was not sufficient to form the basis of a cohesive group. Rather it was a trend permeating various forms of sectarian thought, and making an important contribution to the development of Sunnism.

The chief figure among the upholders of 'postponement' was undoubtedly Abū-Ḥanīfa. He was a non-Arab, who was born in Kufa about 700, lived there for most of his life, and died in Baghdad in 767. He was associated with a group of legal scholars in Kufa, of whom some at least had accepted 'postponement'. About 737 on the death of his principal teacher he seems to have been recognized as head of the group, and the vigour and originality of his mind directed their legal thinking along lines which led in the next generation to the formation of the Ḥanafite legal school, named after him. There was also a Ḥanafite theological school, which was in part identical with the legal school. The doctrine of 'postponement' had been popular in Kufa long before Abū-Ḥanīfa, but his was presumably the main responsibility for giving it and the definition of *īmān* the intellectual form which made them widely acceptable. The majority of the earliest persons named in the sources as 'Murji'ites' came from Kufa, and this may be because Kufa was a stronghold of early Shī'ism, and 'postponement' was felt to be a satisfactory way of expressing opposition to the undue exaltation of 'Alī. In Basra there were some upholders of 'postponement', but the majority there may have preferred to express similar political attitudes by the term *wuqūf*, 'suspension of judgement', as did the Wāqifites and the alleged founder of Mu'tazilism, Wāṣil.

The upholders of 'postponement' are best understood as one current within the main stream of what later became Sunnite Islam. The actual term *irjā'*, 'postponement', was not used in later Sunnism, but the political and practical attitudes based on it were accepted. The Khārijite doctrine of the exclusion of the grave sinner from the community was firmly rejected; and this also meant that 'Uthmān was regarded as a lawful caliph. The early Shī'ite doctrine of the superiority of 'Alī was also rejected; and the eventual Sunnite view was that the first four caliphs ranked in merit in their chronological order, so that 'Uthmān was above 'Alī. Later Sunnism also accepted to some extent the emphasis given to the content of belief by Abū-Ḥanīfa and others, but the Ḥanafite leaning towards an 'orthodoxy' which was purely intellectual was not universally accepted, and an element of performance or 'works' was required by other equally Sunnite theological schools.

NOTES

1. For 'the general religious movement' and similar matters see *Formative Period*, 63-81.
2. Ignaz Goldziher, *Muhammedanische Studien*, vol.2, Halle 1890 (translated as *Muslim Studies*, vol.2, London 1971). Joseph Schacht, *The Origins of Muhammadan Jurisprudence*, Oxford 1950; summarized in *An Introduction to Islamic Law*, Oxford 1964. Fuat Sezgin, *Geschichte des arabischen Schrifttums*, vol.1, Leiden 1967, 53-84, 'Einführung' to the section on Ḥadīth, summarizing a longer work in Turkish. Further developments are seen in Josef van Ess, *Zwischen Ḥadīt und Theologie*, Berlin 1975, which partly accepts Sezgin's views.
3. *Formative Period*, 265-71.
4. J. van Ess, 'Das *Kitāb al-irǧā'* des Ḥasan b. Muḥammad b. al-Ḥanafiyya', *Arabica* xxi (1974), 20-52. This appeared after *Formative Period*, 119-43, where there is a general account of the 'Murji'ites', but does not necessitate much change in the latter. *Early Muslim dogma, a source-critical study* by Michael Cook (Cambridge 1981), making use of an Ibāḍite source, is severely critical of van Ess, pointing out weaknesses in his arguments, but presents no convincing positive view, so that the authenticity of *Kitāb al-irjā'* may be provisionally accepted.
5. *Formative Period*, 125; cf. Cook, *Early Muslim dogma*, 33.

Chapter Five

GOD'S DETERMINATION OF EVENTS

About the time when Muslim thinkers were showing interest in the idea of 'postponement' the question of God's determination or predetermination of events was also attracting attention. Where opponents gave the nickname of Murji'a to the upholders of 'postponement', we have the curious situation that in the debate about predetermination both sides nicknamed the other Qadariyya, anglicized as Qadarites. Since God's *qadar* is his determination of events, those who believed in it would most naturally be called Qadarites; but in point of fact the opposite has happened. Almost all later Sunnite writers in speaking of Qadarites mean those who *dis*believed in God's absolute *qadar* and asserted the freedom of the human will; and this has become normal usage with Western students of Islam, and will be followed here.[1]

In the discussion of God's *qadar* both the main parties found support for their views in the Qur'ān; but the Qur'ān has many passages which seem akin to the outlook of pre-Islamic Arab 'fatalism', and it is logical to begin with a brief description of this. Information about it comes from the numerous poems by pre-Islamic Arabs which are still extant and also from a few Qur'ānic statements about their beliefs. These Arabs believed that their lives were controlled by Time (*dahr, zamān*). It is Time which brings men their successes and above all their misfortunes. Though Time is said to shoot arrows which never miss the mark, it is primarily conceived as an impersonal force, something like 'the course of events'. It would be natural to identify this force with 'fate' or 'destiny', but what brings misfortunes is sometimes called 'the days' and even 'the nights', and this shows that the aspect of 'time' was uppermost. Time is not something which is worshipped, however, but is rather, like gravitation, a natural phenomenon which one must accept.

The control of human life by Time is limited. It does not determine every act of the individual, but, whatever he decides to do, it fixes the final outcome. In particular his 'term' (*ajal*) or date of death is fixed; whether he decides to take part in a battle or to keep away from it, he will die if his 'term' has come. His good fortune or evil fortune, as the case may be, is also predetermined, and likewise, it would seem, his 'provision' or 'sustenance' (*rizq*)—an important matter in lands where food was often scarce (though also mentioned in the Christian prayer for 'daily bread'). Fatalism of this kind was appropriate to the life of the nomads in the deserts and steppes of Arabia. The regularities of nature found in most other regions of the world are there often replaced by irregularities. To take precautions against all the possible chances of disaster is impossible, and to attempt to do so would make a man a nervous wreck, incapable of sustaining life in the desert. To cultivate the attitude of accepting with equanimity what 'the days' bring was probably the best hope of making a success of one's life in the harsh conditions of the desert.

The monotheistic religious message of the Qur'ān is largely expressed in terms of the thought-world of the Arabs of the period. The control of human life, of course, is regarded as being in the hands of God, not of Time. Thus when some idolaters deny the life to come and say that 'Time alone destroys us', Muḥammad is told to retort, 'It is God who makes you live, then makes you die, then gathers you for a day of resurrection' (45.24, 26). God takes the place of Time as the source of misfortune: 'no misfortune has happened in respect either of the land or of yourselves but it was in a book before we (God) brought it about' (57.22). The idea of some event 'being in a book' or 'being written' before it happens is frequent. The effect of a fatalistic attitude in calming anxiety is even greater, one imagines, when Time is replaced by God—'nothing will befall us except what God has written for us' (9.51). Prominent among the things that are written is man's term-of-life. In a notable verse (3.154) Muḥammad is told to say to those who criticized his decision to fight at Uḥud (where the Muslims had the worse of the battle), 'if you had been in your houses, those for whom killing was written down would have sallied out to the places of their falling'. The predestinarian relevance of the idea of 'provision' or 'sustenance' is not so obvious, yet at least sometimes it is regarded as being predetermined by God, as in 30.40, where God's 'making provision' seems to follow immediately his creating a human being. (This point about the predetermination of *rizq* is made more explicitly in some Ḥadīth.)

It is not surprising that some of these ideas which were present in the minds of those to whom the Qur'ān was addressed were used by the Umayyads and their supporters in defence of the legitimacy of their rule. One of the Umayyad claims was that they had inherited the caliphate from 'Uthmān, in that Mu'āwiya had undertaken the responsibility of avenger of blood when 'Alī refused it, and this justified his position according to old Arab ideas. The Umayyads also claimed, however, that the caliphate had been bestowed on them by God, in much the same way as he was said in the Qur'ān (2.30) to have made Adam his *khalīfa* on earth. This is reflected in, among other places, the verses of court-poets like Jarīr and al-Farazdaq; for example, 'the earth is God's, he has entrusted it to his *khalīfa*'; 'God has garlanded you with the caliphate and with guidance; for what God decrees there is no change'. The word 'decrees' here is *qaḍā* which is frequently used of God's eternal decrees. With such ideas current it was easy to go further and say that to deny that God had given the caliphate to the Umayyads was unbelief and that to disobey them or their agents was sin. This was the intellectual context in which Qadarism appeared.

An important document for the beginnings of Qadarism is the *Risāla* or epistle, said to have been written to the caliph 'Abd-al-Malik by al-Ḥasan al-Baṣrī about the year 700. The ascription is probably correct, but, even if it is not, the document is still important evidence of early Qadarism.[2] Al-Ḥasan al-Baṣrī (642–728), son of a prisoner from Iraq, was born in Medina but went to Basra in 657 and spent most of the rest of his life there. Whether he was a Qadarite or not has been hotly debated, more or less since his own lifetime, but the *Risāla* makes it clear that he believed that human beings can choose freely between good and evil. When the predestinarians supported their case by such Qur'ānic verses as 13.22: 'God sends astray whom he will', al-Ḥasan insisted that this must be interpreted in accordance with other verses like 14.27: 'God sends astray the evil-doers'. In other words he held that, when the Qur'ān is considered as a whole, the determination of human activity by God follows on some act of human choice and is a recompense for it. It is to be noted, however, that in interpreting 57.22 (quoted above) about misfortunes being 'in a book' he asserted that this did not apply to unbelief or disobedience but only to external things like wealth and harvests. Al-Ḥasan also maintained that God creates only good, and that men's evil acts are from themselves or from Satan; but he allowed that God's 'guidance' of men contained an element of 'succour' or 'grace' (*tawfīq*).

From the little we know of the views of Qadarites who were al-Ḥasan's contemporaries or who belonged to the next generation it is clear that al-Ḥasan stood close to them. He might be said to represent a moderate form of Qadarism in which the emphasis was on practical piety. Yet in the context of the age even views such as those described had political implications. A story is told of how two Qadarites said to al-Ḥasan, 'these princes (the Umayyads) shed the blood of the Muslims and seize their goods ... and say "Our acts occur only according to God's determination (*qadar*)"', and he replied that 'the enemies of God lie'. That is to say, al-Ḥasan's teaching that evil acts are from men or from Satan implies a denial of Umayyad claims, so that his undoubted piety did not make him apolitical. He firmly rejected armed revolt, but he strongly maintained that pious men like himself had a duty publicly to voice criticisms of those in authority if they acted contrary to God's law, and he seems on occasion to have done this regardless of consequences.

During the lifetime of al-Ḥasan Qadarism as such was not felt to be a threat by the Umayyad government, though they disapproved of it and the caliph 'Umar II (717–20) wrote a letter criticizing it.[3] Qadarite views, however, could also be combined with Khārijism, and in some of the later revolts against the Umayyads certain participants are said to have been Khārijites and Qadarites at the same time. In Syria a group of Qadarites, who had at first been quietist, seem to have become interested in political reform towards the end of the reign of the caliph Hishām (724–43). One of the leading men in this group, Ghaylān ad-Dimashqī, who had been on good terms with 'Umar II and was also a believer in 'postponement', somehow became involved in subversive activity and was executed. The reform movement continued, however, and was supported by a member of the Umayyad family, the caliph Yazīd III, who reigned for a few months in 744; but after his death the last Umayyad caliph again persecuted the Qadarites.

The replacement of the Umayyad dynasty by the 'Abbāsid in 750 altered the political implications of Qadarite doctrine. 'Abbāsid legitimacy was based on a form of Shī'ite ideas and not on the claim that all they did was determined by God; and indeed for much of the first half of the ninth century influential positions at the caliphal court were held by several of the Mu'tazilite theologians who had taken over the Qadarite belief in free will. It was also now possible to oppose Qadarism without appearing to support unjust rulers. The precise timing of the various changes is somewhat conjectural, but certain general trends are clear. Those upholding a definite doctrine of human free will, apart from a few who were Khārijites, came to be merged into the Mu'tazilite sect (to be described later). There were thus no Qadarites, properly speaking, after the eighth century, but certain later writers use the term as a nickname for those who are normally called Mu'tazilites. Those followers of al-Ḥasan and other members of the general religious movement whose concern was to insist that human beings are capable of avoiding sins may have tended towards a moderate anti-Qadarite position. In particular many predestinarian Ḥadīth began to have a wide circulation. In al-Ḥasan's time these may have been known to some scholars, but they do not seem to have had much currency since he does not feel any need to discuss them in his *Risāla*. The arguments, too, of 'Umar II in his letter are mainly from the Qur'ān. In the early 'Abbāsid period, however, many predestinarian Ḥadīth came to be well known. In one such Muḥammad decribed how God instructs the angel in charge of the child in the womb and determines four things: whether it is to be male or female, whether it is to be fortunate or unfortunate, what is to be its 'provision' and what is to be its 'term'. Most Ḥadīth dealing with this question are predestinarian, but there are a few exceptions.

There are two possible forms of predestinarian or anti-Qadarite views. In the moderate form what happens to a person is determined by God, but the person's reaction to these happenings is not necessarily determined. This form is compatible with an article in a creed attributed to Abū-Ḥanīfa and probably representing his views: 'what reaches you (of evil) could not possibly have missed you, and what misses you could not possibly have reached you'. The more extreme form of the belief is that the person's reactions to external happenings are also determined. In another Ḥadīth Muḥammad speaks of a primordial Pen created by God which writes everything that is to happen until the Day of Judgement. Yet other Ḥadīth assert that an individual's place in heaven or hell is predetermined. The main stream of Islamic thought finally rejected Qadarism, even in a moderate version, and accepted one or other of these forms of predestinarian belief, though responsible theologians always found a place in their theories for moral effort. To this extent Qadarism, unlike the belief in 'postponement', made little contribution to the final position of Sunnite Islam.

The nickname applied by opponents to believers in some form of predestination was Mujbira or, less frequently, Jabriyya—anglicized as Mujbirites and Jabrites. Many of these persons were the forerunners of the main body of later Sunnites and in no sense heretics. The Ash'arites later developed the theory that their special view on the matter (expressed by the term *kasb*, 'acquisition') was a mean between 'compulsion' (*jabr, ijbār*) and the free will of the Qadarites, and some writers on sects found Jabriyya a useful term to designate those holding views at the opposite pole from Qadarism; but it is doubtful if any actual persons ever held the more extreme Jabrite views described.

Many Western scholars have regarded Qadarism as due to Christian influences on Islam.[4] In other areas of Islamic thought scholars have found the influence of Neoplatonism and other forms of Hellenistic philosophy. In general it may be agreed that such influences are present, even if the details are not always clear. Syria and Iraq were permeated by Christian conceptions, and some Jewish and Christian ideas had even penetrated into Arabia. The Qadarite Ghaylān ad-Dimashqī was of Coptic descent, and it may be surmised that many of the other early Muslim thinkers came from a Christian background. The real problem, however, is to understand the precise nature of this

Christian or Hellenistic influence. The persons 'influenced' were not academics isolated in an ivory tower but were actively involved in the life of a dynamic community. This involvement was both religious and political, but may for convenience be called simply 'political' provided it is remembered that politics is not a compartmentalized segment of the life of the community. Most of the Qadarites and other members of the general religious movement accepted that part of Khārijite views which insisted that the activity of the state should be based on Islamic principles. It was when Umayyad policies went against Islamic principles that men in the general movement questioned the Umayyad claim that their acts were 'determined' by God. Qadarism was indeed thought by its adherents to be true, but in adopting it they were more impressed by its usefulness as an argument against what they saw as false Umayyad claims. Similarly the idea of 'postponement' or 'suspension of judgement' may well have come from Hellenistic sources, but it was adopted because it fitted in well with the situation of a community which was being torn apart by the hostility between supporters of ʿAlī and supporters of ʿUthmān.

One of the main differences between Christianity and Islam is that for three centuries the Christian Church was a purely religious community without political power, whereas from the time of the Hijra in 622 Islam was identified with a political community. Until about the tenth century all the Islamic sects are religio-political. Even when arguments appear to be hair-splitting theological subtleties, such as whether the Qur'ān is the created or the uncreated Speech of God, there are political implications. This means that, while it is interesting to find foreign or extraneous sources for Islamic theological ideas, the source does little to explain the place of the idea in Islamic thought, just as the 'sources' of Shakespeare's plots fail to explain the greatness of the plays. The main explanation comes from understanding the import of the idea within the Islamic religio-political context. In so far as emphasis on sources is suggesting that Islam is nothing but a revision of Christian or Jewish or Hellenistic ideas, this is misleading and a belittling of the uniqueness and originality of Islam.

NOTES

1. General bibliography on Qadarism: Josef van Ess, art. Ḳadariyya in *EI*², which includes the results of a number of other studies by him: *Traditionistische Polemik gegen ʿAmr b. ʿUbaid* (Beiruter Texte und Studien, 7), Beirut 1967; 'ʿUmar II and his Epistle against the Qadarīya', *Abr Nahrain*, xii (1971), 19-26; 'Maʿbad al-Ǧuhanī', in R. Gramlich (ed.), *Islamwissenschaftliche Abhandlungen* (Festschrift Fritz Meier), Wiesbaden 1974, 49-77; 'Les Qadarites et la Gailānīya de Yazīd III', *Studia Islamica*, xxxi (1970), 269-86; *Zwischen Ḥadīt und Theologie, Studien zum Entstehen prädes-*

tinatianischer Überlieferung, Berlin 1975; *Anfänge Muslimischer Theologie, zwei antiqadaritische Traktate aus dem ersten Jahrhundert der Higra* (Beiruter Texte und Studien, 14), Beirut 1977. Michael Cook, *Early Muslim Dogma* (n.4/4), criticizes van Ess's studies of the Qadarites but has no firm suggestions of positive alternatives except in respect of 'influences'. *Formative Period*, 77-118.

2. Hellmut Ritter, 'Studien zur Geschichte der islamischen Frömmigkeit: Ḥasan al-Baṣrī . . .', *Der Islam*, xxi (1933), 1-83, has the text of the *Risāla* and discusses doctrines; Michael Schwarz, 'The Letter of al-Ḥasan al-Baṣrī', *Oriens*, xx (1967), 15-30; Cook, op. cit., 117-23. Further reference in Sezgin, *GSA*, i.591-4; *Formative Period*, 334, n.3/37.
3. Text, translation and discussion in van Ess, *Anfänge*, 113-76, Arabic 43-54; also an earlier article (see n.5/1).
4. Carl H. Becker, *Christianity and Islam*, London 1909; translation of a German article in his *Islamstudien*, Leipzig 1924, i.386-431; also an article 'Christliche Polemik und islamische Dogmenbildung', reprinted in *Islamstudien*, i.432-49, from *Zeitschrift für Assyriologie*, xxvi (1911), 175-95. Morris S. Seale, *Muslim Theology, A Study of Origins with Reference to the Church Fathers*, London 1964. Cook, *Early Muslim Dogma* (n.4/4).

Part Two

THE FIRST WAVE OF HELLENISM

CHAPTER SIX

POLITICS AND THEOLOGY UNDER THE ʿABBĀSIDS

When the ʿAbbāsid dynasty came to power in 750, their claim to the caliphate was based on the assertion that the imamate had passed from ʿAlī to Muḥammad ibn-al-Ḥanafiyya, then to his son Abū-Hāshim, and that the latter had designated as his successor the father of the first two ʿAbbāsid caliphs. Before long, however, this particular claim to legitimacy seems to have been found unsatisfactory, and the caliph al-Mahdī (775–85) replaced it by the claim that the rightful successor of the Prophet had been his uncle al-ʿAbbās, and that the succession had then continued in his family, the ʿAbbāsids. How long this claim was maintained is not clear.

An important feature of the new dynasty was the growth of Persian influence. Persian clients had rallied in large numbers to the black banners of the ʿAbbāsid revolt, and so it is not surprising that many of the subordinate officials in the new administration were Persians or persianized Aramaeans and exercised considerable power. Outstanding was the Persian family of Barmak (the Barmakids or Barmecides), whose head was vizier from 786 to 803. The transfer of the capital of the caliphate eastwards from Damascus to Iraq—to Baghdad after its foundation in 763—affected the internal distribution of power in favour of the eastern provinces. It also meant that the main work of administration was in the hands of the class of 'secretaries' or civil servants, who had continued to exist as a class in Iraq since before the Muslim conquest, and had retained much of the technique of government used in the Persian empire under the Sasanians. These men, too, were the bearers of the Persian or rather persianized culture of Iraq. Some were Christians, most probably nominal Zoroastrians, because Zoroastrianism, officially recognized and almost a department of government, was in decline as a religion. Thus the secretaries had a culture of which they were proud, including important Hellenistic elements, but, apart from the Christians, they had little vital religion. When they saw the best appointments in their profession going to Muslims, many of them accepted Islam outwardly.

Prominent among the Persian secretaries was Ibn-al-Muqaffa' (d.c.759).[1] He is regarded as one of the creators of Arabic prose through his numerous translations into Arabic from Persian. These included works on administrative practice and court ceremonial, as well as a history of the Persian kings. His best-known book is *Kalila and Dimna,* a collection of Indian fables in which much practical wisdom is put into the mouths of animals. He expressed his dislike of the dominant Islamic and Arab tradition by adopting a standpoint which may be labelled Manichaean, and among his works is one attacking the Qur'ān. For a time other Persian secretaries also found Manichaeanism a useful way of emphasizing their distinct identity. From about 779 to 786, however, there was an official persecution of Zindīqs or 'dualistic heretics', which was largely directed against Manichaeanism of this type. The traditional Manichaeans, of whom there were a few, seem to have been little affected by the persecution. Some secretaries then found a less dangerous way of expressing their position; they produced literary works aimed at the depreciation of all things Arab. This is known as the Shu'ūbite movement, and is mainly a literary phenomenon.

The class of secretaries had rivals for power in the class of religious intellectuals which was emerging within the 'general religious movement' and may by anticipation be called the class of ulema (*'ulamā'*). Many of these men, especially those interested in legal questions, had supported the 'Abbāsids against the Umayyads. The 'Abbāsids respected their views and were prepared to select judges from their ranks, though they also brought pressure to bear on them to overcome their disagreements and adopt common principles. The rivalry between the secretaries and the ulema came to be linked with that between the Persian and Arabic cultural traditions and also with that between Shī'ism and what eventually became Sunnism. The essential difference between Shī'ism and Sunnism with regard to this rivalry is that, where the Shī'ites in difficulties sought a divinely-inspired leader, an imam, their opponents held that salvation came through carefully following the divine law as expressed in the Qur'ān and in the *sunna* or example of the Prophet. Since the ulema were accepted as the accredited interpreters of the divine law, the Sunnite position gave them great power.

By the reign of the caliph al-Ma'mūn (813–33) the unity of the empire was felt to be threatened by the opposition of the rival groups of interests—the secretaries, Shī'ites and Persians on the one hand, and the ulema, the Sunnites and the Arabs on the other.[2] Al-Ma'mūn in 817 tried to reconcile the opposing groups by designating as his heir the man recognized as imam by many Shī'ites, but unfortunately this man died in the following year. Later al-Ma'mūn tried to find a theological compromise by demanding that many persons in important positions (such as judges and court officials) should publicly profess their belief in the doctrine that the Qur'ān was the created word of God, not his uncreated word. This piece of apparent hair-splitting is relevant to the conflict just outlined. If the Qur'ān is created, God could presumably have created it other than it is, whereas, if it is uncreated it presumably expresses something of his own being which is unchangeable. If the Qur'ān could have been created other than it is, the work of the ulema in interpreting it loses much of its authority; and a divinely-inspired imam (caliph) would be entitled to say how the law was to be changed. In practice this would almost certainly mean more power for the caliph's ministers and secretaries. The policy of demanding a profession of belief in the createdness of the Qur'ān continued in force until about 850, and is known as the Miḥna or 'inquisition'. The reason for its abandonment is probably that it failed to reconcile the opposing groups, despite the fact that nearly all the ulema made the profession, apparently out of fear.

Al-Maʾmūn's views were very like those of the Zaydites.[3] These are spoken of as a sect by the heresiographers, but they were a trend of thought rather than a closely-knit sect. One of their doctrines was that the rightful imam must be a member of the family of the Prophet (or more precisely a descendant of ʿAlī and Fāṭima) who had publicly claimed the imamate and had made good his claim by the sword. Al-Ma'mūn, though not a descendant of ʿAlī, had made good his claim by the sword. Moreover, besides being the first caliph to make use of the term 'imam' with its Shīʿite flavour, he seems to have held that the imam should be the 'most excellent' (*afḍal*) of the community; and another point of Zaydite teaching was that ʿAlī was the rightful successor of Muḥammad because he was the 'most excellent' and not simply because he was 'designated'. This formulation enabled the Zaydites to say that Abū-Bakr and ʿUmar were truly caliphs, since they had been accepted as such by ʿAlī despite their 'inferiority' to him. The Zaydites are classified among the Shīʿites because of their views about ʿAlī. Their name is derived from a great-grandson of ʿAlī and Fāṭima called Zayd who led an unsuccessful revolt against the Umayyads in 740. Several revolts against the ʿAbbāsids led by descendants of ʿAlī and Fāṭima are also reckoned as Zaydite, but the elaboration of Zaydite doctrine was chiefly the work of persons not involved in revolts. There is also some obscurity about the dividing line between Zaydism and Muʿtazilism (to be discussed in chapter 8). Some leading Muʿtazilites were closely associated with al-Maʾmūn's administration, and Muʿtazilites were chiefly responsible for the doctrine of the createdness of the Qur'ān which was at the centre of the 'inquisition'.

The main body of Shīʿites in the ninth century, though much divided among themselves, are mostly called by the nickname of

Rāfiḍites ('deserters') by their opponents, because they 'deserted' Abū-Bakr and 'Umar, the two shaykhs, that is denied that they were rightful caliphs, or because they 'deserted' Zayd. It is preferable to call them Imāmites, since those who called themselves by this name after about 900 (see chapter 9) accepted these earlier men as their theological predecessors. It is difficult to know what were the political aims of such persons during the first century or so of 'Abbāsid rule. Later Imāmites held that the imamate was handed on from father to son in the line of al-Ḥusayn until the 'occultation' of the twelfth imam in 874; and this suggests that each of these imams in turn claimed to be the legitimate ruler of the Islamic empire. This cannot be the case, however, since the 'Abbāsids would have put dangerous rivals to death, whereas they only placed one imam under house-arrest. On the contrary it is recorded that a scholar defended Imāmite views against a Zaydite in the presence of al-Ma'mūn himself. The most likely view is that the early Imāmites were not arguing on behalf of a particular imam but in favour of an absolutist conception of the caliphate, one in which the imam or caliph, because he has been 'designated' by his predecessor, receives his authority from above, as it were, and not from any electors or from the oath of allegiance of the Muslims.[4]

NOTES

1. *EI*[2], art. Ibn (al-)Muḳaffa' (F. Gabrieli); *Formative Period*, 171f.
2. *Formative Period*, 173-9.
3. Ibid., 162-6.
4. Ibid., 157-62.

Chapter Seven

THE ATTRACTION OF GREEK THOUGHT

Within the culture associated with the Islamic religion there has always been a tendency to maintain that Islam is self-sufficient and that in Qur'ān and Ḥadīth it contains in essentials all the religious and moral truth required by all humanity to the end of time. Muslims have accordingly been hesitant about accepting ideas from other intellectual traditions, and especially from the Judaeo-Christian tradition because of the theory they developed that the Jewish and Christian scriptures had been 'corrupted'. Even material derived from Biblical sources—such as the genealogy from Abraham back to Adam in Ibn-Hishām's life of Muḥammad—is not acknowledged as such. It is thus all the more noteworthy to find it openly admitted that much was borrowed from the Hellenistic tradition. Yet even here the actual influence was more extensive than was admitted, while in the end much of what was borrowed was rejected or treated as of minor importance. The admitted borrowings came by way of translations of Greek works and original compositions in Arabic in the Greek philosophical and scientific tradition. The unadmitted borrowings are found in the development of the discipline of 'philosophical theology' or Kalām.

A system of Hellenistic education had been established in Iraq under the Sasanians and was continued under the Muslims. The main subject of instruction was probably medicine; but philosophy and other 'Greek sciences' were always taught as well. The teaching was mainly in the hands of Christians, and the best-known college was at Gundē-Shāpūr (about 150 km north-east of Basra). Later, when a hospital was set up in Baghdad, there were probably philosophical lectures in connection with the medical teaching. This system of Hellenistic education was thus complete in itself, and was spread over a number of institutions.

Even before the inauguration of the 'Abbāsid caliphate a beginning had been made of translating Greek scientific and philosophical works into Arabic. At first the choice of works depended probably on the individual scholar or his patron, but the caliph al-Ma'mūn (813–33) or his advisers realized the importance for the whole empire of the Greek sciences and organized the work of translation on a large scale. An institution was set up called the 'House of Wisdom' (*bayt al-ḥikma*), where books were translated and copied, and where a library was kept for reference. For a period of a century or two translations continued to be made, and the older translations revised. The greatest name is that of Ḥunayn ibn-Is'ḥāq (809–73), a Christian from al-Ḥīra who became a teacher of medicine in Baghdad and court physician to the caliph al-Mutawakkil (*regnabat* 847–61). He had something like a bureau for translation, with several well-qualified colleagues. Unlike most of the earlier translators—nearly all Iraqian Christians—who had translated from Syriac, Ḥunayn had learnt Greek and was in the habit of collating a number of manuscripts before making his translations. This was the highest level reached by the translators from the technical and linguistic standpoint. Later, however, with the growth of independent philosophical thinking in Arabic, the translations were revised to express the arguments with greater clarity, precision and accuracy; but this was usually done from Syriac versions and not from the Greek originals.

The vast extent of the work of translation is impressive. Many translations are still extant and an even greater number are known by title only.[1] At first sight it looks as if all Greek works on science and philosophy had been translated into Arabic; but this is not so. Recent studies have shown that what in fact was translated was that section of Greek scientific and philosophical literature which was still valued in the late Hellenistic schools. This includes the whole of Aristotle except the *Politics*; even the *Poetics* was translated, though one wonders how intelligible it was to men who had no acquaintance with drama. The pre-Socratics were neglected, but some later writers received more attention than has been the case in the modern European tradition; indeed philosophical works of Galen have been preserved in Arabic which are not extant in Greek. Thus the translations of Greek works throw light not merely on the origins of philosophy in Arabic, but also on the later history of Greek science and philosophy in Hellenistic times.

All this work of translation was only possible because at various points there was contact with a living tradition.[2] Most important was the school of Gundē-Shāpūr.[3] From 765 to 870 the Persian-Nestorian family of Bokhtīshū' from this centre supplied the court physician to the caliphs, and at the same time were responsible for a teaching hospital in Baghdad. Besides the strictly medical curriculum there must also have been some work in philosophy here. Secondly there was the philosophical tradition of Alexandria. The fact that before the Arab conquest Syriac had been replacing Greek suggests that it was not in a healthy condition—perhaps because of the rising 'nationalism' of the Copts or their unmetaphysical outlook. Whatever the reason—and it may be connected with the weakness of Islamic intellectual life in Egypt—about 718 the college was moved to Antioch. Here it remained for over a century, but about 850 migrated eastwards to Ḥarrān, along the road to Mosul, and then about half a cenntury later was attracted to the metropolis, Baghdad. These migrations were primarily migrations of the teachers and also to some extent of the library. In Baghdad they seem to have taken a full share in the intellectual life of the capital or at least that section of it which was sympathetic to philosophy.

There were also other lines of philosophical tradition, but we are not so well informed about them. Besides the Alexandrian college in Ḥarrān, which was under Christian direction, there was a pagan centre belonging to the sect known as the Ṣābi'ans. Their religion included star-worship, but it had a basis in Greek philosophy, and in consequence of this they made important contributions to the arabizing of the Hellenistic intellectual tradition. In 872 one of their leading scholars, Thābit ibn-Qurra (d.901), who had already studied at Baghdad, quarrelled with other members of the sect and left Ḥarrān for the capital. Here with support from the caliph he devoted himself to translating and to composing original works, chiefly in medicine and mathematics; he also collected round him some younger Ṣābi'ans. It was not only in Baghdad, however, that philosophy was cultivated. The biographies of some of the leading philosophers makes it clear that there was also considerable interest in it in the eastern part of the caliphate; but it is not possible to say anything definite about this.

How exactly the transition was made from translation to the composition of original works is not altogether clear. It would be natural, however, for some of the scholars engaged in translation to want to write something original, either to add something to what was in the Greek works, or to provide a simple introduction for those unfamiliar with the Greek sciences. There was also a need to bring philosophical conclusions more into line with Islamic doctrines. This transition and these motives are exemplified in Abū-Yūsuf Ya'qūb ibn-Is'ḥāq al-Kindī (*c.*800–70). He is usually known as al-Kindī, and, as the first of the notable Islamic philosophers and the only one of Arabic descent, he is also called the 'philosopher of the Arabs' (*faylasūf al-'Arab*). The last reason for original philosophical writing was perhaps the most important, and his production has been described as essentially 'Greek philosophy for Muslims'.[4]

Al-Kindī's family had held a number of official posts in Arab parts of the caliphate; the chief of these had been the governorship of Kufa. He himself became attached to the caliphal court, and during the reign of al-Muʿtaṣim (833–42) was tutor to the latter's son. This was during the period of the Muʿtazilites' ascendancy (to be described in the next chapter), and al-Kindī seems to have shared their views on dogmatic questions. In this respect he was much closer to the main body of Islamic theological thought than most of the other philosophers. Early in the reign of al-Mutawakkil (847–61) there was a reversal of government policy and the Muʿtazilites fell from favour. This may have contributed to an unfortunate experience which befell al-Kindī; by the intrigues of two hostile courtiers his library was taken from him and removed to Basra for a time, but in the end he got it back again.

From this incident we know that al-Kindī had what was for the time a huge library. He must have spent the greater part of his time in study, and was an acknowledged expert in nearly all the Greek sciences. His numerous short writings suggest that he was an effective agent in spreading the knowledge of these sciences among the Muslims. The philosophical position which he adopted was by and large Neoplatonic, as was that of most of the Islamic philosophers. This was mainly the result of the form taken by the later Greek philosophical tradition when the Muslims came into contact with it. Though Aristotle was studied carefully, he was seen through Neoplatonic eyes. To increase the confusion there was a work in circulation among the Muslims known as *The Theology of Aristotle*, which has now been recognized as consisting of extracts from the Neoplatonic philosopher Plotinus. This work had a considerable vogue in its Arabic version. Its Neoplatonic doctrine of God must have seemed sufficiently close to Qur'ānic monotheism. At any rate al-Kindī accepted Neoplatonism with what must have seemed to him minor modifications. He felt capable of asserting that the truths revealed through prophets were metaphysical knowledge, and that there was no contradiction between philosophy and revelation. Presumably he meant that philosophy could be developed in a way that was both in accordance with its own nature and also compatible with revelation. He did not simply take over the views of others, but into the Neoplatonic doctrine of emanation quietly inserted a creation out of nothing, as if there was no difficulty in reconciling the two.

The other chief scholar in the Greek tradition during the early ʿAbbāsid period was ar-Rāzī (that is, the man from Rayy), well known in Europe as Rhazes. His full name is Abū-Bakr Muḥammad ibn-Zakariyyā' ar-Rāzī, and he is said to have been born in 865 and to have died in 923 or 932. His early life was spent in his native town of Rayy (near modern Teheran), and it was only after his thirtieth birthday that he began to study medicine in Baghdad. He practised as a physician and taught both at Rayy and Baghdad and also for short periods at some of the minor courts in the eastern regions of the caliphate.

His chief claim to fame is as a physician, and his medical works were long read and valued in Europe. Yet like most physicians of this period he was also something of a philosopher. Indeed philosophy might be said to take the place of religion for him, as it did for Plato, whom he greatly admired and tended to follow. It was through philosophy and the use of reason, he believed, that human life could be improved. This outlook finds expression in a simply written little book on ethics and the art of living, which has been translated into English under the title of *The Spiritual Physick.*[5] The translator speaks of his attitude as one of 'intellectual hedonism', which 'reflects very characteristically the outlook of the cultured Persian gentleman'. He had little use for religion, Islamic or any other. Doubtless he shared something of the outlook of the Persian secretary class, of whom he must have known many; but, though he is said to have had Manichaean sympathies, there is no clear evidence of this in his writings. Likewise, he is said to have had connections with the Ṣābi'an philosophical school of Ḥarrān; but his philosophy is more Platonic than either Neopythagorean (like that of the Ṣābi'ans) or Neoplatonic. Its precise source is, indeed, still something of a mystery, and he stands apart from the other Islamic philosophers. His ideal of life was of one devoted to intellectual pursuits, and his philosophy was of a piece with this. The ideal could not be made universal, but the philosophy justified his own use of his talents in helping to raise the level of Islamic culture, even if it was not a satisfactory account of what he in fact achieved.

The attraction of Greek science and philosophy for the Muslims seems to have been due in the first place to practical interests. The caliphs were concerned for their own health and that of those around them, and believed that the practitioners of Greek medical science could do something to help them. In this milieu, too, a high practical value was attached to astrology, which was not distinguished from astronomy. Astrological-astronomical works had an important place in the translation programme, and those competent in this discipline were received with favour at court. Since philosophy was closely associated with these sciences in teaching, it was natural that attention should be paid to it also. It is important to realize, however, that all this cultivation of the Greek tradition took place largely in isolation from the main stream of Islamic thought represented by the 'general religious movement'.

The contacts of this latter with the living Hellenistic tradition came about chiefly in two ways. Some men came to realize the usefulness of logical methods and of philosophy as a whole through having arguments with members of other religions. Such arguments seem to have been common. Among the works of St John of Damascus (d.750) is a 'Disputation between a Christian and a Saracen' which shows Christians the arguments they were likely to meet and possible lines of reply.[6] A record has also been preserved of the speech made by the Nestorian patriarch Timothy in 781 in a public discussion in the presence of the caliph.[7] In Iraq there were also Buddhists and members of Indian sects. Thus from an early date Muslims must have realized that they were living among people of high intellectual culture who criticized and rejected some of their religious beliefs, and the needs of polemics and apologetics would encourage them to pay some attention to philosophical concepts and methods.

The other form of contact was through the conversion to Islam of men who had been brought up in the Hellenistic tradition of Iraq. This is difficult to document exactly, but it is known that many of the most prominent religious scholars of the early ʿAbbāsid period were converts or the sons of converts. Allowance must be made, however, for the fact that in Iraq—in contrast to Egypt—many men, even when they had not received explicit Hellenistic teaching, seem to have had a natural penchant towards the use of reason. Discussions of legal questions were prominent in the general religious movement, and some of the scholars involved, notably Abū-Ḥanīfa and his followers, favoured rational forms of argument. When such scholars turned to theology, it was natural that they should make use of reasoning in this sphere also. Other scholars, and in particular the Ḥanbalites, strenuously opposed rational methods in both jurisprudence and theology. The discipline of rational, philosophical or speculative theology was known as Kalām (literally 'speech'), and must have been well established before the end of the eighth century, since we hear of discussions in the salon of the Barmakids.

One of the prominent early Mutakallimūn or exponents of Kalām was Ḍirār ibn-ʿAmr, whose *floruit* was about the reign of Hārūn ar-Rashīd (786–809).[8] He is known to have visited Baghdad, but spent most of his life in Basra, where he is reported to have been the leader of the discussions on Kalām before the Muʿtazilite Abū-l-Hudhayl. Only brief accounts of his views on various points have survived, but these cover all the matters discussed at the time from politics to physics. His political position may be described as moderate, and he was sufficiently versed in the Greek tradition to write a book on the Aristotelian doctrine of substances and accidents. In respect of theology in the narrower sense he was broadly speaking a Sunnite, and he seems to have been the first exponent of a conception later regarded as characteristic of Ashʿarism, the conception of *kasb* or 'acquisition'. This was an attempt to reconcile the individual's responsibility for his acts with God's omnipotence. All Muslims held that God was omnipotent and also that he was a just judge; but to condemn people to Hell for acts for which they were not responsible would be unjust. Ḍirār's solution of the problem was that God creates our acts, whereas we 'acquire' them. Obviously any human act, such as shooting an arrow, presupposes that all the things involved will continue to function according to their natures. All, however, are created by God, as indeed is also the agent's power to initiate the act. Yet despite this the act is in some sense *his* act, and the term *kasb* is an attempt to indicate this relationship between the human agent and his act. It probably had a commercial connotation and meant 'having it credited to him' rather than simply 'acquiring'. Other renderings would be 'appropriating it' or 'making it his'.[9]

Another scholar who was a contemporary of Ḍirār's and participated with him in theological debates in the salon of Yaḥyā the Barmakid, was Hishām ibn-al-Ḥakam. In many respects his views were similar to those of Ḍirār, but in politics he was an Imāmite (or Rāfiḍite). While Ḍirār seems to have been an Arab, Hishām was probably a non-Arab, and moreover in Kufa, where he spent most of his life, was in touch with at least one of the groups which mingled dualistic speculations with Greek ideas.

The names are preserved of half a dozen other scholars who seem to have been followers of Ḍirār and to have constituted something like a school. They are sometimes referred to collectively as Ahl al-Ithbāt, 'the upholders of the affirmation' (*sc.* of God's omnipotence). One or two others are also known to have engaged in Kalām who were neither Muʿtazilites nor followers of Ḍirār. In the period after Ḍirār and Hishām the development of Kalām was largely in the hands of the Muʿtazilite sect, but some of the earliest Muʿtazilites worked closely with these two men and seem to have been influenced by them. Indeed for a time the term 'Muʿtazilite' (originally a nickname) was used loosely and was applied to Ḍirār and others who employed Greek ideas in theological discussions. It is clear that all the early theologians mentioned were very interested in Hellenistic thought and had a wide knowledge of it, though they were perhaps not as expert as the translators and the philosophers like al-Kindī. During the excitement of the pioneer exploration of Hellenistic philosophy men of diverse views and interests seem to have mixed freely with one another, but before the end of the ninth century the philosophical theologians and the philosophers proper were working in complete isolation from one another.

The phrase 'the first wave of Hellenism' used as the title of Part 2 describes this first period of enthusiasm for the study of the Greek tradition, and also indicates that it was limited in certain respects. Though the theologians sometimes discussed questions that were essentially philosophical, more and more they lost interest in such matters. What they continued to use was certain methods of argument they had learnt and a few ideas which were found helpful in arguments with other Muslims and with members of other religions. By about 850, however, this 'first wave' had subsided, and no fresh Greek elements were taken into Kalām until the late eleventh century with al-Ghazālī.

Ḍirār and his followers have been described as a 'forgotten school'. The Muslim writers of books on heresies could not conceive of a development of doctrine but thought that it remained static and unchanging. All they did therefore was to mention heretical views and to classify theologians on that basis. Though Ḍirār was in fact working his way towards some of the formulations of Sunnite Kalām, the heresiographers failed to appreciate this, and recorded some of his incidental speculations, such as the suggestion that on the day of resurrection the faithful would receive a sixth sense by which they would perceive God's essence. The modern historian, thinking in terms of development, is able to see that Ḍirār and his associates made important contributions to the elaboration of Kalām in both its Sunnite and Muʿtazilite versions.

NOTES

(The chapter corresponds to *Formative Period*, ch.7, 180-208.)

1. Translations: See *GAL*, i.219-29; *GALS*, 1.362-71; Graf (B/A), ii.109-14, 122-32, etc. The basic work is Moritz Steinschneider, *Die arabischen Übersetzungen aus dem Griechischen*, Graz 1960; reprinted from various journals dated 1889 to 1896. Other manuscripts have since been discovered. See also Ibn-an-Nadīm, *Kitāb al-Fihrist*, part 7, section 1: translation by Bayard Dodge, *The Fihrist of al-Nadīm*, New York 1970, vol.2. Franz Rosenthal, *The Classical Heritage in Islam*, London 1975; a volume of translations from Arabic.
2. See especially Richard Walzer, 'Islamic Philosophy' in *Greek into Arabic*, Oxford 1962, 1-28; other important articles are also reprinted here. Max Meyerhof, 'Von Alexandrien nach Bagdad: ein Beitrag zur Geschichte des philosophischen und medizinischen Unterrichts bei den Arabern', *Sitzungsberichte der preussischen Akademie der Wissenschaften*, Berlin 1930, Phil.hist.Kl., 389-429. F. E. Peters, *Aristotle and the Arabs, the Aristotelian Tradition in Islam*, New York 1968; the same author's *Allah's Commonwealth, a History of Islam in the Near East 600-1100 A.D.*, New York 1973, deals in some detail with Hellenistic influences in intellectual history.
3. *EI*², art. Gondēshāpūr (Aydin Sayili).
4. *EI*², art. al-Kindī (J. Jolivet, R. Rashed). George N. Atiyeh, *Al-Kindī, the Philosopher of the Arabs*, Rawalpindi 1966. Afred L. Ivry, *Al-Kindī's Metaphysics*, Albany 1974; translation with commentary.
5. His book *The Spiritual Physick* has been translated by A. J. Arberry, London 1950.
6. 'Disceptatio/Disputatio Christiani et Saraceni', in Migne, *Patrologia Graeca*, 94.1585-96; 96.1336-48.
7. Syriac text edited and translated by A. Mingana in *Woodbrooke Studies*, ii, Cambridge 1928, 1-162.
8. Josef van Ess, 'Ḍirār b. ʿAmr und die 'cahmīya': Biographie einer

vergessenen Schule', *Der Islam*, 43 (1967), 241-79; 44 (1968), 1-70, 318-20; also art. Ḍirār b. ʿAmr in *EI*², Supplement.

9. M. Schwarz, '"Acquisition" (*Kasb*) in Early Kalām', in S. M. Stern et al., edd., *Islamic Philosophy and the Classical Tradition* (Richard Walzer Festschrift), Oxford 1972, 355-87.

Chapter Eight

THE MU'TAZILITES

In the second half of the nineteenth century European scholars were attracted by some of the views of the Mu'tazilites and studied them with great sympathy. In an account of them published in 1865 Heinrich Steiner of Zürich spoke of them as 'the free-thinkers of Islam'. At this period the later Sunnite philosophical theology or Kalām was little known in Europe and still less appreciated. The Mu'tazilites were seen as standing for freedom of the will and human responsibility; in other respects they adopted sensible, almost nineteenth-century liberal attitudes. It was felt that Islam would have been ever so much more congenial to the European if only the Mu'tazilites had not been replaced by the dry-as-dust, hide-bound, hair-splitting Ash'arites and their like. In the twentieth century, however, Western scholars gradually realized that this whole conception of the Mu'tazilites was inaccurate. They were not free-thinkers but quite definite Muslims, even if they indulged in speculation on some points; and, far from being liberal in outlook, they were behind the unhappy episode of the 'Inquisition' in the ninth century. In other ways, too, their theological views were linked with the politics of the day. Finally it was realized that some at least had been zealous apologists for Islam towards members of other religions.

The Mu'tazilites who attracted the European scholars and who were important in the history of Islamic theology were those who were involved in the process of bringing Greek conceptions into the discussions of Islamic dogma, that is, in the first elaboration of the discipline of Kalām. As has just been indicated, the name 'Mu'tazilite' was at first used in a fairly wide sense to include men like Ḍirār ibn-'Amr, but was later restricted to those who accepted the five points of the Mu'tazilite dogmatic position (to be enumerated later). Nowadays 'Mu'tazilite' is normally used only in the restricted sense by both Muslim and Western scholars, and this usage is followed here.[1]

The main founders of the Mu'tazilite school, as it came to be, were four men: Muʿammar, Abū-l-Hudhayl and an-Naẓẓām at Basra and Bishr ibn-al-Muʿtamir at Baghdad. The dates of their deaths are given as 830, 841 (or later), 836 (or 845) and 825, but none appear to have been publicly active after about 820, and their main activity was possibly much earlier. Muʿammar was roughly a contemporary of Ḍirār and is said to have had Bishr as a pupil. Abū-l-Hudhayl was sufficiently well known to take part in a symposium on love in the salon of Yaḥyā the Barmakid (before 803), and succeeded Ḍirār as leader of the discussions on Kalām in Basra. Bishr ibn-al-Muʿtamir was imprisoned because of Shīʿite sympathies during the reign of Hārūn ar-Rashīd (786–809), presumably after the fall of the Barmakids in 803. Thus it is likely that it was during that reign that Muʿtazilite Kalām began to take shape.

This account of the beginnings of Muʿtazilism differs from that given by ash-Shahrastānī, which has been widely accepted as the standard one, not least by occidental scholars. His account places the origin of Muʿtazilism fully half a century earlier in the circle of al-Ḥasan al-Baṣrī (d.728). On one occasion al-Ḥasan was asked whether the grave sinner should be regarded as a believer or as an unbeliever. When he hesitated, one of the circle, Wāṣil ibn-ʿAṭāʾ, broke in with the assertion that the grave sinner was neither but was in an 'intermediate position' (*manzila bayn al-manzilatayn*—literally, 'a position between the two positions'). On Wāṣil's leaving the circle, accompanied by some of the members, and establishing himself at another pillar of the mosque, al-Ḥasan remarked 'he has withdrawn (*iʿtazala*) from us'; and this gave rise to the collective name Muʿtazila, 'withdrawers'.

There are strong reasons for rejecting this story. There are numerous versions of it, some much earlier than ash-Shahrastānī, and the versions differ at important points. The person who withdrew is sometimes said to be ʿAmr ibn-ʿUbayd, not Wāṣil, and the circle from which he withdrew to be not that of al-Ḥasan but of his successor Qatāda. The phrase with *iʿtazala* is also ascribed to various people. A further difficulty is that Wāṣil and ʿAmr are both sometimes spoken of as Khārijites, and their views—to judge from the little that is recorded of them—seem at least as close to those of some moderate Khārijites as to those of the Muʿtazilites. Moreover there is nothing to suggest that Wāṣil and ʿAmr had any special knowledge of Greek thought or were interested in it; they died in 748 and 761 respectively.

One point in the story which may be accepted, however, is that there was some connection between Muʿtazilism and the disciples of al-Ḥasan al-Baṣrī, among whom ʿAmr was prominent. The scholars in al-Ḥasan's following seem to have remained on friendly terms with one another for at least forty years, even when their views diverged. Wāṣil and others may have held something like the five principles of the Muʿtazilites, though in an embryonic form. Even if this is so, however, the implicit doctrinal (and political) position was not the distinctive contribution of the Muʿtazilites to the growth of Islamic theology; it was their embracing of Kalām.

Such considerations make it probable that it was Abū-l-Hudhayl who put forward the story about 'withdrawing' and who insisted that the only true Muʿtazilites were those who accepted the five principles, which by this time had been theologically elaborated. Insistence on the five principles excluded some of the followers of Ḍirār and gave doctrinal cohesion to most of the practitioners of Kalām, so that they could now be said to be a genuine school. The use of the story had also advantages. It gave the term 'withdrawers' an unobjectionable meaning, of which those so called need not be ashamed; originally it had probably been a nickname meaning those who had 'withdrawn' from both ʿAlī and his opponents in the first civil war. The story also presented the Muʿtazilites as having genuine roots in Islamic life, and so met the objection that they were introducing foreign un-Islamic ideas. At some point they seem to have been taunted with being followers of Jahm ibn-Ṣafwān—a man with a bad reputation, perhaps because he had fought along with infidels against Muslims. Some verses ascribed to Bishr ibn-al-Muʿtamir, which are probably authentic, speak of Ḍirār as a follower of Jahm and himself of 'Amr ibn-ʿUbayd. Both Wāṣil and ʿAmr would be preferable to Jahm as intellectual figure-heads for the school, and there were similarities between their political attitudes and those of the Muʿtazilites in the early ninth century.

In the 'Inquisition' begun by al-Ma'mūn the doctrine of the createdness of the Qur'ān, of which public profession had to be made, was a doctribe proclaimed by the Muʿtazilites. Several Muʿtazilites had high positions in al-Ma'mūn's administration and must have supported his policy of attempting to reconcile opposing interests by the 'Inquisition'. In other respects, too, the views implicit in al-Ma'mūn's policies were close to those recorded of Bishr ibn-al-Muʿtamir and the other Muʿtazilites of Baghdad. The Muʿtazilites of Basra, following Abū-l-Hudhayl, were less favourable to ʿAlī but seem also to have been interested in reducing tensions within the community.

The first of the five principles of the Muʿtazilites was that of 'unity', or, more correctly, 'assertion of unity', since the Arabic word *tawḥīd* means literally 'the making one'. This implied much more than the mere statement that God is one and that there are not many gods. Muslims enumerate ninety-nine 'beautiful names' (*al-asmā' al-ḥusnā*) of God mentioned in the Qur'ān, and of these seven received special attention from the early theologians: the Knowing (or omniscient), the Powerful (or Almighty), the Willing, the Living, the Hearing, the Seeing, the Speaking. Some theologians held that God had attributes (*ṣifāt*) corresponding to these names, such as Knowledge, Power, Will. To the Muʿtazilites, however, this was seen as introducing an element of multiplicity into the unity of God's nature or essence (*nafs, dhāt*), and in insisting on 'unity' they were asserting that these attributes had no sort of independent or hypostatic existence, but were merged in the unity of God's being. In so far as God knew, he knew by himself or by his essence, and not by any hypostatic Knowledge. (In passing it may be noted that Arabic-speaking Christian theologians commonly identified the three hypostases (or *personae*) of the Trinity with three attributes, such as Existence, Knowledge, Life.)

The discussion of the attributes by Muslims seems to have developed out of discussions about the Qur'ān. These may have begun before 750, but it is more likely that it was only towards the end of the century that there were vigorous arguments about the Qur'ān and that these arose from questions connected with Qadarism. Muslims in general accepted the view that the Qur'ān is the Speech (or Word) of God. The Qur'ān, however, has many references to historical events, and at the same time phrases suggesting its pre-existence on a heavenly 'table' (*lawḥ*—85.21f.). From these points it could be argued that the historical events were predetermined. A contrary argument to this is found in a letter of al-Ma'mūn about the 'Inquisition'. He quotes the verse 'thus we narrate to you accounts of what has gone before' (20.99), and draws the inference that the Qur'ān was produced *after* the happenings of which it gives accounts. Even if the discussions began from Qadarism, however, by the time of al-Ma'mūn (as explained above) what was at issue was rather the relative political powers of the caliph and his ministers on the one hand and the ulema on the other hand.

Arguments were developed on both sides with great subtlety, and the range of topics included in the discussion became ever wider. Central to the arguments was the interpretation of Qur'ānic phrases. Thus from the words 'we have made it (*jaʿalnā-hu*) an Arabic Qur'ān' (43.3) it was argued that this 'making' implies creating. One of the most ingenious arguments was from the passages, of which there are several, where a speech, such as 'I am thy Lord', is addressed to Moses from a bush. The upholders of uncreatedness then insisted that, if this is created, a created thing must have said to Moses 'I am thy Lord', so that Moses became guilty of idolatry in accepting a created thing as his Lord.

From arguments of this kind, which were often only verbal juggling, the discussion passed on to deeper questions. The Muʿtazilites tried to baffle their opponents by asking them about their own 'utterance' of the Qur'ān; when a Muslim recites the Qur'ān, his reciting or 'utterance' of it is surely not uncreated. This puzzle rests of course on the special nature of speech, and in particular on the difference between the relation of speech to the speaker and that of the thing made or created to its maker or creator. Speech is an expression of the character of the speaker to a much greater extent than an artefact is an expression of the character of its maker, and is indeed in a sense one with the speaker, whereas the thing made is separate from its maker. Modern electronic devices have multiplied the puzzles in this field; for instance, when I hear a recording of a speech by a man now dead, am I hearing the man himself?

The conception of the Word or Speech of God as eternal is one of the points which have suggested to European scholars that the development of Islamic theology was largely due to Christian influences. In this case there is the obvious similarity between the Christian belief that Jesus is the eternal Word of God and a phrase about him in the Qur'ān (3.45). The parallel is not exact, however, for the word commonly applied to the Qur'ān is *kalām*, which is properly 'speech', whereas the phrase used of Jesus is *kalima min-hu*, 'a word from him (God)'. Yet, even if the similarity were closer than this, it does not follow that there was direct influence. As has already been explained, the development of Islamic theology came about because of tensions within the community of Muslims. Muslim theologians did not simply copy Christian ideas, but it is possible that a man might adopt a Christian idea if it fitted into his arguments against Muslim rivals.

The transition from discussions about the Speech of God to a general discussion of the attributes is an easy one. Those who say that the Qur'ān is the uncreated or eternal speech seem to an opponent to be asserting that there are two eternal beings, God and the Qur'ān. One of the ways in which they tried to escape from this conclusion was by maintaining that the Qur'ān is God's knowledge or part of his knowledge. They can then say to an opponent, 'Is it possible for God to exist and his Knowledge not to exist?' If it was conceded that his Knowledge existed eternally, then the Qur'ān must also exist eternally. The Mu'tazilites avoided this denial of their doctrine of 'unity' by holding that God had no such hypostatic Knowledge in any way distinct from himself. They then applied this view to the other attributes.

The second of the five principles defining the Mu'tazilite position was that of justice or righteousness (*'adl*), and they liked to speak of themselves as 'the people of unity and justice'. In their concern for the observance of the moral laws of Islam the Mu'tazilites were heirs of the puritan outlook of the Khārijites, which is not surprising in view of the Khārijite sympathies of Wāṣil and 'Amr. This concern, however, is more linked with other principles than with the principle of justice. The latter came to be primarily associated with their belief in the freedom of the human will and the individual's responsibility for his acts, the connection being that, if God condemns men to Hell for acts for which they were not responsible, he is acting unjustly. In this the Muʿtazilites were heirs of that section of the 'general religious movement' which favoured Qadarism.

Since all Muʿtazilites accepted the freedom of the will in general, the views recorded of them tend to be about subordinate questions. The central concern here was the relation of God to the ultimate destiny of human beings—Paradise (Heaven) or Hell. By insisting on human freedom and responsibility the Muʿtazilites made a person's ultimate destiny depend on himself. The basic thought was that God in revelation showed the believers what they ought to do to attain Paradise, and then left it to each of them to do it or not to do it. This gave a tidy rational scheme with Paradise as the reward for obedience and Hell as the punishment for disobedience. It is presupposed that God is bound to reward and punish in this way, in accordance with the third principle. In due course, however, they became aware of complications. What about children? If they had not committed any sins, should they not go to Paradise? But, if they went to Paradise, they had not earned it by their obedience, and was that fair to those who had?

In this connection a reference to the story of the three brothers is not amiss. Though it is usually told to explain al-Ashʿarī's abandonment of the Muʿtazilites, it seems rather to contain a criticism of the Muʿtazilites of Baghdad by those of Basra. According to the story there were once three brothers, one good, one wicked, and one who died as a child; the first is in Paradise, the second in Hell, and the third in something less than Paradise where he is neither rewarded nor punished. The third complains that by being made to die as a child he has been given no chance to merit Paradise by his obedience —the commands and prohibitions of Islam were not applicable to children below a certain age, and so these could not be held either to obey or to disobey. He is given the reply that God caused him to die early because he foresaw that, if he grew up, he would be thoroughly wicked. Upon this the second brother asks why he also had not been made to die young before he committed the sins which brought him to Hell. To this, of course, there is no answer. The whole story is a critique of certain Muʿtazilites who held that God is bound to do what is best (*al-aṣlaḥ*) for human beings. The discussions of such matters have also further ramifications, such as the unmerited sufferings of children and the sufferings of animals. The latter topic may have been introduced as a result of contact with Indian sects, though it was also discussed by Christian theologians.

The remaining three of the five principles, though used to define the Muʿtazilite position, especially in its political aspect, hardly appeared in the theological discussions. In al-Ashʿarī's account of the opinions of individual Muʿtazilites in his *Maqālāt* by far the greater part (about nine-tenths) is concerned with points which fall under the first two principles. The third principle is 'the promise and the threat' (*al-waʿd wa-l-waʿīd*), or Paradise and Hell, and it implies that God is bound to reward the obedient with Paradise as he has promised and to punish the disobedient with Hell as he has threatened. Among the points discussed under this heading were: what is faith? what is the difference between grave and light sins, and ultimately between good and evil? from what kind of men can Ḥadīth be accepted? Such questions arose out of the debates between Murjiʾites and Khārijites. The Muʿtazilites remained close to the Khārijite position and, for example, opposed the view common among followers of Abū-Ḥanīfa with Murjiʾite sympathies that sinners of the community would ultimately be transferred from Hell to Paradise at the intercession of the Prophet.

The fourth principle was that of the 'intermediate position', said to have been introduced by Wāṣil. In practice it led to political compromise on the basis of leaving certain questions undecided. One did not decide whether ʿUthmān was a believer or an unbeliever, or whether some of those who participated in the civil war after his death were in the right and others in the wrong. The aim seems to have been that Muslims should in some sense accept the whole of their past history and so avoid a situation in which some identified themselves with one strand in it and others with another. This aim is commendable, but the 'intermediate position' had a negative aspect; one neither wholly identified oneself with, say, ʿAlī, nor wholly disassociated oneself from him. The eventual Sunnite position was one of more whole-hearted acceptance, and probably owed more to the conception of 'postponement' (*irjāʾ*).

The fifth principle is that of 'commanding the right and forbidding the wrong' (*al-amr bi-l-maʿrūf wa-n-nahy ʿan al-munkar*). This was understood by the Muʿtazilites and others as the obligation to maintain justice and oppose injustice by tongue, hand and sword, where one was able to do so successfully. It could cover both moral exhortation of one's fellow-Muslims and moral criticism of unjust rulers and even revolt against them. For the earlier Muʿtazilites, at least, it implied supporting the ʿAbbāsids.

Enough is known about the leading Muʿtazilites to make it possible to give an account of their distinctive individual views, but such a detailed study would be out of place in the present survey. The following is a brief sketch of the developments up to about 950.

The Muʿtazilite school of Basra is probably earlier than that of Baghdad, and grew out of the teaching of men like al-Ḥasan al-Baṣrī and Ḍirār. As already mentioned, Muʿammar seems to have been a contemporary of Ḍirār. Because he explored the use of Greek conceptions in a somewhat idiosyncratic way, he may have had less direct influence on later developments.[2] The man who did most to give a definite shape to Muʿtazilism in Basra was the slightly younger Abū-l-Hudhayl, also known as al-ʿAllāf, said to have been born between 748 and 753. He probably remained active in Basra until about 818 when he settled in Baghdad. In his thinking he made considerable use of the Aristotelian conception of substance and accident, but, in accordance with the atomism which came to dominate Islamic theology, he regarded each accident as lasting for only a single (atomic) moment.[3] Also at Basra was an-Naẓẓām (Ibrāhīm ibn-Sayyār), a follower of Abū-l-Hudhayl but probably not much younger. He seems to have been more interested in the scientific side of Greek thought, perhaps as a result of the teaching of the non-Muʿtazilite Hishām ibn-al-Ḥakam, whose lectures he is said to have attended.[4] In the generation after Abū-l-Hudhayl and an-Naẓẓām none of the Muʿtazilites of Basra was outstanding.

The founder of the school of Baghdad was without question Bishr ibn-al-Muʿtamir. He presumably studied in Basra, since he wrote refutations in verse of several of the leading scholars of Basra, Muʿtazilites and others. Along with some of these he participated in the Barmakid symposium on love. It was presumably after the fall of the Barmakids that he was imprisoned by Hārūn ar-Rashīd for alleged Rāfiḍite sympathies; but it is unlikely that he was a Rāfiḍite in the strict sense, though he certainly thought highly of ʿAlī. He and some of his disciples are found at the court of al-Maʾmūn in Khorasan in 817, and presumably returned to Baghdad in 819 along with the caliph. Bishr may have begun Muʿtazilite teaching in Baghdad in the Barmakid period, but the real founding of the school of Baghdad may not have been until 819. The other Muʿtazilites prominent at the court of al-Maʾmūn made little contribution to theological discussion, but a little later there was a notable triad: al-Iskāfī (d.854) and the two Jaʿfars, Jaʿfar ibn-Ḥarb (d.850) and Jaʿfar ibn-al-Mubashshir (d.848). About the time when they were active the doctrine became popular in Baghdad that God is bound to do what is best (*aṣlaḥ*) for human beings. The two Jaʿfars were also noted for their ascetic way of life.

With these three men the great creative period of Muʿtazilism, its Golden Age, may be said to have come to an end. When the policy of the 'Inquisition' was abandoned about 850, they lost their political influence and their contacts with the caliphal government. Gradually they were transformed into a small coterie of academic theologians in touch neither with the masses of the people nor with the main streams of Islamic thought. There were all the marks of a Silver Age; the zest and excitement of the previous period had been lost, and thinkers, instead of exploring fresh fields, were seeking to introduce greater refinement into the answers to old questions. Round about the year 900 this trend is partially reversed and an element of originality is found in three men, two in Basra and one in Baghdad.

Somewhere about 885 the headship of the school of Basra fell to al-Jubbā'ī (Abū-'Alī Muḥammad).[5] Against the Mu'tazilites of Baghdad he argued that it is only in respect of religion that God is bound to do what is best for human beings, namely, by sending prophets to bring his messages to them. He saw that God's dealings with individuals cannot be rationally explained but remain inscrutable; and he may have made some use of the story of 'the three brothers'. The only obligation upon God, he insisted, is that he should be consistent with himself. On his death in 915 he was succeeded by his son Abū-Hāshim ('Abd-as-Salām ibn-Muḥammad al-Jubbā'ī). Abū-Hāshim is chiefly remembered for a novel theory of 'states' (*aḥwāl,* sing. *ḥāl*). When one says 'God is knowing', 'knowing', he held, expresses the 'state' of God's essence distinct from that essence. This was in effect an attempt to maintain that in an attribute like 'knowledge' there is nothing hypostatic or quasi-substantive. Thus baldly stated the theory is not impressive, but one or two later Ash'arite theologians found something attractive in it. Abū-Hāshim died in 933.

About the same time the head of the school of Baghdad was a man who is known both as al-Ka'bī and as Abū-l-Qāsim al-Balkhī. He discussed the attributes of God and the question of what God is bound to do for his creatures, but he is noted above all for his working out of the atomistic view of nature. He held, for example, that an accident does not endure for two successive moments of time, but that every substance and every accident is created afresh by God in each moment. God's omnipotence implies that he can do what he likes without anything resembling a stable policy. Despite the idea of causal continuity in nature implicit in Greek science and philosophy a dominant place in their thought was given to atomism by Islamic thinkers and not least by the Ash'arites. This may be due in part to the experience of Arabian nomads in the desert, where the irregularity of nature can be more obvious than its regularity, or to sedentary peoples' experience of the whims of autocratic rulers.

While it may be difficult for the Western scholar of the last quarter of the twentieth century to share the enthusiasm for Mu'tazilism of the scholars of a century earlier, it certainly made an outstanding contribution to Islamic thought by the assimilation of a large number of Greek ideas and methods of argument. This was essentially the achievement of the great Mu'tazilites of the Golden Age. It must be constantly emphasized, however, that this was no simple acceptance of Greek beliefs because they seemed true and superior to Arab or Qur'ānic beliefs. It is rather the case that whatever was taken from the Greeks was accepted because it was useful, that is, useful in their arguments with other Muslims and with non-Muslims. Since the Muʿtazilites were regarded as heretics, however, by the Sunnites, many of their ideas and doctribes could not be taken over directly by Sunnism; but what could happen was that, when Sunnite theologians were arguing against Muʿtazilites, they might find themselves forced by the course of the argument to adopt some of the ideas of their opponents. Perhaps it could be said that the function of the Muʿtazilites was to take over all Greek ideas that seemed even remotely useful to the formulation of Islamic doctrine, so that it could then be left to others to sift these ideas in order to discover which were genuinely assimilable. In the end many ideas were retained, but seldom in precisely the form in which the Muʿtazilites had presented them.

NOTES

1. Muʿtazilism generally: *Formative Period,* chs 8 and 10,2 (pp.209-50, 297-303); Sezgin, *GAS,* i.613-24, good bibliography; Albert N. Nader, *Le systeme philosophique des Muʿtazila,* Beirut 1956 (also in Arabic), presents Muʿtazilite theology as a system without considering historical development; H. S. Nyberg, 'Zum Kampf zwischen Islam und Manichäismus', *Orientalische Literatur-Zeitung,* xxxii (1929), 425-41; do., *EI*[1], art. Muʿtazila, now out-of-date in some respects, and the conjecture that the early Muʿtazilites were propagandists for the ʿAbbāsids is to be rejected; Josef van Ess, *Frühe muʿtazilitische Häresiographie,* Beirut 1971, texts with introduction; Watt, 'Was Wāṣil a Khārijite?' in *Islamwissenschaftliche Abhandlungen* (Fritz Meier Festschrift), ed. R. Gramlich, Wiesbaden 1974, 306-11.
2. H. Daiber, *Das theologisch-philosophische System des Muʿammar b. ʿAbbād as-Sulamī* (Beiruter Texte und Studien, 19), Beirut 1975; Anwar G. Cheyne, 'Muʿammar ibn ʿAbbād al-Sulamī . . .', *Muslim World,* li (1961), 311-20; Harry A. Wolfson, 'Muʿammar's Theory of *Maʿnā*', *Arabic and Islamic Studies in honour of Hamilton, A. R. Gibb,* ed. G. Makdisi, Leiden 1965, 673-88.
3. R. M. Frank, 'The Divine Attributes according to the Teaching of Abūl Hudhayl al-ʿAllāf', *Museon,* lxxxii (1969), 451-506.
4. J. van Ess, *Das Kitāb an-Nakṭ des Naẓẓām,* Göttingen 1972.
5. *EI*[2], art. (al-) Djubbāʾī (L. Gardet); D. Gimaret, 'Matériaux pour une bibliographie des Ǧubbāʾī', *Journal Asiatique,* 264 (1976), 277-332.

Chapter Nine

THE POLARIZATION OF SUNNISM AND SHĪʿISM

In the history of Islamic religion the main feature of the century from 850 to 950 was that it became polarized into definite Sunnite and Shīʿite forms. The Muslim scholarly tradition has no conception of development, and so the Sunnites see Sunnism as having been the belief of Muslims from the beginning. Modern scholars using the concept of development, on the other hand, can show how Sunnism gradually attained a fuller and more precise formulation of its beliefs, as circumstances forced the Muslims to decide between rival interpretations of basic texts.

It was in the aftermath of the Inquisition that Sunnism may be said to have become the official religion of the caliphate. The policy of the Inquisition was abandoned by a series of measures in the first two or three years of the reign of al-Mutawakkil (847–61), and from this time onward Sunnism was the form of religion followed, at least *de facto,* by the ʿAbbāsid caliphs. Apart from this political decision, however, various other processes were taking place which together led to the consolidation of Sunnism in something like its final form.[1]

One of these processes was a clearer formulation of the basic principles or 'roots' of jurisprudence, and a widening area of agreement between jurists.[2] Previously each of the main centres of legal thought had tended to go its own way and had merely said, 'The teaching of our school is . . .', or had supported it by reference to a distinguished earlier member of the school. In time, however, some points of law came to be justified by quoting a Ḥadīth about something Muḥammad had said or done; this, of course, was in those cases where there was no clear Qur'ānic statement, or where the interpretation of the Qur'ān was disputed. As a result of the work of the jurist ash-Shāfiʿī (767–820) the methodological superiority of justifying legal principles by Ḥadīth came to be generally recognized and all the schools began to claim that their teachings were in accordance with Qur'ān and Ḥadīth as two 'roots' of law (*uṣūl al-fiqh*). Ash-Shāfiʿī also introduced other two 'roots', 'analogy' (*qiyās*) and 'consensus' (*ijmāʿ*), but not all the schools recognized these. By about 900 the four Sunnite schools or rites (*madhāhib*) which still exist—Ḥanafites, Ḥanbalites, Mālikites and Shāfiʿites—had a fairly definite shape, and there were also some minor schools which subsequently faded away. No new school with a distinctive methodology was founded after this date.

The development of jurisprudence led to advances in the study of Ḥadīth.[3] Much care was taken in distinguishing 'sound' Ḥadīth from others by scrutiny of the *isnāds,* and great collections of Ḥadīth were formed for legal purposes. The best known are those of al-Bukhārī (d.870) and Muslim (d.875), and in the course of the tenth century these and four others came to be accepted as specially authoritative, and are sometimes described by the occidental term 'canonical'. This was another aspect of the consolidation of Sunnism.

Something similar was happening in Qur'ānic studies.[4] The interpretation of the text of the Qur'ān had always received much attention from Muslim scholars, and by about 900 there was wide agreement about the interpretation of many verses. All that was best in the work of the previous two and a half centuries was taken up into the great Qur'ān-commentary of aṭ-Ṭabarī (d.923), which faithfully preserves the more important divergent views on questions of interpretation. Another scholar Ibn-Mujāhid (d.935) devoted himself to the study of the variants in the Qur'ānic text, and as a result of his work seven sets of readings came to be accepted as equally correct.

In the elaboration and formulation of Sunnite dogma there was also a growing measure of agreement. This came about despite the fact that there were two opposing trends in respect of what might be called theological method. Something has already been said about Kalām or rational theology, and an account has been given of the views of men like Ḍirār and the Muʿtazilites. Vehemently opposed to these Mutakallimūn were the Ahl al-Ḥadīth, the 'people of the Ḥadīth', who probably included most of the serious scholars of the period and not merely the specialists in the study of Ḥadīth. The Ahl al-Ḥadīth contained many shades of theological opinion, but the majority of them were in a general sense 'conservative'. In contrast many of the Mutakallimūn, especially the Muʿtazilites, might be called 'liberal' or 'radical'. Earlier Western students of these matters tended to think that all practitioners of Kalām were Muʿtazilites up to the time of al-Ashʿarī; but the researches of the last forty years have made it clear that in the ninth century there were Mutakallimūn whose dogmatic position was closely akin to that of the 'conservatives' among the Ahl al-Ḥadīth.

The foremost representative of the Ahl al-Ḥadīth in the first half of the ninth century was Aḥmad ibn-Ḥanbal (780–855).[5] From him the Ḥanbalite legal school took its name, and there was a distinctive Ḥanbalite theological tradition closely associated with the legal school. His eminence came partly from his outstanding intellectual ability and partly from the fact that in the Inquisition he was one of the few ulema who refused to make a public profession of belief in the createdness of the Qur'ān. Several credal statements have been preserved setting out his position (and that of most of the Ahl al-Ḥadīth) on the doctrinal questions which had hitherto been discussed, such as God's determination of events. Some of these credal statements may have been slightly modified by the later Ḥanbalites who transmitted them, but there is no change of substance. Emphasis was placed on the uncreatedness of the Qur'ān, and Aḥmad ibn-Ḥanbal insisted that even the human utterance (*lafẓ*) of the Qur'ān was uncreated. The close relation of religion and politics in Islam is shown by the fact that there is an article to the effect that 'the best of the community after the Prophet is Abū-Bakr, then 'Umar, then 'Uthmān, then 'Alī'. Despite earlier questioning of the position of 'Uthmān this became the final Sunnite position.

Throughout the ninth century and later the Sunnite position was also being given fuller formulation by the Ḥanafites, the followers of Abū-Ḥanīfa in law and, to a great extent, also in theology.[6] Though the Ḥanafites believed in the use of reasoning in legal matters (and are prominent among the Ahl ar-Ra'y, the upholders of individual reasoning in law), not all of them allowed the use of reasoning in questions of doctrine. This did not greatly affect their credal statements, however. These are ascribed to Abū-Ḥanīfa himself, but are clearly later. Thus the creed called the *Waṣiyya* or 'Testament' of Abū-Ḥanīfa appears to date from about 850, whereas that known as *Al-fiqh al-akbar II* is possibly half a century later, since it expresses a more developed doctrine of the attributes of God. The latter also asserts that man's utterance of the Qur'ān is created, whereas the earlier *Waṣiyya* is silent on this point and in general closer to the views of Aḥmad ibn-Ḥanbal. Both have an article about the four caliphs. Perhaps the most important difference between the Ḥanafites and the Ḥanbalites is that the Ḥanbalites maintain that faith increases and decreases, while the Ḥanafites deny this; the point at issue seems to be whether faith is taken to include activity (acts of obedience) or is thought of primarily as involved in membership of the community.

There were also Mutakallimūn during the ninth century whose doctrinal position was not far removed from that of the Ḥanbalites and Ḥanafites. The most influential seems to have been Ibn-Kullāb, who died shortly after 854, and who was remembered for his elaboration of the doctrine of the attributes (*ṣifāt*) of God.[7] For a time there was a group of Sunnite Mutakallimūn known as the Kullābiyya, and it was apparently to this group that al-Ashʿarī attached himself when he abandoned the Muʿtazilites (as will be described in the next chapter).

Another group took shape in the eastern provinces in the later ninth century with its centre at Nishapur. These were the Karrāmites, the followers of Ibn-Karrām (d.869).[8] In the tenth and eleventh centuries they were a political force of some importance and appear in general histories of the region and period. It is difficult to reconstruct Ibn-Karrām's doctrines from the few scattered statements that have been preserved, but he seems on many points to have been close to the Ḥanafites, though also opposing them on a few.

Despite the cleavage between the Mutakallimūn or rational theologians of a Sunnite persuasion and the Ahl al-Ḥadīth who objected to 'rational' arguments, there was increasing agreement about the doctrinal or dogmatic statements constitutive of Sunnism. These agreements arose out of the discussions described in previous chapters. Against the Khārijites (and with the Murji'ites) it was agreed that sinners whose intellectual belief was sound were not excluded from the community because of their sin. Against the Shīʿites it was agreed that the first four caliphs were genuine caliphs, and that the chronological order was the order of excellence. Against the Qadarites and Muʿtazilites it was agreed that all events are determined by God. It was also agreed that the Qur'ān was the uncreated word or speech of God, though there were differences of opinion about the human utterance of the Qur'ān.

While there was thus a consolidation by the early tenth century of the main ingredients of Sunnism, it was only somewhat later that the various groups recognized one another as fellow-Sunnites. Part of the difficulty was that there was for long no Arabic term with the precise connotation of the English word 'Sunnites'. The nearest equivalent is the phrase Ahl as-Sunna wa-l-Jamāʿa, 'the people of the Sunna and the community', but it was perhaps only towards 1100 that this was widely accepted as including all those whom we would call Sunnites. At earlier dates when the phrase Ahl as-Sunna or some variant is used it may have a different sense or refer to only one of the groups now included among the Sunnites. The same applies to the adjective *sunnī*. Yet, even if full Sunnite self-awareness and mutual recognition only came about in the later eleventh century, there are good grounds for holding that the essential polarization of Islam into Sunnite and Shīʿite happened in the early tenth century.

While the most important event during this period from a Shīʿite standpoint was the creation of Imāmite Shīʿism, the other two main branches gained greater definiteness by becoming associated with particular political entities. In 909 an Ismāʿīlite dynasty, the Fāṭimids, managed to establish itself in Tunisia, and then in 969 conquered

Egypt and moved its centre of government to the new city of Cairo. Before the Ismāʿīlites had their success in Tunisia, the Zaydite form of Shīʿism had become virtually restricted to two small independent states, one to the south of the Caspian Sea and the other in the Yemen. An account of the theological elaboration of Ismāʿīlism and Zaydism will come more appropriately a little later (ch.16).

The distinctive feature of Imāmite Shīʿism is the recognition of a series of twelve imams, and for this reason they are sometimes called 'Twelvers', in Arabic Ithnāʿashariyya.[9] The earlier imams appear to have been recognized in some sense by those Muslims of Shīʿite sympathies usually called Rāfiḍites by their opponents; but it was argued above that neither the imams themselves nor their followers claimed that they were the rightful rulers of the whole Islamic empire. The followers were in fact divided into many rival groups. One Shīʿite writer describes fourteen groups as existing after the death of the Eleventh Imam, and another as many as twenty. Some seventy years later, however, virtually all these rival factions had been welded together into a single Imāmite sect. It is for this remarkable fact that we now seek an explanation.

The following are the twelve imams eventually recognized:

1. ʿAlī ibn-Abī-Ṭālib (d.661)
2. al-Ḥasan ibn-ʿAlī (d.669)
3. al-Ḥusayn ibn-ʿAlī (d.680)
4. ʿAlī Zayn al-ʿĀbidīn (d.714)
5. Muḥammad al-Bāqir (d.733)
6. Jaʿfar aṣ-Ṣādiq (d.765)
7. Mūsā al-Kāẓim (d.799)
8. ʿAlī ar-Riḍā (d.818)
9. Muḥammad Jawād at-Taqī (d.835)
10. ʿAlī an-Naqī (d.868)
11. al-Ḥasan al-ʿAskarī (d.874)
12. Muḥammad al-Qāʾim (in occultation).

In each case son follows father, except that al-Ḥusayn followed his brother al-Ḥasan.

Al-Ḥasan al-ʿAskarī died on or about 1 January 874, apparently leaving a son Muḥammad who mysteriously disappeared either about that time or a year or two later. The details are obscure and much disputed. What is certain is that before long a group of the followers of the imams asserted that the Twelfth Imam had gone voluntarily into concealment or occultation (*ghayba*), that he was no longer subject to mortality, and that at the appropriate time he would return as the Mahdī to right all wrongs. They also asserted that he was represented on earth by a *wakīl* or 'agent', one of their number, who was possibly held to be in contact with the imam. There were disputes as to who was *wakīl* at a given time, but it came to be generally accepted that the fourth *wakīl* in the series died in or about 940 and was not replaced by a fifth. This marks the beginning of the greater occultation (*al-ghayba al-kubrā*) which still continues, during which period there is no *wakīl*. The previous period, during which there was a *wakīl*, is known as that of the lesser occultation.

The public declaration of the lesser occultation was a deliberate political act which had several advantages for those responsible. It put an end to the bickering between rival claimants to the imamate and their supporters, and so offered the possibility of a united movement. It removed the control of this movement from the imams, whose political competence was slight, into the hands of men with experience of public affairs and considerable political skill. It cleared these men of the suspicion of plotting against the ʿAbbāsids, and yet permitted them to be critical of ʿAbbāsid policies. The fact that the Imāmites referred to themselves as 'the élite' (*al-khāṣṣa*) and to the Sunnites as 'the common people' is in keeping with the further fact that the establishment of Imāmism is known to have been the work of a few wealthy and influential families. Prominent among these was the Āl Nawbakht, from whom came the second *wakīl* and also the man credited with the intellectual formulation of Imāmite beliefs, Abū-Sahl an-Nawbakhtī (d.923), as well as the author of an important work on 'The Sects of the Shīʿa', al-Ḥasan ibn-Mūsā an-Nawbakhtī (d.*c.*922).

The passage from the lesser to the greater occultation, which is linked with the death of the fourth *wakīl* in or about 940, is also, it would seem, a deliberate political act. Because of the date it is presumably connected with the final loss of political power by the ʿAbbāsid dynasty. For over a century governors of distant provinces had been asserting a degree of autonomy and insisting that the caliph nominate their sons (or other relatives) to succeed them. In due course governors of less distant provinces followed, and finally in 936 the caliph of the day was unable to avoid nominating one Ibn-Rāʾiq, governor of Basra, as 'chief emir' (*amīr al-umarāʾ*) to be in charge of the army, police and civil administration at the centre of the caliphate. In 945 he was followed, as effective ruler of the central Islamic lands, by the Buwayhid (or Būyid) dynasty of emirs. There was still an ʿAbbāsid caliph (until 1258), but he had no political power, only certain ceremonial and spiritual functions.

One result of proclaiming the greater occultation was to put an end to the office of *wakīl*, and this was presumably intended. Rivalries for the position of *wakīl* had certainly hindered the unification of the various potentially Imāmite groups. It may also be that the office of *wakīl* had proved less influential in practice than had originally been hoped for, perhaps because of the decline of caliphal power and the increase of that of military commanders. Many of the leading

Imāmites were financiers who had been involved in the money affairs of the ʿAbbāsids, and they may have been adversely affected by the financial breakdown which accompanied the decline of ʿAbbāsid power. All in all it looks as if the doctrine of the greater occultation led to the abandonment of an active political role by the Imāmites. There had always been a quietist strain in Shīʿism, as was seen in the application of messianic ideas to ʿAlī and his descendants during the Umayyad period. Now it was possible for Imāmites, while waiting for the hidden Imam, to tolerate and give some support to the actual ruler without becoming deeply involved in politics. This would seem to make of Imāmite religion a personal and private affair.

It may be that the creation of Imāmite Shīʿism by proclaiming the doctrine of the occultation of the Twelfth Imam was in some sense a response to the consolidation of Sunnism as described above. What is certain is that most of the vague and divergent beliefs of a Shīʿite character which had been prevalent up to this time disappeared through being taken up into the unified belief of Imāmism. The Imāmites, to judge from various facts such as their use of the term 'the élite', were not nearly so numerous as the Sunnites. Yet it seems likely that most of the populations of the main provinces of the Islamic empire were either Sunnite or Shīʿite, and thus there is some justification for speaking of polarization.

During the late ninth and early tenth century the ṣūfī (mystical) movement experienced a period of advance, and this might appear to constitute a third element in Islamic thought along with Sunnism and Shīʿism.[10] This is not so, however. Each ṣūfī certainly had his own theological position; for example, Louis Massignon in his great study of the ṣūfī al-Ḥallāj (d.922) had a long chapter on his dogmatic theology (ch.12). In most cases, however, these views of the ṣūfīs were those of one or other of the Sunnite (or, less frequently, Shīʿite) groups. Apart from 'mystical theology', which was of no concern to dogmatic theologians, there was no sufficiently coherent body of distinctively ṣūfī theology to be argued against. Massignon suggests, however, that the theologians' discussions of apologetic miracles, found from the time of al-Bāqillānī (d.1013) onwards, were triggered off by the claims of al-Ḥallāj. The group of ṣūfīs who came nearest to being a school of dogmatic theology were the Sālimiyya, who came into existence shortly before 900 and can be traced for about two hundred and fifty years. They take their name from Ibn-Sālim (880-967), who was a follower of the ṣūfī Sahl at-Tustarī (d.896).[11] Their views will be mentioned later.

NOTES

1. For the chapter generally: *Formative Period*, ch.9, esp. 256-71.
2. Legal schools: N. J. Coulson, *A History of Islamic Law*, Edinburgh 1964; Schacht, *Introduction to Islamic Law* (n.4/2).
3. *EI*², art. Ḥadīth (J. Robson).
4. Watt, *Bell's Introduction to the Qur'ān*, Edinburgh 1970, 167-70, 45-50.
5. *EI*², art. Aḥmad b. Ḥanbal (H. Laoust); *Formative Period*, 291-5.
6. *Formative Period*, 131-4, 285f.; Wensinck, *Muslim Creed* (B/E), has translations of the Ḥanafite creeds *Al-fiqh al-akbar I* and *II* and the *Waṣiyya*.
7. Ibn-Kullāb: *EI*², supplement, art. Ibn Kullāb (J. van Ess); *Formative Period*, 286-9.
8. Ibn-Karrām: *EI*², art. Karrāmiyya (C. E. Bosworth); *Formative Period*, 289-91.
9. Massignon, *Passion*², i.350-68 (E.T., i.307-22), the fullest account of the period from 874 to 941; Watt, 'The Significance of the Early Stage of Imāmite Shīʿism', in N. R. Keddie (ed.), *Religion and Politics in Iran*, New Haven 1983, 21-32; also in German in K. Greussing (ed.), *Religion und Politik im Iran*, Frankfurt am Main, 1981, 45-57.
10. Ṣūfism: A. J. Arberry, *Sufism*, London 1950; Annemarie Schimmel, *Mystical Dimensions of Islam*, Chapel Hill 1975; J. van Ess, *Die Gedankenwelt des Ḥārit al-Muḥāsibī*, Bonn 1961; Louis Massignon, *Passion*² and *Essai*² (as in B/E).
11. Ibn-Sālim: (Abū-l-Ḥasan or Abū-l-Ḥusayn Aḥmad ibn-Muḥammad al-Baṣrī); Massignon, *Passion*², i.631; ii.140f. (E.T. i.582; ii.130f.), correcting statements in *Passion*¹, 361f. and *Essai*², 294-300. See also pp.109-10 and n.14/29.

Chapter Ten

AL-ASH'ARĪ

Al-Ash'arī is one of the outstanding figures in the history of Islamic theology, but it is only recently that scholars have been able to form a clear idea of the precise nature of his achievement and its importance. Until about the middle of this century it was generally supposed that before the 'conversion' of al-Ash'arī the only rational or philosophical theology was that of the Mu'tazilites and some similarly-minded people; from this supposition it followed that the beginning of Sunnite philosophical theology or Kalām was when al-Ash'arī changed allegiance from Mu'tazilism to Ḥanbalism and resolved to defend Sunnite (Ḥanbalite) doctrines by Mu'tazilite methods. It is now realized that there were forms of Sunnite Kalām before al-Ash'arī, notably among the Kullābiyya (as described in the last chapter), and it is probable that on his 'conversion' al-Ash'arī attached himself to the Kullābiyya. In this group he was doubtless prominent, but another man, al-Qalānisī, was, if anything, more prominent. It was possibly nearly a century later before this group of theologians began to think of themselves as Ash'arites, and to be so regarded by others. The publication of a book by the Ash'arite Ibn-Fūrak (d.1015), entitled 'The Difference between the two Shaykhs, al-Qalānisī and al-Ash'arī', may have contributed to this result. What is certain is that by the eleventh century the main branch of Sunnite Kalām thought of itself as Ash'arite.

Abū-l-Ḥasan 'Alī ibn-Ismā'īl al-Ash'arī was born at Basra in 873, and studied under the head of the Mu'tazilites there, al-Jubbā'ī.[1] As a distinguished pupil he sometimes took the place of the master, and might conceivably have succeeded him, it is said. On the other hand, al-Jubbā'ī had a very intelligent son, Abū-Hāshim, who did in fact succeed him; and it may be that the rivalry between this man and al-Ash'arī was a factor contributing to the latter's abandonment of the Mu'tazilites, which took place about 912, shortly before the death of the master in 915. The positive side of this 'conversion' was the acceptance of Sunnite dogma in its Ḥanbalite form; and for the rest of his life al-Ashʿarī devoted himself to the defence of this position and the critique of Muʿtazilism. He moved to Baghdad towards the end of his life, and died there in 935.

Some sources suggest that the story of the 'three brothers' (mentioned above) provided a theological motive for the change; but this is unlikely, since al-Jubbā'ī and other Muʿtazilites of Basra already felt dissatisfaction with the attempts to give a rational account of the variations in men's destinies. It looks as if al-Ashʿarī, carrying his master's line of thought a little farther, came to the conclusion that revelation was superior to reason as a guide to life, and decided to attach himself to those who explicitly gave first place to revelation.

Al-Ashʿarī doubtless also saw that Muʿtazilism in general was becoming increasingly irrelevant to the contemporary situation. Earlier Muʿtazilites had been associated with attempts to work out a compromise which would help to overcome the cleavage between Sunnites and Shīʿites. With the abandonment of the policy of the 'inquisition' about 850 the caliphal government became pro-Sunnite, and what has been called the consolidation of Sunnism followed. At the same time many vague strands of Shīʿite feeling were replaced by the more definite Imāmite form of Shīʿism. By 912 it must have been clear to an acute observer that the prospects of anything being achieved by the Muʿtazilite compromise were rapidly declining. The Muʿtazilites had in fact become a group of academic theologians who had retired to an ivory tower remote from the tensions and pressures of ordinary life.

The actual decision to change allegiance is said to have been made after a series of three dreams during the month of Ramaḍān, in which the Prophet Muḥammad appeared to him. In the first of these the Prophet told him to defend what had been related from himself, that is, the Ḥadīth, and in the second asked how he had been fulfilling this task. Other versions speak of him first studying Ḥadīth about seeing Muḥammad in dreams (since he doubted the reality of his experience), about intercession (by the Prophet on the Last Day) and about the vision of God in Paradise. At some point, in all versions of the story, he completely gave up rational methods, and confined himself to studying Qur'ān and Ḥadīth. In the third dream, however, the Prophet, when told about this, angrily said that he had commanded him to defend the doctrines related from himself, but had not commanded him to give up rational methods. On the basis of this conception al-Ashʿarī worked out his new theological position, which may be described as the support of revelation by reason. The doctrines he accepted were more particularly those of Aḥmad ibn-Ḥanbal, but because of the use of rational methods the Ḥanbalites rejected both him and his followers.

His main differences from the Muʿtazilites may be brought under four heads. First, he held that the Qur'ān was uncreated and was the very Speech of God, and that it, like the other attributes, was eternal and in some sense distinct from God's essence. Secondly, with regard to the anthropomorphic expressions in the Qur'ān, he insisted that these must simply be accepted 'without specifying how' (*bi-lā kayf*). The Muʿtazilites, on the other hand, had held that, for example, where the Qur'ān speaks about God's 'hand' what is meant is his 'grace'; this could be supported by metaphorical usages of the word 'hand' in Arabic comparable to the English 'lend a hand'. Thirdly, al-Ashʿarī insisted that various eschatological matters must be taken as they stand and not explained as metaphors. The Muʿtazilites had tended to say that the vision of God by the faithful in Paradise meant that they would know him in their hearts (the heart being the seat of knowledge); but al-Ashʿarī argued forcibly that the Qur'ānic phrase (75.23), 'looking to their Lord', could mean only looking in the normal sense, though this had to be understood 'without specifying how' and without implying anything resembling corporeality in God. Fourthly, he rejected the Muʿtazilite doctrine of free will, or man's ability to do an act or its opposite, and asserted the doctrine of 'acquisition' (*kasb, iktisāb*) previously held by Ḍirār, according to which God creates the acts of individuals but the individuals 'acquire' them; the act is God's creation in that it is only at the moment of action that he creates the power to act in the individual, and in that it is power to do only this act, not either this act or its opposite.

Besides the lengthy book on 'the Views of the Islamic Sects' (*Maqālāt al-islāmiyyīn*) there are extant several shorter works by al-Ashʿarī, of which the most important are those usually referred to as the *Ibāna* and the *Lumaʿ*. Both deal with a number of questions currently being discussed by theologians, but it is thought that the *Ibāna* was intended to meet criticisms by Ḥanbalites while the *Lumaʿ* was directed against those from Muʿtazilites. A. J. Wensinck was the first Western scholar to examine the *Ibāna* and he could not understand how such a book could have been written by the father of rational theology, since the arguments appeared to be chiefly quotations from Qur'ān and Ḥadīth. Wensinck's difficulties are understandable, but they disappear completely when it is realized that the Muʿtazilites of the time also argued from Qur'ānic verses (as can be seen from some extant material), and when the precise character of al-Ashʿarī's arguments is carefully examined. When he quotes a verse and argues from it, he is not simply quoting (as some other writers did) but is placing the verse within a setting of rational conceptions, and he has other arguments which do not depend on quotations; for example, in defending the reality of the vision of God in Paradise, he argues in effect: 'whatever exists God may show to us; but God exists, and so it is not impossible that he should show himself to us'.

One is thus justified in concluding that these later theologians had good grounds for taking al-Ash'arī as eponym of their school.

Along with the supposition that al-Ash'arī was the initiator of the main school of Sunnite Kalām there went a second supposition, namely, that about the same time a second school of Sunnite Kalām was founded in Samarqand by the Ḥanafite scholar al-Māturīdī, and that these were two parallel schools of roughly equal importance. This second supposition is not so erroneous as the first, but it requires some qualification. It is true that al-Māturīdī was leader of a school of Sunnite Kalām in Samarqand, but this school remained obscure and little known for centuries; thus it is not mentioned in Ibn-Khaldūn's account of Kalām written in the late fourteenth century. Though the Māturīdites knew about the Ash'arites by about the year 1000, it is not until about 1200 that a few scattered references to Māturīdites appear in Ash'arite writings. By the sixteenth century, however, it was possible for an Ottoman scholar to write that 'at the head of the science of Kalām among the Ahl as-Sunna wa-l-Jamā'a were two men, one a Ḥanafite and the other a Shāfi'ite', namely, al-Māturīdī and al-Ash'arī. This resurrection of al-Māturīdī doubtless owes something to the fact that the official legal rite in the Ottoman empire was the Ḥanafite.[2]

Despite this exaltation of his position al-Māturīdī (Abū-Manṣūr Muḥammad ibn-Muḥammad ibn-Maḥmūd) remains obscure. He must have been roughly a contemporary of al-Ash'arī, since he died in Samarqand in 944, but virtually nothing is known of his life. A general work on theology, *Kitāb at-Tawḥīd,* has now been edited, and this makes it possible to speak authoritatively about his views. Earlier European statements about thirteen differences between Ash'arites and Māturīdites are derived from a late and unreliable source, and are in part mistaken. The differences between the Māturīdite-Ḥanafite position and the Ash'arite may now be discovered from the primary texts which have been edited and are readily available. They are conveniently arranged under four heads.

First, for al-Ash'arī and his followers, as for the Ḥanbalites, faith (*īmān*) consists of word and act, that is, profession of belief and fulfilment of the prescribed duties. Since the level of the performance of duties varies, faith is subject to increase and decrease. For the Ḥanafites, on the other hand, faith consists in word only, or, as they phrased it, belongs to the heart and the tongue. It is thus the inner conviction accompanying the formal profession of belief, and so cannot be said to increase or decrease. Secondly, with regard to the freedom of the will al-Māturīdī was close to the Mu'tazilites and held that men had the ability (power) to do either an act or its opposite; but other Ḥanafites were closer to al-Ash'arī. Thirdly, al-Māturīdī, following the Murji'ite views of Abū-Ḥanīfa, held that a believer does not cease to be a believer because of a grave sin, and so will not be eternally in Hell. Al-Ashʿarī's position was similar, but he was not prepared to assert that no believer will be eternally in Hell. Fourthly, both schools held that God has attributes (*ṣifāt*), such as knowledge, and they held that it is by his attribute of knowledge that God knows, not, as the Muʿtazilites had said, by his essence. They accepted the distinction between active (*fiʿliyya*) and essential (*dhātiyya*) attributes, but, whereas al-Māturīdī considered all alike to be eternal, al-Ashʿarī maintained that an 'active' attribute like creativity cannot be eternal since it only exists when God is actually creating.

The work of al-Ashʿarī and of al-Māturīdī marks the ebbing of the first wave of Hellenism. A number of Greek concepts had been eagerly seized upon by a small section of the more educated Muslims. Some, especially those hostile to the nascent Sunnism, committed themselves entirely to the guidance of reason as that was understood in Greek philosophy, and gave no more than lip service to Islamic religion. More important was the attempt of the Muʿtazilites and others to effect a fusion of Islamic dogma and the Greek intellectual tradition. Though the first enthusiasts may have made too great concessions to the Greek outlook, they undoubtedly raised the level of intellectual activity among the Muslims. The service of Sunnite Kalām was to discern ways of assimilating the Greek conceptions and methods so far adopted without compromising any of the central dogmas. Thus Islam emerged from the first wave of Hellenism still recognizably itself, even if changed in some, perhaps only peripheral, matters.

NOTES

1. Al-Ashʿarī: *Formative Period,* 303-12; Sezgin, *GAS,* i.602-4; R. J. McCarthy, *The Theology of al-Ashʿarī,* Beirut 1953, has texts and translations of important works, including the *Lumaʿ*; Walter C. Klein, *Al-Ašʿarī's Al-Ibānah,* New Haven 1940; George Makdisi, 'Ashʿarī and the Ashʿarites in Islamic Religious History', *Studia Islamica,* xvii (1962), 37-80 and xviii (1963), 19-39; Michel Allard, *Le problème des attributs divins dans la doctrine d'al-Ašʿarī et de ses premiers grands disciples,* Beirut 1965, esp. 173-285.
2. Al-Māturīdī: *Formative Period,* 312-16; Sezgin, *GAS,* i.605-6; *EI*[1], art. al-Māturīdī (D. B. Macdonald); edition of *Kitāb at-tawḥīd* by Fathalla Kholeif, Beirut 1970.

Part Three

THE SECOND WAVE OF HELLENISM

CHAPTER ELEVEN

THE FLOWERING OF PHILOSOPHY

After the first enthusiastic acceptance of Greek ideas in the years round about 800 the majority of Muslim religious scholars made no further explorations of the Greek heritage but contented themselves with criticizing or assimilating what was already present in Islamic works. It was this lull in exploration which justified the metaphor of a first wave of Hellenism. Before long, however, the beginnings could be observed of a second wave. During the tenth century small groups continued to cultivate philosophy, and this was closely connected with the study of Greek medicine and the other Greek sciences. The Muslim students of philosophy were far from being fanatical adherents of Islam, and, in philosophical discussions and even in teaching, Muslims and Christians seem to have associated on equal terms. The work of these groups culminated eventually in the outstanding achievements of Avicenna in both philosophy and medicine, and these in turn led to the acceptance into Islamic theology of further Greek conceptions and methods through the work of al-Ghazālī.

In the first half of the tenth century philosophy was dominated by the figure of al-Fārābī (*c.*875–950).[1] He is known as 'the second teacher', Aristotle being the first. Though born in Turkistan, he eventually studied philosophy and the 'Greek sciences' in Baghdad, where his chief teacher of philosophy was a Nestorian Christian, while he was in contact with others of the Christian Aristotelians there, such as the philosopher Yaḥyā ibn-ʿAdī (d.974). How he gained a livelihood is not clear, but, since he lived an ascetic life, his needs were doubtless few. In 942 he accepted an invitation to the court of the Ḥamdānid prince Sayf-ad-dawla in Aleppo, and spent the remainder of his life there.

His philosophy may be described as having a foundation of Aristotelianism and a superstructure of Neoplatonic metaphysics. To this he added a political theory based on the study of Plato's *Republic* and *Laws.* The last element seems to be an original contribution of his own, but in the former two he is developing the line of thought of al-Kindī. In the centre of his metaphysics is the First Being or absolute One, which was understood to be identical with God as proclaimed in Islamic doctrine. From him emanated all other existing things in hierarchical order. Similarly in the state there is a head, the *ra'īs*, from whom all authority in the state emanates in that he assigns men to their appropriate grades (in something the same way as the 'Abbāsid caliph assigned men to various posts in the court and administration). The grades are described as grades of commanding and obeying or of controlling and being controlled; at the foot in the lowest grade are those who are themselves controlled, but do not control any others below them, while at the top is the *ra'īs* who control others but is not himself controlled. The intermediate grades control others and are themselve controlled in varying degrees.

Al-Fārābī uses perfectly general terms (like 'head' rather than imam or caliph) which could be applied to non-Islamic states as well as to the Islamic empire, but he is thinking primarily of the Islamic world. The 'first head' of his ideal state is a prophet who has also the best qualities of the true philosopher. He is to be followed by a 'second head' who should have slightly different qualities. If the qualities requisite for the 'second head' are not all found in one man, then rule may be divided among those who share the qualities. Some of the descriptions of such persons could apply to the ulema and students of Ḥadīth as they existed in his time, while the 'second head' might just conceivably be an imam as conceived by the Imāmites. Perhaps al-Fārābī was deliberately vague, and was chiefly concerned that philosophy should contribute to ordering the affairs of the caliphate.

In the second half of the tenth century we hear of a philosophical coterie in Baghdad which met in the house of Abū-Sulaymān al-Manṭiqī, 'the logician' (d.985 or later). Unlike most philosophers this man seems to have had no official position, though he was in favour at the Buwayhid court. Some of the discussions at his house have been recorded by his younger friend Abū-Ḥayyān at-Tawḥīdī (d. 1023), who was an important literary figure, though he earned his living as a secretary to viziers and other court-officials in Baghdad and the provinces.[2] Both men had studied under the Christian philosopher Yaḥyā ibn-'Adī (d.974).

Another man who combined philosophy and literature was Miskawayh (or Ibn-Miskawayh) (d.1030), a Persian who served as secretary to members of the Buwayhid reigning family and their viziers. He is best known for a lengthy universal history, of which the concluding part has been translated into English as *The Eclipse of the 'Abbāsid Caliphate.* (Incidentally this reproduces Abū-Ḥayyān's account of the discussion of 'Aḍud-ad-Dawla's death in 983 at the house of Abū-Sulaymān.) Among Miskawayh's other extant works is a book of philosophical theology, *Al-Fawz al-aṣghar,* dealing with the being of God, the being of the soul and the nature of prophethood. It is not an important book in the intellectual history of Islam, but it is an interesting example of how thinkers who were primarily philosophers nevertheless accepted a framework of Islamic conceptions; the last section of this book, for example, explains in terms of a philosophical account of the soul how prophethood is possible. More influential philosophically was *The Refinement of Character,* which is the exposition of a complete system of morals on a mainly Platonic basis. The book was used by al-Ghazālī and other writers.[3]

Philosophy must have been cultivated at many centres in the Islamic world. By chance we hear of men versed in the philosophical sciences at a small town near the south coast of the Caspian Sea. At least it was a man from this town who gave the first instruction in philosophy to a boy who later became in the opinion of many the greatest of all the philosophers writing in Arabic. This was Avicenna, or Abū-ʿAlī ibn-Sīnā (980–1037). He was mainly of Persian stock, it would seem, but may also have had Turkish blood. He grew up in Bukhara, and began his education by memorizing the Qur'ān and Arabic poetry, before passing on to jurisprudence. He was possibly only about fourteen when the visiting scholar mentioned above introduced him to Aristotelian logic, and found to his surprise that the boy soon had a better grasp of the subject than his teacher. With an insatiable thirst for knowledge Avicenna then devoured all the scientific and philosophical books he could get hold of. He studied medicine, apparently by himself, and obtained so thorough a theoretical grasp that practising physicians came to read medical books under his guidance. According to the autobiographical fragment from which we derive this information all this happened before he was seventeen; and he also tested out and increased his medical knowledge by treating patients.

In this course of omnivorous study the one subject which gave him trouble was metaphysics. He says he had read over Aristotle's *Metaphysica* forty times and had the text by heart, and yet he was baffled by it, until he chanced to come on a little book by al-Fārābī which brought him full illumination. This anecdote indicates that it was the direct influence of the older Islamic philosopher which led him to adopt so similar a general position in philosophy. For the next year or so he had access to a remarkable library of Greek works belonging to the sultan of Bukhara, and made the fullest use of his time. Before he was eighteen, he reckoned, he had assimilated all the scientific and philosophical knowledge available, so that thereafter he added nothing to his store of information, though his understanding of it deepened. Perhaps it was well that he had read so widely while he had the opportunity, for about 998 his circumstances changed. On his father's death he had to seek a civil service appointment to make a living. The political conditions of the region also altered for the worse; and the rise and fall of small dynasties and administrations meant that he had constantly to move from place to place. From about 1015 to 1022 he was in Hamadhan, and for part of this time occupied the difficult and dangerous post of vizier or chief minister to the local Buwayhid prince. From about 1023 until his death he was in Ispahan, under the patronage of the local prince.

In considering Avicenna as a philosopher, it must also be remembered that his *Canon of Medicine* holds an outstanding place in medical science, and that his writings on other sciences were also influential. His philosophy is contained chiefly in two books, the *Shifā'* and the *Najāt*, of which the first is a great compendium including sciences as well as philosophy, while the second is an abridged version of the philosophical parts of the longer work. This second is divided into three parts, one dealing with logic, one with 'natural philosophy' (really questions about such matters as substance and accident and the nature of the human soul), and one about 'theology' (including cosmology). The general position is Neoplatonic. God is the One, the 'necessarily existent' (*wājib al-wujūd*), from whom everything emanates. Beneath him are the pure intelligences and the spheres. The conception of the human soul is essentially Aristotelian, but modified apparently in accordance with the discussions and interpretations of later Greek platonizing philosophers. Like most of the other Islamic philosophers he explains the possibility of prophethood; but where al-Fārābī had connected prophethood with the highest form of imagination, Avicenna links it with the highest part of the soul, the intellect.

It is also worth noting that in contrast to al-Fārābī, there is no trace of Shī'ism in Avicenna, that is, no attempt to show that the actual ruler receives a more than ordinary portion of divine wisdom. He is mainly concerned to explain how through a prophet a state based on divine wisdom may be established in the first place. This change of emphasis and apparent avoidance of Shī'ism is perhaps chiefly due to the fact that by this time Fāṭimid propaganda was active in the east of the Islamic world. Avicenna himself remembered how when he was a boy propagandists had arrived in Bukhara and how he had overheard heated discussions about the teaching they gave. In his maturity even Imāmite-Shī'ite rulers must have realized that this propaganda was a threat to their power; and anything resembling it would therefore be suspect. Another relevant point is that Avicenna had as much political power as he wanted, and does not seem to have felt in any way the rivalry of Sunnite ulema. Thus there was nothing to lead him to exaggerate the importance of philosophy. In this respect he was in a similar position to the Mu'tazilites during the period of their political ascendancy; and like them he took for granted that his philosophical interpretation of Islam was the true one. An identification of their own interpretation with the true Islam was likewise common among mystics; and Avicenna had also a mystic side.

The final questions concerning Avicenna are about the relation of his philosophy to his mysticism and to his religious outlook generally. To begin with the latter, he was brought up as a good Muslim, he memorized the Qur'ān and he studied the Sharīʿa or revealed law. In the autobiographical fragment he tells us that he went to the mosque and prayed about his intellectual problems, and he says nothing about any conscious change in his views. He probably felt that the Greek scientific and philosophical learning belonged to a different sphere from Islamic doctrine, and that there was no fundamental opposition between them. In his philosophy he seems to have thought of himself as supporting and elucidating what he considered to be the central doctrines of Islam—the existence of God who is the source of all being, and the possibility of men becoming prophets and receiving revelations. Avicenna's conception of prophethood and his conception of the soul's journey to God are closely linked both with one another and with his philosophy. Nineteenth-century European scholars thought that his mysticism was extraneous to his philosophy, but fuller acquaintance with his writings makes it clear that this is not so. His mysticism and his philosophy constitute a single integrated system. The extent of his mystical writings shows that the mystical life meant much to him. It was presumably the source of his intellectual energy. Because of this personal religious attitude Avicenna has been held by one of the leading modern scholars to come closer to the spirit of Plato than other philosophers whose style is more Platonic and less Aristotelian. 'He understood something which is the very essence of Plato's thought, and it may be that for this reason he appealed to religious Muslims—as Plato himself has conveyed religious truth, to people open to religion, at all times.'[4]

While on the subject of philosophy mention may be made of Ikhwān aṣ-Ṣafā' or Brethren of Purity. They have been called Neoplatonists, but they were not exactly Neoplatonic philosophers. They have been called Ismāʿīlites, but, while they may have had some connections originally with Ismāʿīlism, they did not share the political concerns of the Ismāʿīlites we know. They seem to have been a secret society engaged in a mystical quest for the purification of the soul with a view to attaining happiness in the life of eternity. Modern scholars have tried to discover their identity, but none has found a convincing solution of the problem. What we have is a collection of fifty-two epistles dealing with mathematics, natural sciences, philosophical disciplines and theology. Nineteenth-century European scholars were greatly impressed by the epistles and regarded them as a kind of encyclopaedia of the sciences of the day (as known in Basra in the tenth or eleventh century); but further study has shown that the learning is superficial, that there are many contradictions and that the disparate materials have not been shaped into a unified system. Though one or two later writers quote from the epistles, they cannot be said to have been an important formative influence in Islamic thought.[5]

NOTES

1. Al-Fārābī: *GAL*, i.232-6; *GALS*, i.375-7, 957f.; *EI*^{2}, art. (al-)Fārābī by R. Walzer; his book 'On the Principles of the Views of the People of the Excellent State', often called for short *Al-Madīna al-fāḍila*, has been translated into German by F. Dieterici as *Der Musterstaat* (Leiden 1900) and into English by R. Walzer as *Al-Farabi on the Perfect State*, Oxford 1982; a short work on politics is *Fuṣūl al-madanī: Aphorisms of the Statesman*, edited and translated by D. M. Dunlop, Cambridge 1961.
2. *EI*^{2}, arts. Abū Sulaymān al-Manṭiqī, Abū Ḥayyān al-Tawḥīdī (both by S. M. Stern); I. Keilani, *Abū Ḥayyān at-Tawḥīdī: introduction à son oeuvre*, Beirut 1950; Marc Bergé, *Pour un humanisme vécu: Abū Ḥayyān al-Tawḥīdī*, Damascus 1979.
3. Miskawayh: C. K. Zurayk, *The Refinement of Character*, Beirut 1968 (translation of *Tahdhīb al-akhlāq*); M. Arkoun, *Contribution à l'étude de l'humanisme arabe au IVe/Xe siècle: Miskawayh . . . philosophe et historien*, Paris 1970; *Al-Fawz al-aṣghar* is translated in J. W. Sweetman, *Islam and Christian Theology*, London 1945, i/1.93-185; *The Eclipse of the 'Abbāsid Caliphate*, translated by H. F. Amedroz and D. S. Margoliouth, Oxford 1920, etc. (the passage referred to is vi.76-8).
4. Avicenna: A.-M. Goichon, art. Ibn Sīnā in *EI*^{2} with extensive bibliography; also *La Philosophie d'Avicenne et son influence en Europe médiévale*, Paris 1944, and *La Distinction de l'essence et de l'existence d'après Ibn Sīnā*, Paris 1937; G. M. Wickens (ed.), *Avicenna: Scientist and Philosopher*, London 1952, six lectures delivered at Cambridge to celebrate the millenary, including one by A. J. Arberry on his life: Louis Gardet, *La Pensée religieuse d'Avicenne*, Paris 1951, studies his relation to Sunnite theology and his mysticism; Henry Corbin, *Avicenna and the Visionary Recital*, London 1961, explores his mystical and theosophical thought and the relation to him of later Imāmite Shī'ism; F(azlur-) Rahman, *Avicenna's Psychology*, London 1952, translation of a section of *K. an-Najāt* with notes; also *Prophecy in Islam*, London 1958, on the philosophical conception of prophethood; Soheil M. Afnan, *Avicenna, his Life and Works*, London 1958, with an important section (pp.233-57) on his influence in the east. The closing quotation is from Richard Walzer, *Greek into Arabic* (B/D), 26.
5. Ikhwān aṣ-Ṣafā': Yves Marquet, art. Ikhwān al-Ṣafā' in *EI*^{2}; also *La Philosophie des Ihwān al-Ṣafā'*, Algiers 1975; Ian R. Netton, *Muslim Neoplatonists: an Introduction to the Thought of the Brethren of Purity*, London 1982; Geo. Widengren, 'The Pure Brethren and the Philosophical Structure of their System', in Alford T. Welch and Pierre Cachia (eds), *Islam: Past Influence and Present Challenge*, Edinburgh 1979, 57-69.

Chapter Twelve

THE PROGRESS OF ASH'ARITE THEOLOGY

Before giving an account of some of the leading figures in the Ash'arite school it will be helpful to say something about the difficulty of seeing the Ash'arites in an adequate perspective. For long Western scholars tended to identify Ash'arism with theological orthodoxy. It was only with the growth of interest in Ḥanbalism stimulated by Henri Laoust that this identification was seen to be inadequate. Under the inspiration of Laoust, George Makdisi published an article in 1962 entitled 'Ash'arī and the Ash'arites in Islamic Religious History'. In this he called attention to the fact that Western Islamists had relied almost exclusively on Ash'arite sources. This began with the publication in London in two volumes (1842, 1846) of ash-Shahrastānī's work on sects and religions, *Kitāb al-milal wa-n-nihal,* followed by its translation into German in 1850/1. This was a balanced scholarly work and rightly had an immense influence on Western thinking about Islam, but it was not without some bias in favour of Ash'arism. Towards the end of the century two other works, both Ash'arite, came to be used for the later history of the school. These were the biographies of Ash'arite theologians by Ibn-'Asākir (d.1175) and the biographies of Shāfi'ite jurists by as-Subkī (d.1370). Makdisi pointed out that both of these, despite an appearance of objectivity, are skilled apologetic works whose aim was to get Ash'arism acknowledged as having a right to exist within the Shāfi'ite legal school. In all the legal schools there were 'traditionalist' majorities bitterly opposed to Kalām or rational theology. The article concluded that the importance of the Ash'arites had been exaggerated and the contribution of the 'traditionalists' overlooked.

This conclusion is in the main to be accepted, and an attempt will be made here to preserve a balance between the various groups of theologians, though there is little material on which to base an assessment of the relative strengths. It must also be pointed out that within the Ash'arite school undue importance has been attached to al-Ghazālī. This may have been because many Western scholars have been attracted by his intellectual autobiography; but they have also been followed by contemporary Muslim scholars. The articles about him, at least up to about 1960, easily outnumbered the articles about all other Islamic theologians taken together. It is as a theologian and mystic, too, that these were concerned with him. Yet this was not his importance for his contemporaries and successors. The majority of the references to his works by Muslim writers in the two centuries after his death were to books on jurisprudence. This brings in another Western misconception—to suppose that the place of theology in Islam is identical with its place in Christianity. The central discipline in Islamic higher education, however, was not theology but jurisprudence. The *madrasa,* college, was essentially a place for teaching jurisprudence, and its head was the professor of jurisprudence. This is why it was important to get the legal schools to acknowledge Kalām as a permissible study.[1]

(a) *al-Bāqillānī*

The first important figure in the Ashʿarite school after al-Ashʿarī himself is al-Bāqillānī.[2] According to Ibn-Khaldūn it was he who perfected the methodology of the school; and, though the atomism attributed to him by Ibn-Khaldūn is now known to be earlier, it is probable that it was in his time and through his work that the school took definite shape. His contemporary Ibn-Fūrak was possibly responsible for getting al-Ashʿarī accepted as eponym of the school.

Little is recorded of the life of al-Bāqillānī. His name is given as Abū-Bakr Muḥammad ibn-aṭ-Ṭayyib ibn-al-Bāqillānī. No date is given for his birth, but it was probably about 940. He was born in Basra, spent his earlier years there, and is said to have studied under two of the immediate pupils of al-Ashʿarī. From Basra he was summoned to take part in theological discussions at the court of the Buwayhid emir ʿAḍud-ad-dawla, then at Shiraz. That was probably about 970. He then seems to have gone with the emir to Baghdad, since he was sent on an official embassy to Constantinople in 982. His dealings with the court seem to have come to an end with the death of ʿAḍud-ad-dawla in 983, but it is also possible that his conduct of the embassy had not been satisfactory. The rest of his life, until his death in June 1013, was spent in Baghdad, except that for a time he was *qāḍī* (judge) in some place other than Baghdad. In jurisprudence he was a Mālikite and so contributed to the spread of Ashʿarism in Mālikite circles in North Africa. Most of the other well-known Ashʿarites belonged to the Shāfiʿite school, but there were also some Ḥanafites among them.

A general account of the theological views of al-Bāqillānī is to be found in his *Kitāb at-tamhīd,* 'The Book of the Introduction', which belongs to the class of *summae theologicae,* of which several will be mentioned subsequently.[3] The plan of the book is instructive and may be set out as follows:

1. Prolegomena dealing with the nature of knowledge and its objects, and with the existence and names of God (6–34 in McCarthy's edition).

2. Refutation of other religions, including Zoroastrians, Christians, 'Barāhima' and Jews (34–190).

3. Refutation of certain deviant Muslim groups: Mujassima (Corporealists) (191–6); Mu'tazilites (197–377); Shī'ites (160–239 of Egyptian edition).

The first point to be noticed about this is that the choice of topics is not irrelevant to the current situation in Baghdad. The rulers there since 945 had been the Buwayhid dynasty of emirs, and, though in most respects they aimed at being neutral between the various sects and schools, they sympathized with the Imāmite Shī'ites and gave them a measure of support. In consequence some of the Sunnite groups, such as the Ash'arites and the Ḥanbalites, were brought closer to one another through the common threat. Thus in the *Tamhīd* there is no attack on the 'traditionalist' Sunnite position as held by many Ḥanbalites, and only five pages directed against the Mujassima (possibly meaning the Karrāmites) who insisted on applying the term *jism*, 'body', to God, though possibly meaning rather 'substance'. The length of the section against the Mu'tazilites is possibly due to the fact they and the Imāmites had many doctrines in common and shared in the favours of the Buwayhids. The section on other religions reflects the presence in Baghdad of Zoroastrians, Christians and Jews; the Barāhima (cf. Brahmin), probably of Indian origin, were known as a group who acknowledged no prophets.

Much of what al-Bāqillānī says follows along the lines of the teaching of al-Ash'arī as it is known from his *Luma'* and *Ibāna*. Michel Allard, who studied his views on the attributes of God, found that his chief originality lay in his insistence on the reality of the attributes and in his development of a theory of language. This last seems to have been forced upon him by the assertion of Mu'tazilite opponents that the 'name' (*ism*) is different from 'the named' (*al-musammā*) and also from 'naming' (*tasmiya*), whereas some of his own party, doubtless influenced by old Semitic ideas, wanted to identify the name and the named. The matter was complicated by the fact that the word translated 'attribute' is *ṣifa* from the root *waṣafa*, 'describe', which gives us the verbal noun *waṣf*, 'describing', and *al-mawṣūf*, 'the described'. Al-Bāqillānī insisted above all that a *ṣifa* like 'knowledge' or 'power' is different from the *ism*, 'knowing', 'powerful', but at the same time belongs to God. (The adjectival 'names' are prominent in the Qur'ān and in popular piety.)

Two other works of al-Bāqillānī deal with topics which attracted the attention of theologians only after the time of al-Ashʿarī himself. One is *Iʿjāz al-Qurʾān,* 'The miraculous character of the Qurʾān', that is, its inimitability, especially in respect of literary style. The other was given the English title of 'Miracle and Magic: a Treatise on the Nature of the apologetic Miracle and its differentiation from Charisms, Trickery, Divination, Magic and Spells'. The two works are closely connected in subject-matter. The term *muʿjiza,* 'translated apologetic or evidentiary miracle', is the active participle of *aʿjaza,* 'render incapable', and is not used of any miraculous happening but only of one granted by God to a prophet to prove the truth of his claim to prophethood and silence his opponents. The word *iʿjāz,* literally 'rendering incapable' or 'silencing', is the verbal noun from the same verb.

The Muslims had been facing the underlying problem since the time of Muḥammad himself, and it was not surprising that it now thrust itself upon the rational theologians. The Jews of Medina had in effect argued that Muḥammad's claim to be prophet in the Biblical tradition must be false, since some of his revelations contradicted the Bible. So the question was raised how one could be certain that Muḥammad was a prophet. When the Muslims conquered Syria, Iraq and Egypt they were constantly mixing with Christians and others who denied the prophethood of Muḥammad. For popular consumption the preachers discovered or invented miracles for Muḥammad, but the serious theologians took the line that the miracle proving that Muḥammad was a prophet was the Qurʾān itself. In the Qurʾān (2.23; 10.38; 11.13) his opponents had been challenged to produce comparable suras, and they had failed to do so. The miraculous character of the revelations was enhanced by interpreting the word *ummī* to mean that Muḥammad could not read (though its original meaning was probably 'Gentile').

The problem became more urgent after the mystic al-Ḥallāj (d.922) asserted that certain miraculous happenings showed that his account of his spiritual experiences was true. Opponents alleged that the happenings in question were due to trickery or sorcery. Al-Bāqillānī insisted that the apologetic miracle must be something which only God can bring about and which he does in fact bring about after a prophet has predicted that God will do this to substantiate his prophethood. The prophet's claim and prediction ruled out mere conjuring. To rule out deliberate trickery and deception al-Bāqillānī argued that the happening must be one contrary to the normal course of events and such that only God had power to bring it about. There was a basis for this in the Qurʾānic accounts (7.103–36; etc.) of how, when Pharaoh asked Moses for a sign to show that his claim to bring a message from God was true, Moses flung down a staff which turned into a serpent and swallowed the serpents produced by the staffs which Pharaoh's sorcerers had also flung down. The arguments about the nature of the *mu'jiza* are in terms which apply to all prophets, but they are complemented by the assertion that the miraculous character of the Qur'ān is in its eloquence or sublime literary quality. Elsewhere al-Bāqillānī makes clear his view that the essential speech of God is not the Arabic text of the Qur'ān but its 'meaning' (*ma'nā*); and in accordance with Islamic tradition he holds that it was the same 'meaning' that was revealed to Moses in the Torah in the Hebrew language and to Jesus in the Evangel in Syriac.

(b) *the Ash'arites of Nishapur*

While there continued to be exponents of Ash'arite theology in Baghdad and other centres, it so happens that during the eleventh century the best known Ash'arites are associated with Nishapur (in the east of modern Iran). In the tenth century this was an extensive and populous city, sometimes the seat of the local ruler. For most of the tenth century the leading power in eastern Iran and further east was the Sāmānid dynasty—autonomous princes giving nominal allegiance to the 'Abbāsid caliph in Baghdad. They were patrons both of traditional Arabic and Islamic learning and of the new Persian literature which was coming into existence. Nishapur thus became a great intellectual centre, in prestige falling not much short of Baghdad which lay two months' journey to the west.

Prominent in the intellectual life of Nishapur was the Karrāmite sect (p.59 above), who were noted for their ascetic and pietistic practices. Their leaders in the later tenth century, the family of Banū Maḥmashādh, had for a time the support of the Sāmānid governor Sebüktigin and then of his son Maḥmūd, who had become autonomous sultan of Ghazna; but they lost this support about 1011. Later, in 1095 and 1096, they are recorded as involved in fighting against both the Ḥanafites and the Shāfi'ites in both Nishapur and Bayhaq. It is not clear why the legal and theological schools were so bitterly opposed to them. The point most often mentioned is their use of the term *jism*, 'body' (or 'substance'?), in respect of God; but they also appear to have been opponents of the Mu'tazilites. Apart from the Karrāmites the people of Nishapur seem to have been about equally divided between Ḥanafites and Shāfi'ites.

Ibn-Fūrak (Abū-Bakr Muḥammad ibn-al-Ḥasan ibn-Fūrak al-Iṣbahānī) was born about 941, possibly in Ispahan, but studied in both Basra and Baghdad.[4] In 982 or 983 admirers in Nishapur persuaded the Sāmānid emir Ibn-Sīmjūr to invite him there as a teacher. A *madrasa* or college was built for him, and his presence in Nishapur is said to have led to a great flowering of various studies there. He died in 1015 by poisoning on his way back from Ghazna, whither he had been summoned by Sultan Maḥmūd. It was probably the Karrāmites who poisoned him after he had defeated them in argument; but Ibn-Ḥazm, who criticized him bitterly, alleged that the poisoning was by order of Maḥmūd because of a view he had expressed about Muḥammad's prophethood.

While he seems to have been the chief source for the early history of Ash'arism, his main work in the eyes of later generations was one about the application to God in Ḥadīth of anthropomorphic terms. Against the Karrāmites he argued that these must be interpreted allegorically; and he asserted as a general principle that it is better to interpret these texts in accordance with the conception of God as transcendent, for which there is a clear basis in revelation, than to do the opposite and, by interpreting literally texts which have not been fully understood, to endanger the conception of God's transcendence. In this Ibn-Fūrak may have gone beyond the views of al-Ash'arī himself.

Al-Baghdādī (Abū-Manṣūr 'Abd-al-Qāhir ibn-Ṭāhir) was probably born in Iraq.[5] Some time before 975 he came to Nishapur with his father, a wealthy man and a scholar, and studied under the teachers there. He was said to have mastered seventeen different disciplines, and a book of his on arithmetic was highly praised. He was apparently the outstanding teacher in Nishapur in his later years, and argued personally with the Karrāmites, on one occasion (in 980) in the presence of the emir. Shortly before his death in 1037 a Turkmen invasion caused him to leave Nishapur for Isfarāyin, where he died almost immediately and was buried beside another Ash'arite, al-Isfarāyinī.[6]

His book *Al-Farq bayn al-firaq*, 'The Differences between the Sects', is an important heresiographical source (p.164 below), both descriptive and polemical. In the last section of some forty pages he presents the fifteen basic principles of Islam, as the Ash'arites understand them. In another book, *Uṣūl ad-dīn*, 'The Principles of Religion', he has a chapter for each of the basic principles, and each chapter is divided into fifteen sections. This has been characterized by Allard as an extended creed rather than a work of theology, since there is little detailed argument. The main heretical views are briefly mentioned. Many of the positions he himself adopts are similar to those of al-Bāqillānī, though he is closer to Ibn-Fūrak on the question of anthropomorphic terms.

Al-Bayhaqī (Abū-Bakr Aḥmad ibn-al-Ḥusayn) was born in 994 in the district of Bayhaq, about 100 km west of Nishapur.[7] Apart from travelling to other centres for study he spent most of his life in Bayhaq until 1049 when he was requested to go to Nishapur. This request arose out of the persecution of the Ash'arites by al-Kundurī, vizier of the Seljūq sultan Ṭughril Beg, who had been ruling from Nishapur since 1040. The reason for this attack by al-Kundurī was probably his rivalry for the position of vizier with Abū-Sahl ibn-al-Muwaffaq, the head of the municipality of Nishapur; the latter was a Shāfi'ite in law, whereas al-Kundurī was a Ḥanafite. It would have been difficult to attack the Shāfi'ite law-school as such, but many Shāfi'ites were Ash'arites in theology, and Ash'arism had many critics. About 1049 two distinguished Ash'arites, al-Qushayrī and al-Juwaynī, were excluded from the mosques, and an order came from the sultan for their imprisonment, along with that of Abū-Sahl ibn-al-Muwaffaq and others. Eventually the two theologians left Nishapur and went to the Hijaz. Meanwhile al-Bayhaqī had written to al-Kundurī a long letter, which has been preserved, in which he showed the Ash'arites were above suspicion of heresy and asked for the end of the persecution. It was about a year later that al-Bayhaqī went to Nishapur, and he may have spent some years there before he too went to the Hijaz. The return of the exiles to Nishapur took place after the imprisonment and death of al-Kundurī about 1063 and 1064. Al-Bayhaqī died in 1066.

Although reckoned an Ash'arite, al-Bayhaqī was primarily a student of Ḥadīth and not a speculative theologian. This made his defence of Ash'arism specially valuable, since he was universally accepted as an authority in the field of Ḥadīth. His 'Book of Names and Attributes' consists to a great extent of the citation from Qur'ān and Ḥadīth of the sources which justify the ascribing to God of the various names and attributes. Underlying his treatment, however, are certain rational principles, as Michel Allard has shown in his careful study, and this makes the book a work of theology. In the Ash'arite tradition he accepted the distinction between the essential and active attributes, but above all he steered a middle course between the *ta'ṭīl* (denial of distinct attributes) of the Mu'tazilites and the *tashbīh* (anthropomorphism) of the Karrāmites. In other words, names of God properly vouched for in the sources represent real attributes, such as the name *'ālim*, 'Knowing', and the attribute *'ilm*, 'knowledge'; but they are not to be understood either in a literal, material sense or in a purely metaphorical sense. All this applies even to such terms as 'hand', 'face' and 'eye' when used of God. Al-Bayhaqī is the most noteworthy representative among the Ash'arites of this non-speculative line.

Al-Qushayrī (Abū-l-Qāsim 'Abd-al-Karīm ibn-Hawāzin) was born in a village near Nishapur in 986 and died in the town itself on the last day of 1072.[8] As a young student in Nishapur he was attracted to ṣūfism by the teaching of the leading master of the time, ad-Daqqāq, whose daughter he married. He excelled in all the religious disciplines, especially in theology, the exegesis of the Qur'ān and the study of Ḥadīth. In jurisprudence he was a Shāfi'ite. For Ash'arite theology his teachers were Ibn-Fūrak and al-Isfarāyinī. On one occasion the latter is said to have scolded him for not taking notes of the lectures, but, when the student showed that he had remembered the lectures perfectly the teacher took a fancy to him and said that in his case it would be enough to read his books and discuss them with him privately. He suffered with other Ash'arites under the persecution of al-Kundurī, and for a time taught Ḥadīth in Baghdad. His most famous work is his *Risāla* or 'Epistle', which is a full account of early ṣūfism and has been much read and studied. The theological aspect of the work of al-Qushayrī has not been adequately examined, but Louis Massignon has indicated how he used Ash'arite principles to defend ṣūfism from charges of heresy.

Al-Juwaynī (Abū-l-Ma'ālī 'Abd-al-Malik ibn-'Abd-Allāh), known as Imām al-Ḥaramayn, was the son of a distinguished jurist and was born on the outskirts of Nishapur in 1028.[9] He was a very industrious student and, when his father died in 1046, succeeded to his chair of jurisprudence. The year 1048, however, saw the beginning of the persecution of the Ash'arites by the vizier al-Kundurī (described above). Al-Juwaynī is said to have fled from Nishapur just as the sultan's police were publishing a document condemning him. Some sources suggest that he went immediately to the Hijaz, but it is more likely that he went first to Ṭughril Beg's camp, which was also his court, and was also for a time in Baghdad before spending four years in Mecca and Medina. From this period of teaching in the two holy cities he received the honorific title of 'the imam of the two sanctuaries' (Ḥaramayn). After al-Kundurī's fall from power in 1063 and his replacement as vizier by Niẓām-al-mulk the latter reversed the policy of persecuting Ash'arism and gave it some governmental suppport by establishing a series of colleges, each known as a *madrasa Niẓāmiyya.* One of the first was at Nishapur, where al-Juwaynī was appointed professor, continuing until his death in 1085.

Despite the careful study by Michel Allard of al-Juwaynī's views on the attributes of God, further work must be done on other aspects before we have a clear picture of the development of al-Juwaynī's thought. Allard's study was based on four books, now easily available. The chief of these is the *Irshād,* a general work covering the main theological doctrines. At the end of this al-Juwaynī promises to write a fuller account of the subject in another book called *ash-Shāmil,* 'the comprehensive (book)'; and at least part of this appears to be extant, though there are some problems about identification. A third work with the brief title of *al-Luma'* appears to be a simplified summary of the *Irshād,* while a fourth, *Al-'Aqīda an-Niẓāmiyya,* 'the Niẓāmian creed', though thought to be genuine, expresses views which differ in some respects from those of the *Irshād.*

The general position adopted in the *Irshād* is similar to that of al-Bāqillānī, but the arguments are more elaborate and take account of the numerous discussions with opponents in the intervening period. There is a great interest in the philosophical preliminaries to theology, and this interest is even more marked in the Cairo partial manuscript of the *Shāmil*. It seems likely that it was al-Juwaynī who encouraged al-Ghazālī to study philosophy, but he himself shows little awareness of the details of the thought of al-Fārābī and Avicenna. Apart from this matter there are some indications in the *Irshād* of a slight shift from the position of al-Ash'arī himself. Whereas al-Bāqillānī, probably following a work by al-Ash'arī, had refuted Abū-Hāshim's theory of *aḥwāl*, 'modes', al-Juwaynī is prepared to adopt the term and to identify the 'modes' with the 'attributes' as understood by the Ash'arites. At the same time he abandoned the distinction between essential and active attributes, and distinguished instead between 'essential' (*nafsiyya*) and 'entitative' (*ma'nawiyya*) attributes. The former were those which belonged to the *nafs*, the 'essence' or 'self', and were inseparable from it, while the latter were those derived from a 'cause', *'illa*, subsisting in God; for example, the attribute 'knowing' is derived from 'knowledge', a *ma'nā* or 'quasi-substantive entity' which subsists in God. Similarly, when he comes to speak of 'modes', he distinguishes between those which are 'caused' and those which are 'not caused' in this special sense. Thus, despite his use of the term 'modes', he avoids anything like the Mu'tazilite *ta'ṭīl* or denial of God's attributes, and remains within the Ash'arite tradition.

He also moves away from al-Ash'arī, as some of his predecessors in Nishapur had done, by admitting the *ta'wīl*, 'metaphorical interpretation', of certain of the anthropomorphic terms applied to God in Qur'ān and Ḥadīth. Where al-Ash'arī, following the Ḥanbalites, had held that a term like 'hand' as applied to God was to be understood neither literally nor metaphorically but *bi-lā-kayf*, 'without (asking) how', al-Juwaynī argued that, since the literal or corporeal meaning of the term is impossible in the case of God, it must be understood as 'power'.

At the end of his life, after having sought truth even in philosophical books of which strict theologians disapproved, he came back to something like a child-like faith, and summed up the results of his whole experience of life in the advice, 'Hold to the religion of the old women'.

In a sense the Ash'arite school of Nishapur reached its culmination in al-Juwaynī's great pupil al-Ghazālī, and it was the labours of the men just mentioned that made possible the achievement of al-Ghazālī. He also went beyond them, however, so that in important ways his work marks a new beginning.

NOTES

1. George Makdisi, 'Ash'arī and the Ash'arites in Islamic Religious History', *Studia Islamica*, xvii (1962), 37-80 and xviii (1963), 19-39; also *The Rise of Colleges: Institutions of Learning in Islam and the West*, Edinburgh 1981; Ibn-'Asākir, *Tabyīn kadhib al-muftarī . . .*, *GAL*, i.404; as-Subkī, *Ṭabaqāt ash-Shāfi'iyya*, *GAL*, ii.110.
2. Al-Bāqillānī: *EI*², art. (al-)Bāḳillānī, (R. J. McCarthy); Allard, *Attributs* (n.10/1), 290-312; Rudi Paret, 'Der Standpunkt al-Bāqillānīs in der Lehre vom Koran', in Paret (ed.), *Der Koran* (Wege der Forschung), Darmstadt 1975, 417-25 (from *Studi Orientalistici* in onore di Giorgio Levi della Vida, Rome 1956, ii.294-303).
3. Works of al-Bāqillānī: *GAS*, i.608-10; *K. at-Tamhīd*, ed. M. al-Khuḍayrī, M. Abū-Rīda, Cairo 1947 (from incomplete ms.); also ed. R. J. McCarthy, Beirut 1957 (from complete mss. but does not repeat pp.160-239 of Cairo edition, on imamate); *I'jāz al-Qur'ān*, various editions, and partly translated by G. von Grunebaum as *A Tenth-Century Document of Arab Literary Theory and Criticism*, Chicago 1950; *K. al-Bayān 'an al-farq bayn al-mu'jizāt wa-l-karāmāt . . .*, ed. R. J. McCarthy, Beirut 1958 ('Miracle and Magic . . .').
4. Ibn-Fūrak: *GAS*, i.610f.; *GAL*, i.175f.; Allard, *Attributs*, 314f., 326-9; *EI*², art. Ibn Fūrak (Watt).
5. Al-Baghdādī: *GALS*, i.666; Allard, *Attributs*, 316f., 329-42; *EI*², art. (al-)Baghdādī (A. S. Tritton).
6. Al-Isfarāyinī: *GALS*, i.667; *EI*², art. (al-)Isfarāyinī (W. Madelung).
7. Al-Bayhaqī; *GAL*, i.446f.; *EI*², art. (al-)Bayhaḳī (J. Robson); Allard, *Attributs*, 342-72.
8. Al-Qushayrī: *GAL*, i.556f. and *GALS*, i.770-2; *EI*², art. (al-)Ḳushayrī, Abū l-Ḳāsim (H. Halm); R. Hartmann, *Al-Kuschairis Darstellung des Ṣūfitums*, Berlin 1914; Massignon, *Passion*², ii.110f. (E.T., ii.104f.); Schimmel, *Mystical Dimensions* (n.9/10), 88.
9. Al-Juwaynī: *GAL*, i.486-8 and *GALS*, i.671-3; *EI*², art. (al-)Djuwaynī (C. Brockelmann/L. Gardet); Allard, *Attributs*, 372-404; *Al-Irshād*, ed. J. D. Luciani with French translation, Paris 1938 (cf. review by G. Vajda, *Journal Asiatique*, 230 (1938), 149-53), and ed. M. Y. Musa and A. M. 'Abdalhamid, Cairo 1950; *al-'Aqīda an-Niẓāmiyya*, ed. M. Z. al-Kawthari, Cairo 1948, and translated into German as *Das Dogma des Imām al-Ḥaramain al-Djuwainī u. sein Werk al-'Aqīdat an-Niẓāmīya*, Cairo and Wiesbaden 1958.

Chapter Thirteen

AL-GHAZĀLĪ AND LATER ASHʿARITES

Al-Ghazālī has been acclaimed by both Western and Muslim scholars as the greatest Islamic theologian and indeed as the greatest Muslim after Muḥammad. It is now realized that this is not so, and that there were other theologians of comparable importance though in different ways. Something has already been said about the difficulty of arriving at a due appreciation of the achievements of al-Ghazālī owing to the fact that Western scholars found him congenial and approachable, and studied his works to the exclusion of those of most other theologians. Another difficulty consists in the great volume of his writings. Thus his greatest work, *Iḥyāʾ ʿulūm ad-dīn,* 'The Revival of the Religious Sciences', consists of forty books or chapters, of which each, when translated into a European language, forms a sizable book.

A further difficulty is that of the seventy or so works attributed to him, which are still extant, a number are agreed by scholars to be falsely so attributed; but there is only partial agreement about which works belong to this group. Since many of the works of dubious authenticity are heterodox or heretical works of Ṣūfistic teaching, the acceptance of these as genuine alters the general picture of al-Ghazālī. Those who accept some of the dubious writings as genuine suggest as an explanation either that, besides the exoteric teaching which he gave to all, he had esoteric teaching which he communicated only to a select few, or else that towards the end of his life he completely changed his views and abandoned Ashʿarism. This second suggestion is shown to be impossible by the discovery of an early manuscript of a short work of Ashʿarite-Shāfiʿite tendency, in which it is stated that this was completed by al-Ghazālī less than a fortnight before his death. It is also highly improbable that a lucid and upright thinker like al-Ghazālī could hold and teach esoterically views which contradicted those which he publicly professed. In the present state of scholarship the wisest course is to base any account of al-Ghazālī solely on the works universally accepted as genuine; and that will be done here. Naturally the other works, even if not by al-Ghazālī, are important as illustrating trends in ṣūfism.[1]

(1) *Life.* Abū-Ḥāmid Muḥammad ibn-Muḥammad ibn-Muḥammad al-Ghazālī was born in 1058 in Ṭūs, a town near modern Meshhed in north-east Iran. Almost since his own lifetime there have been arguments whether his *nisba,* 'relative name', should be Ghazālī or Ghazzālī. The latter would relate to a *ghazzāl,* 'spinner (or seller of spun yarn)', the former to a village or woman called Ghazāla; but there is no certainty about the ancestor who was a spinner, since he had a grand-uncle (or less probably uncle) also called Ghazālī, and the village or woman is otherwise unknown. The form Ghazālī is here preferred on the basis of the principle *difficilior lectio potius.*

Al-Ghazālī's early education was in Ṭūs itself. His father died while he and his brother Aḥmad (who became a distinguished jurist and mystic) were still boys, but left some money for their education with a ṣūfī friend. When the money was exhausted, the friend arranged for them to go to a *madrasa,* where they received free food and lodging as well as instruction. At some time not later than 1074 al-Ghazālī went for purposes of study to Gurgan, some 300 miles away at the south-east corner of the Caspian Sea. On the return journey his party was attacked by brigands who among other things took away his notebooks; on his pleading for their restoration this was done, but he was also taunted with claiming falsely to know what was in fact only in his notebooks. At Ṭūs he therefore spent three years committing the material to memory.

In 1077 he went to Nishapur (about 50 miles to the west) to study under al-Juwaynī at the recently founded Niẓāmiyya college. Here he remained until the death of al-Juwaynī in August 1085. Jurisprudence was presumably central in his studies, with Ash'arite theology in second place. Al-Juwaynī may also have encouraged him to read the works of the philosophers al-Fārābī and Avicenna. In his later years at Nishapur he helped with teaching and was recognized as a rising scholar, so that on the death of al-Juwaynī the great vizier Niẓām-al-mulk invited him to his court, which was also a camp and moved about. He seems to have remained at this court until July 1091 when he was appointed professor at the Niẓāmiyya college in Baghdad. Thus at the age of 33 he went to one of the most prestigious positions in the Sunnite Islamic world.

In his book *Al-Munqidh min aḍ-ḍalāl,* 'The Deliverer from Error', he tells us about his intellectual development and about some of the external details of his life from 1091 to 1106. This book is best described as an *apologia pro vita sua,* since in it he is concerned to justify his abandonment of his professorship at Baghdad in 1095 and his return to teaching at Nishapur in 1106; but the plan of the book is roughly autobiographical. He decribes his intellectual journey as beginning with a period of complete scepticism and then consisting of an examination of the four chief 'classes of seekers' of his time, namely, the Ashʿarite theologians, the Neoplatonic philosophers, the Ismāʿīlites (whom he calls the party of *taʿlīm*, 'authoritative instruction') and Ṣūfīs. He speaks of his encounter with each group as a separate stage chronologically, but the stages must have overlapped. It is virtually certain that he commenced the study of ṣūfism at Ṭūs and Nishapur before 1085, while his study of philosophy probably began under al-Juwaynī. It is unlikely, too, that the period of scepticism, though it was a real experience which lasted 'almost two months', came until after he had some familiarity with philosophy, since philosophical considerations are mentioned in his account of it. Thus the course of his intellectual quest has been somewhat schematized in the interests of the literary presentation.

Some books about jurisprudence seem to have been written before he went to Baghdad, and presumably his lectures there were mainly about jurisprudence. His main work of Ashʿarite theology presupposes the study of philosophy and so cannot be dated much before the end of the Baghdad period, but the so-called 'Jerusalem Epistle' (*ar-Risāla al-Qudsiyya*), a brief statement of Ashʿarite doctrine later incorporated in Book 2 of the *Iḥyāʾ*, may have been composed before 1091. He himself tells us that much of his time in Baghdad between 1091 and 1095, after lecturing to three hundred students and doing some writing, was devoted to the study of philosophy. He read the books himself without an instructor, presumably because it was difficult for a person in his position to have contact with heretical philosophers. Though he places the period of scepticism much earlier, it is possible that it was connected with this intense study of philosophy. The scepticism consisted in doubting whether it was possible for man to have any certain knowledge at all, and it came to an end, not through any argument, but when 'God cast a light into his heart'; this 'light' was the realization that there are basic truths which cannot be proved but must simply be accepted.

The first encounter in his quest for truth, according to the scheme of the *Munqidh*, was with the rational theologians (*mutakallimūn*). These are in fact the Ashʿarites, among whom he had been numbered both at Nishapur and at the court of Niẓām-al-mulk. From his new standpoint he regards these theologians as operating on the basis of certain assumptions or presuppositions, which they do not discuss but take for granted, whereas it is precisely for these that he now wants a rational justification. Since these theologians cannot give him this justification, he passes to philosophy. This second encounter will be described more fully in what follows.

The third encounter was of a somewhat different character. It was with those whom he calls Taʿlīmites, the party of *taʿlīm*, who got their 'teaching' or 'instruction' in an authoritative form from their imam. These were in fact the adherents of Ismāʿīlism, which was at this time the official religion of Egypt under the Fāṭimid dynasty and also the inspiration of a secret revolutionary movement in the provinces acknowledging the ʿAbbāsid caliph. As a scholar al-Ghazālī was concerned with Ismāʿīlism, which was occasioning some talk among his contemporaries as a result of Fāṭimid propaganda; and when the caliph commanded him to write a refutation he readily obeyed. There is nothing, however, to suggest that he was as deeply involved personally in this encounter as in the second and fourth, despite his writing at least five books on the topic. The main point which he criticized was the Ismāʿīlite claim that, if one wants infallible knowledge on any point, one must consult the infallible imam.

The fourth encounter was with ṣūfism. In the end al-Ghazālī had been disappointed with philosophy, for he had come to realize that there is a limit to the knowledge that can be obtained by rational methods. He therefore decided to make a more thorough study of ṣūfism than he had hitherto done. As he himself puts it in the *Munqidh*: 'I realized . . . that I had already advanced as far as was possible by way of knowledge. What remained for me was not to be attained by instruction and study but only by immediate experience and by living as a ṣūfī.' At the same time he became dissatisfied with the manner of his life in Baghdad. He felt that he was motivated by personal ambition rather than the desire to serve God, and he thought he might be in danger of going to Hell. Eventually in July 1095 his internal struggles and perplexities resulted in what would now be regarded as a psychosomatic illness. His tongue dried up, and he was unable to lecture or even to eat. The doctors could do nothing. Relief came only when he decided to give up academic work completely and to lead the life of a ṣūfī. He made arrangements for his family and their education, then gave away the rest of his wealth. He left Baghdad in November 1095, ostensibly to make the pilgrimage to Mecca; but this was to prevent obstacles being placed in the way of his carrying out his real intention of becoming a ṣūfī. Actually he went only as far as Damascus, and settled there for some months.

The statements in the *Munqidh* about the next ten years are not altogether clear, and have led to varying accounts of what he did; but when they are supplemented from other sources the following picture emerges. From Damascus he made the pilgrimage in November and December 1096, passing through Jerusalem and Hebron. It is sometimes said that he visited Egypt at that time, but this is improbable. From Damascus he returned to Baghdad not later than June 1097, though he probably did not remain long there but proceeded to his native town of Ṭūs by way of Hamadhān. In Ṭūs he established a *khānqāh* (hostel or convent) where young men came and joined him in leading the ṣūfī life as a community. The genuineness of his conversion to ṣūfism has sometimes been questioned by Muslim scholars, and it has been suggested, for example, that after the coming to power in early 1095 of the Seljūq prince Barkiyāruq his life was in some danger, since he had been involved in supporting the rival prince Tutush, now dead. A political factor may indeed have been present, but al-Ghazālī himself seems to have thought of his position mainly in religious terms.

In 1105 or early in 1106 Fakhr-al-mulk, son of Niẓām-al-mulk and now vizier of the Seljūq prince governing Khurasan, prevailed on al-Ghazālī to accept the professorship at the Niẓāmiyya college in Nishapur. One of the factors which led him to reverse his earlier decision to give up teaching was a Ḥadīth to the effect that at the beginning of each century God would send a *mujaddid*, 'renewer', of his religion. The Islamic year 500 began on 2 September 1106, and many of those he consulted assured him that he was undoubtedly the *mujaddid* for the sixth century. He may have felt too that he would be able to combine teaching at Nishapur with most of the ṣūfī practices he had been engaging in at Ṭūs, which were presumably those which he describes in his book *Bidāyat al-hidāya*, 'The Beginning of Guidance'. He took up his duties at Nishapur in July or August 1106, and continued teaching until at least August 1109. At some point after that date he retired to Ṭūs, possibly because of ill-health, and died there on 18 December 1111. His brother Aḥmad tells how on the day of his death, after making his ablutions and performing the dawn prayer, he asked for his shroud, kissed it, laid it on his eyes and said, 'Obediently I enter into the presence of the King'; then facing Mecca he stretched out his feet and was dead before sunrise.

(2) *His study of philosophy.* Although al-Ghazālī's decision to study the 'sciences' of the philosophers arose out of his own intellectual problems, he was also aware that theology was in a weak position because of its inability to answer philosophical criticisms. For over two centuries the religious scholars had kept all Greek learning at arm's length as something foreign and dangerous, or had tried to attack it without an adequate understanding of the problems and had thereby incurred the ridicule of the philosophers. Al-Ghazālī set about his task with an open mind, ready to follow the argument wherever it led him, but he was also trying to discover how far the results of the Greek sciences are compatible with the beliefs of Muslims. He soon realized that there was nothing in mathematics, logic and physics contrary to Islamic dogma, but he noted as a drawback that the clarity and certainty of mathematical arguments led some people to suppose that all the arguments of the philosophers had the same clarity and certainty, and so to accept without question their metaphysical assertions. After spending 'less than two years' on these studies al-Ghazālī devoted another year to reflecting on what he

had read. In this way he obtained such a grasp of the philosophy of al-Fārābī and Avicenna that his account of it—chiefly following Avicenna—in his *Maqāṣid al-falāsifa,* 'The Aims of the Philosophers', is usually reckoned to be a clearer and more concise account than any written by the philosophers themselves.

For al-Ghazālī, however, this was only a preparation for another work entitled *Tahāfut al-falāsifa,* 'The Inconsistency of the Philosophers', in which he criticized the weaknesses of their metaphysical views. With great subtlety he discussed twenty points of doctrine in which he regarded the philosophers as mistaken and as involved in contradictions. Three of these points he regarded as more serious than the others and amounting to 'unbelief', with the corollary that those who held them were outside the community of Muslims. The three doctrines are: that for bodies there is no resurrection, only for bare spirits; that God knows universals but not particulars; and that the world has existed from all eternity (and so was not created).

Al-Ghazālī's study of philosophy undoubtedly had far-reaching results. What may be called the positive results are easiest to describe. By showing that the disciplines associated with philosophy are largely neutral with regard to Islamic doctrine he made it possible for at least the more rationally-minded theologians to accept much of their content. This included metaphysical conceptions other than the twenty points; and, more importantly, it included Aristotelian logic. He himself was greatly impressed by the logical works of Aristotle, especially those on the syllogism. Previous Muslim theologians and jurists had used various forms of argument other than the syllogism, and their arguments were valid for those who shared their assumptions but were employed in a somewhat haphazard fashion. What attracted al-Ghazālī to this logic was possibly not the single syllogism but the ordering of a series of arguments in such a way that the conclusion of one syllogism became the premiss of the next. He devoted some seventy pages to logic in his *Maqāṣid al-falāsifa,* and wrote two short works on Aristotelian logic intended for those with a traditional Islamic education, and using examples from materials with which they were familiar. He hmself made use of syllogistic reasoning in his exposition of Islamic doctrine, *Al-Iqtiṣād fī-l-iʿtiqād,* 'The Just Mean in Belief'.

As a result of all this one finds later rational theologians in Islam tending to give their theology more and more of a philosophical basis, as will be seen in what follows. Parallel with this was the growth of logic as a distinct discipline, but one whose exponents were no longer philosophers but persons trained in Islamic theology or jurisprudence. The neutrality of philosophical ethics is not so clear, but al-Ghazālī felt able to take over some of its ideas. Indeed it has recently been established that much of his ethical work *Mīzān al-*

ʿamal, 'The Criterion of Action', closely follows an obscure early-eleventh-century philosopher ar-Rāghib al-Iṣfahānī. When the implications of this fact have been further studied, interesting results may be obtained; but it seems unlikely that al-Ghazālī's influence on ethics will prove as important as that on logic. So much for the positive results of al-Ghazālī's study of philosophy. It is these above all which constitute 'the second wave of Hellenism'.

Negative results of his study would be chiefly some weakening of the philosophical movement as a result of his attack on it in the *Tahāfut*. Since there are no pure philosophical works in the eastern provinces after his time, it is tempting to conclude that his attack on the philosophers had been so devastating that philosophy was killed off; but such a conclusion is not justified. It is true that there were no outstanding philosophers in the east after 1100 who stood within the 'pure' Aristotelian and Neoplatonic tradition; but it is also true that the last great philosopher there, Avicenna, had died in 1037, twenty years before al-Ghazālī was born; and so the decline of philosophy may have begun long before the *Tahāfut* appeared. In the western Islamic world Averroes was able to write a critique of the *Tahāfut*, but the tradition virtually came to an end with his death in 1198.

The end of a particular philosophical tradition, however, did not mean the end of all philosophizing. Though the traveller Ibn-Jubayr (d.1217) could still find people who professed to follow al-Fārābī and Avicenna, it would appear that the main study of philosophy had been transformed so that most of the activity was along two fresh lines. One of these, as already noted, was the incorporation of philosophical conceptions and methods into rational theology or Kalām, especially by the Ashʿarites; indeed certain aspects of philosophy became a kind of prolegomena to theology proper. This was mainly found among Sunnite Muslims. The second line was the fusion of philosophy with Shīʿite ideas or with non-Islamic mystical ideas. In the century after al-Ghazālī the philosophy, or perhaps rather theosophy, of the Ishrāq, 'Illuminative Wisdom', was developed by Shihāb-ad-dīn as-Suhrawardī, also known as Suhrawardī Maqtūl, 'the killed Suhrawardī' (d.1191).[2] It was and still is influential, especially in the Iranian world, as will be seen later.

Al-Ghazālī's critique of philosophy, then, by no means put an end to philosophizing, but it may have contributed to the transformations. He certainly encouraged Sunnite theologians to become more philosophically minded, and his attack on Avicennian metaphysics may have led those who still followed Avicenna to combine his teaching with some form of mystical belief and practice.

(3) *His practice of ṣūfism.* In previous centuries ṣūfism had sometimes been associated with heretical beliefs and with a neglect of the common duties of Muslims such as the five daily prayers. In

consequence it had become suspect among many jurists and theologians, even though some jurists and theologians, like al-Qushayrī, had themselves been ṣūfīs. The main aim of al-Ghazālī in his greatest work, the *Iḥyā'* ('The Revival of the Religious Sciences'), was to show how a punctilious observance of the duties imposed by the Sharī'a could be the basis of a genuine ṣūfī life. The much shorter work *Bidāyat al-hidāya* describes the basic rule of life which results from the principles explained in detail in the *Iḥyā'*. This was presumably the rule which he himself followed after leaving the Baghdad professorship and which was also followed in the monastery-college which he established at Ṭūs.

In the *Munqidh* al-Ghazālī speaks of the defects he found in the theologians, but there is nothing to suggest that he ever abandoned Ash'arite doctrine, even if he supplemented it with philosophical considerations. An Ash'arite creed, the 'Jerusalem Epistle', is included in the *Iḥyā'*, and it was after his study of philosophy that he wrote his major theological work, the *Iqtiṣād.* At Nishapur he must have taught Shāfi'ite jurisprudence and probably also Ash'arite Kalām. Certainly while he was there he wrote an important book on the principles of jurisprudence called *Al-Mustaṣfā,* 'The pure (Teaching)'. Finally, a few days before his death he completed a short work (roughly within the field of jurisprudence) in which he maintained that it was wrong to communicate the subtleties of Kalām to ordinary people. From these facts it seems certain that al-Ghazālī remained a Shāfi'ite and Ash'arite to the end of his life, though he was now using philosophical methods to defend Ash'arite doctrine. Consequently those works ascribed to him which make it appear that before his death he abandoned Sunnism and adopted some kind of monism are to be rejected as unauthentic. On becoming a ṣūfī he did not cease to be a Shāfi'ite and an Ash'arite; and thus by his conduct of his own life and by the quality of his writings he helped to allay the suspicions towards ṣūfism felt by many Sunnite scholars, and to make it easier for later Sunnites to adopt a ṣūfī way of life.

(4) *The successors of al-Ghazālī.* The fact that the most important Ash'arites of the eleventh century were connected with Nishapur does not mean that there were no Ash'arites elsewhere. The apologist and historian of Ash'arism, Ibn-'Asākir (d.1176), has biographical notices of thirteen men whose date of death lay between 1111 and 1148, some of whom had been born before al-Ghazālī. Several of these men lived chiefly in Nishapur, and some chiefly or partly in Baghdad; but others were mainly connected with Damascus, Jerusalem, Ispahan and Kirmān respectively. In Ispahan there was a Niẓāmiyya college where Ash'arism was taught and studied. Men travelled easily from one seat of learning to another, and often received an enthusiastic welcome because of their reputation as

scholars. Despite this widespread study of Ash'arite theology, however, there are only two important names in the century and a half after al-Ghazālī.

The first of these is ash-Shahrastānī (Tāj-ad-dīn Muḥammad ibn-'Abd-al-Karīm), who was born in 1086 (or 1076) in Shahrastān, the main quarter of the city of Gurgan in eastern Persia.[3] His education was completed at Nishapur, either before or just after al-Ghazālī's period of teaching there. In 1116 he made the pilgrimage to Mecca, and then spent three years lecturing and preaching at the Niẓāmiyya in Baghdad. The remainder of his life until his death in 1153 was spent in Nishapur and Shahrastān.

It was presumably at Nishapur that he was introduced to philosophy, and he took up the subject with enthusiasm. Almost a third of his work on sects and religions (already mentioned) consists of an exposition of the philosophy of Avicenna in a manner comparable to the *Maqāṣid* of al-Ghazālī; and he also wrote a refutation of Avicenna, perhaps following the model of the *Tahāfut*. His chief work of Ash'arite theology, *Nihāyat al-iqdām fī 'ilm al-kalām* ('The End of Daring about the Science of Kalām'), is called by its editor and translator a Summa Philosophiae, but it is essentially a work of Kalām, treating the same topics and in roughly the same order as the similar works of al-Juwaynī and al-Ghazālī. The invasion of theology by philosophy, however, is marked by the fact that views of Avicenna and other philosophers join those of theological sects among the matters discussed; and the treatment throughout is characterized by new philosophical conceptions and methods.

There was a near-contemporary report that he was suspected of a leaning towards Ismā'īlism and had even been a propagandist for that doctrine. The charge may have arisen out of hostility to philosophy and to theologians who busied themselves with it; or it may be due to the fact that all his books were written for a patron, the *naqīb* or 'dean' of the descendants of 'Alī in Tirmidh. Recently some scholars have tried to show that the charge was justified, and further study is now necessary. What has been shown so far is that there are parallels between some statements made by ash-Shahrastānī and the views of Ismā'īlite authors; but these parallels appear to be not in his main arguments against Avicenna, for example, but in secondary matters. Even when the parallels have been demonstrated, however, there remains the problem of their significance. It may be that they were forms of expression commonly used in the circles in which ash-Shahrastānī mixed and that they did not imply sectarian allegiance; or they may have been introduced to please his patron without indicating a commitment to Ismā'īlism. In the debate so far no cogent reason has been given for thinking ash-Shahrastānī was other than a convinced Ash'arite and Shāfi'ite.

The second important name is that of Fakhr-ad-dīn ar-Rāzī, also known as Ibn-al-Khaṭīb, who was born at Rayy near modern Tehran in 1149 (or 1150) and who died at Herat in Afghanistan in 1210.[4] His father, the *khaṭīb* or official orator of Rayy, was himself a learned man who had been a student at Nishapur. The young Fakhr-ad-dīn studied the whole range of subjects taught at Rayy, partly with his father and partly with other teachers. Shortly after completing his studies he went to the region of Khwarazm (to the south of the Aral Sea) and argued against the Mu'tazilite theologians who were established there; but their hostility forced him to retire to Bukhara and Samarqand. He subsequently went back to Rayy, where he was able to arrange for the marriage of two sons to the two daughters of a wealthy physician. On the death of the latter Fakhr-ad-dīn obtained control of most of his wealth, and from being a poor man became a very wealthy one, who was in a position sometimes to give financial help to local rulers. Eventually, after journeys to Central Asia and India, he settled in Herat, where he was allowed to establish a school within the royal palace of the Ghūrid dynasty. He died there in March 1210.

He is commonly regarded, following Ibn-Khaldūn, as the person who, along with al-Ghazālī, did most to introduce the new philosophical approach into Kalām. He began the study of philosophy at Rayy, but was greatly influenced by another philosopher whom he apparently never met. This was Abū-l-Barakāt al-Baghdādī, also known as Ibn-Malkā, who was born a Jew near Mosul about 1077, became a Muslim late in life, and died in Baghdad, apparently after 1164.[5] He was thoroughly versed in the philosophy of Avicenna, but stood closer to traditional Jewish and Muslim theological doctrine, putting special emphasis on the existence of angels. He thus tended to be critical of Avicenna, and his critical attitude was followed by Fakhr-ad-dīn in *Al-Mabāḥith al-mashriqiyya,* an extensive work on 'metaphysics and physics', although he also borrows freely from Avicenna.

The greatest theological work of Fakhr-ad-dīn ar-Rāzī is his vast commentary on the Qur'ān, entitled *Mafātiḥ al-ghayb,* 'The Keys of the Unseen'. Modern editions contain between 5,000 and 8,000 pages. Critics like Ibn-Taymiyya complained that this work contained everything except *tafsīr* (commentary); but admirers replied that it contained *tafsīr* and everything else as well. He certainly manages to introduce many philosophical discussions. Of his works specifically on theological doctrine the most important is the *Muḥaṣṣal,* whose full title might be rendered 'The Summary of the Ideas of the Scholars, Philosophers and Theologians, ancient and modern'. This work shows clearly the growing importance of philosophy as a basis for theology. It is divided into four roughly equal parts, of which the first deals with logical and epistemological preliminaries, and the second with the objects of knowledge (such as the existent, the possible, the necessary). In this he goes far beyond al-Juwaynī and even beyond al-Ghazālī. In the third part he deals with the doctrine of God, and in the fourth with prophethood, eschatology and similar matters. In these last two parts he is basically an Ashʿarite.

In a long article on Fakhr-ad-dīn ar-Rāzī published in 1912 Ignaz Goldziher called attention to certain points on which his views were close to those of the Muʿtazilites despite the strong criticisms he had made of those in Khwarazm and elsewhere. Among the points mentioned were: the 'metaphorical interpretation', *taʾwīl*, of anthropomorphic terms applied to God, the use and reliability of those Ḥadīths called *āḥād* (that is, with only a single line of transmission), and the impeccability or freedom from sin (*ʿiṣma*) of the prophets. The charge is valid, but the points are minor ones, and Fakhr-ad-dīn's views may well have been due to influences other than Muʿtazilite. Goldziher realized that some previous Ashʿarites had been moving towards the acceptance of *taʾwīl* (as was noted above in the case of al-Juwaynī). Much more is now known about the works of Fakhr-ad-dīn himself and the whole intellectual background (although there are still large gaps in our knowledge); and it seems likely that his intellectual position on such matters was due primarily to his study of philosophy and of the Ashʿarite arguments against Muʿtazilism. It is possible, however, that at a later date he modified his positions somewhat in the course of his controversies with the Muʿtazilites.

Although Fakhr-ad-dīn made more use of philosophy than al-Ghazālī, he was more conservative in questions of dogma and less given to speculating freely. For example, there had been much discussion among theologians of whether God had a *ṣūra*, 'form' or 'image'. Muḥammad was reported to have said on one occasion that 'God created Adam in his *ṣūra*'; and there were other similar Ḥadīths. The one quoted seems to reflect *Genesis* 1.26, but some Muslim scholars resorted to various ingenious devices to avoid making the pronoun 'his' refer to God, since any similarity between God and a man was thought to be at variance with God's transcendence. Where al-Ghazālī had come near to accepting the idea that Adam was made in God's *ṣūra*, Fakhr-ad-dīn found a way of making 'his' refer to God and yet turning the whole saying into an assertion that is entirely about Adam and says nothing about a similarity to God. This combination of philosophy and conservatism was symptomatic of the direction in which Kalām was to develop.

Fakhr-ad-dīn ar-Rāzī was by no means the last of the Ashʿarites, but after him for about a century there was no important figure in any theological school. The gap here is doubtless due in part to the disturbed political conditions in the Iranian provinces and Iraq, especially after the Mongol invasions which culminated in the sack of Baghdad in 1258 and the end of the 'Abbāsid dynasty of caliphs.

NOTES

1. a. Al-Ghazālī—Bibliography, etc.: *GAL*, i.535-46; *GALS*, i.744-56; Maurice Bouyges, *Essai de chronologie des oeuvres de al-Ghazali*, édité et mis à jour par Michel Allard, Beirut 1959 (but written in 1924); Watt, 'A Forgery in al-Ghazālī's *Mishkāt*?', 'The Authenticity of the Works attributed to al-Ghazālī', *Journal of the Royal Asiatic Society*, 1949, 5-22; 1952, 24-45; G. F. Hourani, 'The Chronology of Ghazālī's Writings', *Journal of the American Oriental Society*, 79 (1959), 225-33.
b. Translations of Works: (1) *Iḥyā' 'ulūm ad-dīn*: G. H. Bousquet et al., *Ih'ya 'Ouloūm ed-Dīn, ou Vivification des sciences de la foi*, Paris 1955, summary of contents in detail; Nabih Amin Faris, Books 1 (Knowledge), 2 (Articles of Faith), 3 (Purity), 5 (Almsgiving), Lahore 1962, 1963, 1966 and Beirut 1966; E. E. Calverley, 4 (*Worship in Islam*), Madras 1925; M. Abul Quasem, 8 (Recitation of Qur'ān), Kuala Lumpur 1979; W. McKane, 33 (Fear and Hope), Leiden 1962; other books are translated into French and German. (2) *Al-Munqidh min aḍ-ḍalāl*: W. M. Watt, *The Faith and Practice of al-Ghazālī*, London 1951, also has translation of *Bidāyat al-hidāya*; R. J. McCarthy, *Freedom and Fulfilment*, Boston 1980, with many notes and abbreviated translations of *Fayṣal at-tafriqa*, *Faḍā'iḥ al-Bāṭiniyya*, *Al-Qisṭās al-mustaqīm*, *Al-Maqṣad al-asnā* (On the names of God), and book 21 of the *Iḥyā'* (Wonders of the Heart). (3) *Tahāfut al-falāsifa*: S. A. Kamali, Lahore 1958. (4) *Mishkāt al-anwār*: W. H. T. Gairdner, London 1924. (5) *Jawāhir al-Qur'ān*: M. Abul Quasem, Kuala Lumpur 1977.
c. Works about al-Ghazālī: D. B. Macdonald, 'The Life of al-Ghazālī with especial reference to his Religious Experiences and Opinions', *Journal of the American Oriental Society*, xx (1899), 70-132; Farid Jabre, 'La Biographie et l'oeuvre de Ghazali reconsidérées à la lumière des Ṭabaqāt de Sobki', *Mélanges de l'Institut Dominicain d'Études Orientales du Caire*, i (1954), 73-102; A. J. Wensinck, *La Pensée de Ghazzālī*, Paris 1940; Margaret Smith, *Al-Ghazālī the Mystic*, London 1944; W. M. Watt, *Muslim Intellectual, a Study of al-Ghazali*, Edinburgh 1963; also art. (al-)Ghazālī in *EI*²; Hava Lazarus-Yafeh, *Studies in al-Ghazzali*, Jerusalem 1975; Muhammad Abul Quasem, *The Ethics of al-Ghazālī*, Petaling Jaya, Malaysia, 1975; Vincenzo M. Poggi, *Un Classico della spiritualità musulmana*, Rome 1967, detailed study of the *Munqidh*; Henri Laoust, *La Politique de Gazālī*, Paris 1970; McCarthy, *Freedom and Fulfilment* (above), Introduction, ix-lx; W. Madelung, 'Ar-Rāgib al-Iṣfahānī und die Ethik al-Gazālīs' in *Islamwissenschaftliche Abhandlungen*, ed. R. Gramlich (Fritz Meier zur sechzigsten Geburtstag), Wiesbaden 1974.

2. As-Suhrwardī. Henry Corbin, *Sohrawardi d'Alep, fondateur de la doctrine illuminative (ishrāqī)*, Paris 1939; *EI*², arts. Ishrāḳ, Ishrāḳiyyūn (R. Arnaldez).

3. Ash-Shahrastānī. *GAL*, i.550f.; *GALS*, i.762f.; Alfred Guillaume, *The Summa Philosophiae of al-Shahrastānī*, London 1934, edition and abbreviated translation; W. Madelung, 'Aš-Šahrastānīs Streit-

schrift gegen Avicenna und ihre Widerlegung durch Naṣīr ad-Dīn aṭ-Ṭūsī', *Akten des VII. Kongresses für Arabistik und Islamwissenschaft (1974)*, Göttingen 1976, 250-9; the section of *Al-Milal wa-n-niḥal* dealing with Muslim sects is translated by A. K. Kazi and J. G. Flynn in *Abr-Nahrain* (Leiden), viii (1968/9), 36-68 and following vols.

4. Fakhr-ad-dīn ar-Rāzī. *GAL*, i.666-70; *GALS*, i.920-4; *EI*², art. Fakhr al-Dīn al-Rāzī (G. C. Anawati); I. Goldziher, 'Aus der Theologie des Fachr al-Dīn al-Rāzī', *Der Islam*, iii (1912), 213-47, and in *Gesammelte Schriften*, v (Hildesheim 1970), 237-71.

5. Ibn-Malkā. *EI*², art. Abu 'l-Barakāt (S. Pines); *GAL*, i.602; *GALS*, i.831; Corbin, *Histoire de la philosophie islamique* (B/D), i.247-51; Rescher, *Development of Arabic Logic* (B/D), 169f.

Chapter Fourteen

OTHER SUNNITE THEOLOGIANS, 950–1250

It is now realized by scholars that in the three centuries after al-Ashʿarī there was much theological activity apart from that among the Ashʿarites. Not much of this has been studied in detail, however, and so the treatment here is necessarily sketchy.

(a) *the Ḥanbalites*

Knowledge of the Ḥanbalites has been greatly increased during the last three or four decades through the work of Henri Laoust and his disciples, beginning with his monumental work on Ibn-Taymiyya published in 1939. In the earlier period those who followed Aḥmad ibn-Ḥanbal (pp.57–8), or regarded him as their figurehead, constituted a school that was both legal and theological, and Ḥanbalism has mostly retained this dual character; but especially between 950 and 1250 Ḥanbalites are found who were Shāfiʿite in jurisprudence.

The most distinctive feature of Ḥanbalite theology is its opposition to Kalām, that is, to rational argument in matters of dogma. Ḥanbalite creeds insist that true religion consists in accepting the Qur'ān and Sunna and following the recognized outstanding scholars of later generations, while rejecting certain forms of argument used in Kalām. The emphasis is on the formulation of the dogmas of Islam in a simple and concrete form, so that the general attitude of Ḥanbalism is not unlike that of what is called 'fundamentalism' in Christianity. Not surprisingly the Ḥanbalites had much support from ordinary people, especially from among the populace of Baghdad. The leading Ḥanbalites, however, besides being competent scholars, were very intelligent men, who were capable of giving profound reasons for their opposition to Kalām. To the charge of *tashbīh*, 'anthropomorphism', they responded by showing that Ashʿarism also had an element of *tashbīh*. Where the Muʿtazilites and later Ashʿarites interpreted the anthropomorphic terms in the Qur'ān metaphorically, the Ḥanbalites claimed that they accepted them neither literally nor metaphorically but 'amodally' (*bi-lā kayf*). In this way the Ḥanbalites may be said to have avoided the excessive intellectualism that developed in Kalām and to have preserved the essentials of Islam for ordinary men.[1]

(1) *The period of the Buwayhids, 945–1055.* When the Buwayhid sultans or war-lords became the rulers of Iraq, Iran and other provinces of the Islamic empire, they gave some encouragement to Imāmite Shī'ism and tried to weaken the attachment to Sunnism of the majority of their subjects, though without taking any extreme measures. In this situation Ḥanbalite theologians and preachers appear to have played an important role in propagating and strengthening Sunnism; and they and others were sufficiently successful for it to be possible to speak of a restoration of Sunnism from about the beginning of the eleventh century. Most of the Ḥanbalites of this period are little more than names. Al-Ajurrī (d.970) was a teacher of Ḥadīth and Shāfi'ite jurisprudence in Baghdad until 941, then went to live in Mecca in seclusion;[2] Ibn-Sam'ūn (912–97) was a popular preacher and ṣūfī in Baghdad, but is also claimed by the Ash'arites.[3]

More is known about Ibn-Baṭṭa al-'Ukbarī (917–97), since a work of his has been edited and translated into French by Henri Laoust, and provided with a long and important introduction about the development of credal statements in the Ḥanbalite school.[4] Ibn-Baṭṭa was born at 'Ukbarā on the Tigris 60 km north of Baghdad, but had his early education in Baghdad itself, where his father was a merchant. Later he travelled extensively in search of knowledge of Ḥadīth, visiting among other places Mecca, Basra and Damascus. In Mecca he became friendly with al-Ajurrī. At about the age of forty he returned to 'Ukbarā to lead a secluded life in which he devoted his time to fasting, meditation and study.

The work mentioned was planned as a simple statement of Islamic belief, specially suited for young men and non-Arabs, and it was hoped that by it those who were tending to waver in their faith would be led back to imitation of the Prophet. In the first part Ibn-Baṭṭa speaks about the unity of the community of Muslims and of the need to be loyal to it. As the bases of true belief he names not merely the Qur'ān and the Sunna, but also *ijmā'*, 'consensus'; and by this he understands primarily the consensus of the Prophet's Companions, supplemented by the consensus of the pious and worthy scholars who have followed in their footsteps. The second part treats of the particular doctrines in detail, supporting them by quotations from Qur'ān and Ḥadīth. The order of topics is notably different from that in the Ash'arite doctrinal treatises, and places in the foreground questions about faith (*īmān*), not the doctrine of God and his attributes. This is probably a better order at least for the readers in view. The relatively short third section states precisely what 'following the

Sunna' consists of in respect of various points of ritual and social relationships, while the fourth section mentions the chief heresies to be avoided, and lists the most dangerous exponents of these heretical views. Louis Gardet saw this profession of faith as constituting a kind of hinge between the earlier somewhat formless Ḥanbalite creeds and the later carefully constructed ones.

The teaching and preaching of men like Ibn-Baṭṭa led at the beginning of the eleventh century to what Laoust has called 'la restauration sunnite'. The preachers had produced in many ordinary men a greater awareness of their identity as Sunnites, and this led to popular agitation against rival Shī'ites. Small incidents could lead to violent clashes, as happened in 998 and again in 1007. Meanwhile the position of the 'Abbāsid caliphate—from 991 to 1031 the caliph was al-Qādir—was greatly strengthened by the succession in 997 to part of his father's Sāmānid governorship of a young man who soon became famous as Sultan Maḥmūd of Ghazna. The Sāmānids were autonomous rulers of eastern Persia and neighbouring lands, but nominally were appointed as governors by the 'Abbāsid caliphs. By this time, however, their power was in decline, and within a few years Maḥmūd had made himself the *de facto* ruler of much of the Sāmānid domains as well as of the region of Ghazna in Afghanistan, and he then proceeded to extend his power far into North India. Despite his great power Maḥmūd found it to his advantiage to receive an appointment from the caliph al-Qādir and recognize him as his nominal suzerain, and he also made himself a defender of Sunnism.

Encouraged by the support of Maḥmūd and also of the Sunnite populace in other cities, al-Qādir adopted a policy aimed at increasing his own power and authority and weakening those of the Buwayhid sultan who was still ruling from Baghdad. In 1003 he effectively blocked the nomination of a Shī'ite as chief judge. In 1011 he had a refutation published of the claim of the Fāṭimid dynasty of Egypt to be descended from 'Alī and Fāṭima through their son al-Ḥusayn. In 1017 he invited Maḥmūd to join him in opposing the Mu'tazilites and Ismā'īlites (who included the Fāṭimids). Then in 1018 he had a credal document formally read, probably that known as the Qādiriyya (which is not to be confused with the Qadariyya or Qadarite sect). The policy of formally reading credal statements was continued both by al-Qādir and by the son who succeeded him, al-Qā'im (1031–75), and under the latter it is explicitly stated that what was read was the Qādiriyya.[5]

The Qādiriyya is clearly an expression of Ḥanbalite doctrine. Its formulations are close to those of Ibn-Baṭṭa, though it follows a different order. It speaks of itself as presenting the doctrine of Ahl as-Sunna wa-l-Jamā'a, that is, the Sunnites, and, while it does so in a positive way, the doctrines are so worded that opposing heretical views are definitely rejected, notably those of the anthropomorphists (Mushabbiha), Karrāmites, Imāmites, Ismāʿīlites, Muʿtazilites and Ashʿarites. Al-Qādir was not himself trained in Ḥanbalite theology, but he was friendly with and influenced by one of the most distinguished Ḥanbalite scholars of the day, Ibn-Ḥamīd (d. 1012).[6] Al-Qādir doubtless also realized that a Ḥanbalite type of creed would be the most effective for strengthening Sunnite views among the masses; and in addition to the formal readings in the palace there were frequent readings in the mosques.

The most eminent pupil of Ibn-Ḥamīd was the Qāḍī Abū-Yaʿlā ibn-al-Farrāʾ (d. 1066), who was closely associated with the caliph al-Qāʾim, and present at the formal readings of the Qādiriyya in 1041 and 1053.[7] A recent study, based on the edition of his *Muʿtamad* which deals with *uṣūl ad-dīn*, 'the principles of religion', makes a case for thinking that the Ḥanbalites from Abū-Yaʿlā onwards accepted something of the methodology of Kalām. This view, which appears to be well grounded, will in time lead to some reassessment of the development of Ḥanbalism in the eleventh and twelfth centuries, even though it was already known that Ibn-Taymiyya used forms of argument far beyond those of the early Ḥanbalites.

(2) *The period of the Great Seljūqs, 1055–1157.* The year 1055, when Seljūq forces first occupied Baghdad, may be taken as the date at which power passed to the Seljūqs from the Buwayhids, though the Buwayhids had been in decline for some time and the Seljūqs experienced subsequent set-backs. The Seljūqs were supporters of Sunnism, but to begin with (as seen above) unduly favoured the Ḥanafites and then later strengthened the Ashʿarites, while trying to keep peace between the rival Sunnite factions. It was in the middle of this period that the Crusaders appeared in Syria and conquered Jerusalem; but these events, despite their great significance for western Europe, produced hardly a ripple in Baghdad and nothing further east.

A colourful personage at the beginning of the period was the Sharīf Abū-Jaʿfar, probably the leading exponent of Ḥanbalite jurisprudence in Baghdad at the time.[8] He became famous, or perhaps rather notorious through his forceful opposition to the Muʿtazilites, Ashʿarites and Ṣūfīs. Thus in 1068 he was at the head of a popular demonstration protesting against the renewal of Muʿtazilite teaching and demanding the reading and reaffirmation of the Qādiriyya creed. In the following year and again in 1072 he attacked a younger Ḥanbalite Ibn-ʿAqīl, of whom more will be said presently, for accepting some Muʿtazilite views and being a follower of the condemned mystic al-Ḥallāj. Finally for some five months he led a movement of protest against the public preaching of Ashʿarite doctrines in the Niẓāmiyya college by a visiting professor, Abū-Naṣr al-Qushayrī, son of the ṣūfī and theologian mentioned above. There were several incidents, and peace was only restored between the factions by the death of the Sharīf (September 1077) and Niẓām-al-mulk's recall of al-Qushayrī to Nishapur.

Of other distinguished and less bellicose Ḥanbalite scholars in Baghdad most is known about Ibn-ʿAqīl, who has been the subject of a detailed study by George Makdisi.[9] He was born in Baghdad in 1040 and died there in 1119. Though perhaps originally a Ḥanafite, after the troubles ensuing on the Seljūq conquest of Baghdad in 1055 he became a Ḥanbalite, apparently as a result of the patronage of the influential Ḥanbalite merchant Abū-Manṣūr ibn-Yūsuf. He studied under Abū-Yaʿlā until the latter's death in 1066, but he had broad interests and names twenty-two other teachers (only one a Ḥanbalite) under whom he studied a variety of subjects. For a time he was attracted to Muʿtazilism, like some other scholars who were Ḥanafite in jurisprudence, and he was also interested in the controversial ṣūfī al-Ḥallāj.

In 1066 Abū-Manṣūr was instrumental in having Ibn-ʿAqīl appointed to succeed Abū-Yaʿlā in the chair of jurisprudence in the *jāmiʿ*, 'cathedral-mosque', of al-Manṣūr. This appointment at the early age of 26 incurred the resentment of other scholars, not least the Sharīf Abū-Jaʿfar; and after the death of Abū-Manṣūr some two years later the Sharīf accused Ibn-ʿAqīl of holding heretical Muʿtazilite views and writing in defence of al-Ḥallāj. Ibn-ʿAqīl was fortunate in finding another Ḥanbalite merchant as protector, but had to avoid appearing in public for some years. Then in September 1072 under obscure circumstances the issue was raised again, and Ibn-ʿAqīl was forced to make a public retractation before the Sharīf Abū-Jaʿfar and five official public witnesses. Through the centuries there has been much discussion of the sincerity of this retractation. So far as Muʿtazilism goes, it is likely that he was wholly sincere, since there is no evidence of his having adopted any Muʿtazilite doctrines. On the other hand, he was influenced by the Muʿtazilite spirit of free enquiry, and perhaps also by the methodology. This last point gains some support from the recent discovery of elements of Kalām in the writings of his teacher Abū-Yaʿlā; but it is difficult to be certain since Ibn-ʿAqīl's works on theology are lost. With regard to al-Ḥallāj the position is less clear; the Ḥanbalite school as a whole did not condemn al-Ḥallāj and Ibn-ʿAqīl's writing about him was apparently not destroyed.

Even after his reconciliation with the Sharīf he lived quietly until the latter's death in 1077, though he may have given a few sermons in his own mosque. Then gradually he seems to have taken up again the work of teaching, and the names of several of his pupils are recorded. It is not known whether he continued to teach until the end of his life. He himself, however, describes his feeling that there were no great scholars left, and this saddened him. His sorrow was increased by the death of his sons, the elder aged 14 in 1095 and the younger aged 29 in 1116. He did not complain, but longed for death and was constantly meditating on the life to come.

The most important of his extant works is the single surviving volume of *Kitāb al-funūn*, a gigantic work said to have comprised a hundred or even several hundred volumes. The title means 'The Book of (all) Sorts (of Knowledge)', and the work consists of the author's thoughts on a great variety of topics, from all the fields of knowledge in which he was interested. He apparently set down his thoughts as they came to him and not in any order, but he writes with literary grace, whether the topic occupies only a few lines or extends to a page or two. Clearly he was a very gifted man who may rightly be described as 'standing at the head of the progressive movement within Sunnī traditionalism'.

In the following half-century or so two Ḥanbalite scholars became prominent. One was Ibn-Hubayra (d.1165), who as vizier to the caliphs al-Muqtafī (1136–60) and al-Mustanjid (1160–70) contributed to the 'restauration sunnite', and founded a *madraša* in Baghdad for the teaching of Ḥanbalite jurisprudence.[10] The other, ʿAbd-al-Qādir al-Jīlī or al-Jīlānī (d.1166), is chiefly known as a ṣūfī saint, but was also a theologian, and his chief work *al-Ghunya* includes a theological treatise and a short creed.[11]

(3) *The last century of the ʿAbbāsids, 1157–1258.* Before the death of Sanjar, the last of the Great Seljūqs, in 1157 the dynasty had lost effective control of most of Iraq, and rule was shared by a number of minor dynasties. In Egypt Fāṭimid power had been ended and nominal ʿAbbāsid suzerainty restored in 1171 by the great Saladin (Ṣalāḥ-ad-dīn), founder of the Ayyūbid dynasty. The absence of a strong ruler in Iraq enabled the ʿAbbāsid caliphs of the early thirteenth century to recover a measure of power and influence, and many Ḥanbalites were associated with them, though none is outstanding.

The scholar most worthy of mention is the polymath, Ibn-al-Jawzī (1116–1200), who lived mainly in Baghdad.[12] Over a hundred of his works survive, some admittedly short, and he is said to have written several hundreds more. He was brought into the service of the caliphs by the vizier Ibn-Hubayra, and became prominent as a preacher under al-Mustanjid and still more under his successor al-Mustaḍīʾ (1170–80). For a time he was also the senior professor at five *madrasas*. The next caliph, an-Nāṣir (1180–1225), was less closely associated with the Ḥanbalites, and in 1194 Ibn-al-Jawzī, who had been critical of his policies, was exiled to Wāsiṭ in Iraq, where he remained under house-arrest for five years, and was released only shortly before his death. His most important works are reckoned to be a history and a group of laudatory biographies of leading religious figures of early Islam. In theology he is noted for a polemical work entitled *Talbīs Iblīs*, 'the confusing of the Devil', in which he attacked not only sects such as the Khārijites and the various branches of Shī'ism but also schools and individuals within Sunnism whom he considered to have held heretical views, such as the Ash'arites, including al-Ghazālī, and the ṣūfīs. A son, Muḥyī-d-dīn ibn-al-Jawzī, who perished in the sack of Baghdad by the Mongols, was both a distinguished scholar and the founder of a *madrasa* in Damascus, the Jawziyya. A daughter's son, known as Sibṭ ibn-al-Jawzī, 'the grandson of Ibn-al-Jawzī' (d.1256), settled in Damascus and became well-known as a preacher and historian, but abandoned Ḥanbalism for Ḥanafism.

Long before 1258 Ḥanbalism had established itself in other centres than Baghdad. In Ispahan there was a group, of which a father and son, both known as Ibn-Manda, were prominent members; they died in 1005 and 1077 respectively. There were Ḥanbalites as far east as Herat in Afghanistan, though the most famous there, Al-Anṣārī al-Harawī (1005–89), gained his fame through a work on Ṣūfism.[13] It was above all in Damascus, however, that Ḥanbalism took root. There appears to have been a Ḥanbalite professor there before 945, but it was especially in the later eleventh century that the school became established in Syria and Palestine through the efforts of Abū-l-Faraj ash-Shīrāzī (d.1094), who had been a pupil of Abū-Ya'lā in Baghdad. He had a son, also a scholar, who wrote a refutation of Ash'arism, but is best known as the founder of the first Ḥanbalite *madrasa* in Damascus, the Ḥanbaliyya.[14] Two other Damascene families also produced a succession of scholars, the Banū Munajjā and the Banū Qudāma. The best known of these was possibly Muwaffaq-ad-dīn ibn-Qudāma (d.1223), who wrote a long treatise on jurisprudence which was much commented on and is still highly esteemed. Another book, sometimes called a refutation of Ibn-'Aqīl, is a critique of Kalām; there is an edition and English translation by George Makdisi with the title 'Ibn Qudāma's Censure of Speculative Theology'.[15]

The existence of this strong group of Ḥanbalites in Damascus meant that after the sack of Baghdad by the Mongols leadership in the Ḥanbalite school fell to the scholars of Damascus.

(b) *the Māturīdites*

The Māturīdites are closely identified with the Ḥanafite schools of jurisprudence, and, though there are biographical dictionaries of Ḥanafites, the information given is meagre. Since, too, there has been no extensive study of Māturīdite theological works, all that is possible here is to give brief notices of one or two leading figures.

Al-Ḥakīm as-Samarqandī (d.953) was a pupil of al-Māturīdī, though possibly not much younger, and became *qāḍī* of Samarqand.[16]

His theological work with the short title *As-Sawād al-aʿẓam* gets this from a version of the Ḥadīth about the seventy-three sects in which *al-firqa an-nājiya*, 'the saved sect', is replaced by *as-sawād al-aʿẓam*, 'the greater number'. Al-Ḥakīm here expounds sixty-two articles of belief which he holds must be accepted by all who belong to *as-sawād al-aʿẓam*.

Abū-l-Layth as-Samarqandī—no relative of the above—studied with his father in Samarqand and with other teachers both there and in Balkh.[17] He also taught in both places. His death is assigned to various years between 983 and 1003. About two dozen of his works are extant, some in numerous manuscripts, a fact which shows his high reputation. Among these works are a commentary on the Qur'ān and various books of a juristic or parenetic character. A short *ʿAqīda*, 'creed', composed in the form of question and answer, is still widely used throughout the Islamic world, especially in Malaysia and Indonesia. To him is sometimes attributed *Sharḥ al-fiqh al-akbar*, which is a commentary on the creed ascribed to Abū-Ḥanīfa and known as *Al-Fiqh al-akbar I*. The work mentions the Ashʿarites as a group, however, and since, as noted above, it is doubtful if they constituted a group much before the year 1000, it is more likely that the work is by a pupil of Abū-l-Layth, though he may have been repeating the master's lectures.

Abū-l-Yusr al-Pazdawī (*c.*1030–1100) belonged to a family of scholars, his great-grandfather having been a pupil of al-Māturīdī.[18] He probably spent most of his life in Bukhara, but was *qāḍī* of Samarqand for a period round about 1088. In his book *Uṣūl ad-dīn*, 'the principles of religion', he discusses 96 points of doctrine, giving the Ḥanafite-Māturīdite position on each, and then divergent views and refutations of these. The views are those of Muʿtazilites and other theologians of the 'classical' period prior to al-Ashʿarī, together with those of al-Ashʿarī himself, the Ashʿarites, the Karrāmites and the 'philosophers'. In the case of these three groups no individual names are mentioned. It is noteworthy that the 'philosophers' are mentioned and argued against, but al-Ghazālī would doubtless have found the arguments unsatisfactory. A pupil of his, Najm-ad-dīn Abū-Ḥafṣ an-Nasafī (1068–1142), composed a short creed, *Al-ʿAqāʾid*, which has been the subject of many commentaries and supercommentaries.[19]

Other Māturīdites who composed creeds which have attracted attention were Abū-Muʿīn an-Nasafī (d.1115)[20] and al-Ūshī, who is associated with the region of Ferghana on the Jaxartes, and whose creed, composed about 1173, is a poem of sixty-six lines.[21] There is obviously much work still to be done on the Māturīdites, but from these brief descriptions it would appear that, despite their interest in rational argument in theology, they achieved nothing comparable to the developments among the Ashʿarites.

(c) *the Muʿtazilites*

Before 850 many, perhaps most, Muʿtazilites had Shīʿite sympathies in some form. After 850, however, their doctrines were less relevant to actual politics and their influence with the caliphal government declined, so that Muʿtazilism became a purely theological doctrine, separate from both politics and jurisprudence. Many Muʿtazilites were Ḥanafites or Shāfiʿites in law, and some were Imāmites or Zaydites in politics. Since the Buwayhid sultans favoured Imāmite Shīʿism and also to some extent Muʿtazilism, this may have encouraged the move towards Shīʿism. Most Muʿtazilites, however, accepted some form of Sunnism, and so may now be reckoned among the Sunnite theologians.

The earliest in date of those to be mentioned is something of an exception. The Ṣāḥib Ibn-ʿAbbād (938–95), often referred to simply as the Ṣāḥib, was the son of a Buwayhid official, and himself spent his life in the service of various Buwayhid princes, rising (about 979) to be vizier in Rayy for the surrounding region.[22] Despite this involvement in administrative duties he also distinguished himself as both a scholar and a man of letters. His numerous books range from the fields of theology, history, philosophy and literary criticism to poetry and belles-lettres; and he was also a patron of art and literature. In his theological books he expounds Muʿtazilite doctrine on the basis of the 'five principles' (pp.48–52 above). Later Imāmites claimed that the Ṣāḥib was one of them, and the Qāḍī ʿAbd-al-Jabbār asserts that he was a Rāfiḍite, which amounts to the same thing; and this is in line with some of his own statements, and would not be surprising since he was working for the Buwayhids. Other statements of his, however, suggest that he was a Zaydite; and this may also have been true for a time.

The Qāḍī ʿAbd-al-Jabbār (*c.*935–1025) was the leading Muʿtazilite of his time.[23] Though he was highly thought of by his contemporaries, little attention was paid to him by recent scholars until after 1950–1, when a team of Egyptian scholars discovered in a mosque in Sanaa (Yemen) the greater part of his enormous dogmatic work, *Al-Mughnī*. This discovery, followed by that of most of the remaining parts of the work, has led to widespread interest in his thought. After studying in Hamadhan he went to Basra where under the influence of a Muʿtazilite teacher he changed to Muʿtazilism from the Ashʿarism he had hitherto professed, though in law he remained a Shāfiʿite. He then continued his Muʿtazilite studies in Baghdad. Political factors may have contributed to his change of allegiance, for it is known that at some date after 970 the Ṣāḥib, then vizier in Rayy, invited him to take up a post there, and then about 978 promoted him to be chief *qāḍī* of the region. He lost this post, at least for a time, on the death of the Ṣāḥib, but nothing is known of his life after that point.

Since the discovery and publication of the *Mughnī,* others of his works (previously known) have been published, notably *Sharḥ al-uṣūl al-khamsa,* 'The Exposition of the Five Principles', which is a one-volume compendium of Mu'tazilite theology. The great value of these works of 'Abd-al-Jabbār is that they are the earliest complete Mu'tazilite treatises. Scholars were already familiar with the outlines of Mu'tazilite doctrine, but they now have it in fuller detail and can appreciate the arguments by which it was supported. George F. Hourani, for example, has shown that, although 'Abd-al-Jabbār did not think of philosophical ethics as a subject of study, he and his predecessors had reflected on the questions involved, so that from his works a fairly complete system can be constructed that is not unlike modern British intuitionism.

The general character of the works of 'Abd-al-Jabbār and his style of argumentation are similar to those of Ash'arites such as al-Bāqillānī and al-Juwaynī. Beliefs differing from his own are mentioned and argued against. Sometimes the views are given anonymously, but frequently they are those of earlier Mu'tazilites, who are named, while other opponents are named occasionally. Al-Ash'arī is mentioned by name, but only rarely, whereas the group holding views of an Ash'arite type are normally called the Kullābites, which seems to indicate that al-Ash'arī was not yet recognized everywhere as eponym of the school. The 'philosophers' are sometimes mentioned, but there is no sign of any adoption of philosophical ideas beyond what had been done by the Ash'arites prior to al-Ghazālī. Much further study, however, is still required.

One of the Qāḍī's prominent pupils was Abū-l-Ḥusayn al-Baṣrī (d. 1044), both a Ḥanafite jurist and a theologian who criticized, among others, the Imāmites and the followers of Abū-Hāshim.[24] A more important pupil, however, was Abū-Rashīd (d. 1068?).[25] For a time he had a 'circle' (*ḥalqa*) in Nishapur for the discussion of questions of Kalām; but when the Qāḍī died or retired, he succeeded him as head of the Mu'tazilite school of Baghdad. His chief work dealt with the points in dispute between the Mu'tazilite schools of Basra and Baghdad, and his treatment in it of philosophical conceptions attracted some Western scholars about the beginning of this century; but his study of philosophy was not so thorough as that of al-Ghazālī. Like the Qāḍī he is said to have been originally an Ash'arite in theology.

Az-Zamakhsharī (1075–1144) was born in the province of Khwarazm, but travelled for the purpose of study to Baghdad and Mecca among other places.[26] After many years in Mecca he returned to Khwarazm. Though of Persian stock he became the foremost authority of the day on most of the philological disciplines connected with the Arabic language, and wrote a number of important books. Chief among these is his commentary on the Qur'ān, the *Kashshāf*, which, because of the soundness and extent of his philological knowledge, remains one of the outstanding Qur'ānic commentaries. In theology he accepted the Mu'tazilite views at that time predominant in Khwarazm, but these affected his interpretations of only a small number of verses. Some mainstream Sunnites avoided the *Kashshāf* because of this, but such was its philological excellence that it was widely studied and in many respects followed even by those who disapproved of Mu'tazilite views. In law he is claimed for the Ḥanafite school. At one time, either because of an accident or after frost-bite, he had had to have a foot amputated and replaced by a wooden one; and ever after he seems to have remained very conscious of this disability.[27]

After this brief account of the more prominent later Mu'tazilites the question may be considered whether they represent a new creative period in the history of the school and of Islamic thought, or whether it is correct to think of the 'classical' period as ending with Abū-Hāshim. Goldziher in studying the influence of the Mu'tazilites on Fakhr-ad-dīn ar-Rāzī showed the continuing strength of the school, and George Hourani has claimed that the work of 'Abd-al-Jabbār proves that Mu'tazilism was 'still a living and slightly growing school'. Yet, though there are creative aspects in 'Abd-al-Jabbār, it is doubtful if the school was contributing much to Islamic thought in general. It is not only modern Western scholars who have neglected the Mu'tazilites after Abū-Hāshim. In the twelfth century ash-Shahrastānī speaks of 'Abd-al-Jabbār and Abū-l-Ḥusayn al-Baṣrī as *muta'akhkhirīn*, 'epigons', of the Mu'tazilites, and does not regard their views as sufficiently distinctive to justify separate treatment (though in his *Nihāya* he mentions views of Abū-l-Ḥusayn on five occasions). On the whole, then, there is good reason for taking the period up to Abū-Hāshim as the 'classical' period of Mu'tazilism and of Islamic thought generally.

In effect what the Mu'tazilites were doing after 850 was to elaborate arguments to defend doctrines which had been decisively rejected by most of the Muslim community and were unlikely to be again accepted. They showed great ingenuity and subtlety in their arguments, but they made little impression. Other Sunnites mostly neglected them, and it was only among Imāmites and Zaydites that interest was shown. The Mu'tazilite doctrine of the createdness of the Qur'ān made it possible to place the imam above the Qur'ān (and its interpreters, the ulema); and this fitted in well with the core of Shī'ite belief. This was why the Mu'tazilites had considerable influence on the Imāmites and Zaydites, though, as the Shī'ite theologians became familiar with the methods of Kalām, they ceased to be dependent on the Muʿtazilites. Perhaps the most important achievement of the epigons was to preserve Kalām in such a form that it could be accepted by Imāmites and Zaydites.

(d) *minor schools*

In eastern Iran and Afghanistan from the tenth century to the twelfth some importance attached to the Karrāmites, who have already been mentioned once or twice.[28] Less important were their centres in Jerusalem and Fusṭāṭ (Old Cairo). The heresiographers mention a number of subdivisions, but virtually nothing is known of these except the names. Of the writings of the Karrāmites apparently only one slight work has been preserved, so that the reconstruction of their views and those of their founder, Ibn-Karrām, has to be based on the statements of opponents. Where they were strong they often aroused violent opposition. For a time they had the support of the sultan Maḥmūd of Ghazna, but he withdrew his support about 1012. The fullest information about them comes from Nishapur, where under the leadership of the Maḥmashādh family they had many followers. Despite our limited knowledge of them it appears that they played an important role in spreading a moderate form of Sunnite Kalām in the eastern part of the ʿAbbāsid caliphate.

The Sālimites were ṣūfīs more than theologians, but some of their teaching attracted theological criticism, though only from Ḥanbalites, it would seem.[29] Among the leading members of the school were Abū-Ṭālib al-Makkī (d.990), author of an influential work called *Qūt al-qulūb*, 'the food of the hearts',[30] and Ibn-Barrajān (d.1141), whose ṣūfī commentary on the Qurʾān is partly extant.[31] It is possible that the heretical assertions in *Qūt al-qulūb* have been removed from the text as we have it; but in any case it is difficult to derive theological doctrine from a work of spirituality or a ṣūfistic Qurʾān-commentary. Thus the theological views of the Sālimites have to be reconstructed mainly from the statements of Ḥanbalite opponents. Abū-Yaʿlā in one of his works lists sixteen false doctrines held by them, and ʿAbd-al-Qādir al-Jīlānī repeats ten of these. The first to call attention to the Sālimites was Ignaz Goldziher, and they were later studied to some depth by Louis Massignon because they were among the first to hold that al-Ḥallāj was not heretical. Henri Laoust was aware of their influence on Ibn-Taymiyya through Abū-Ṭālib al-Makkī.

Some of the assertions listed by Abū-Yaʿlā appear to be trivial: Iblīs (Satan), after his refusal to prostrate himself before Adam (Sura 7.11, etc.), did so when asked a second time; Moses prided himself on having been spoken to by God, and then was shown a thousand mountains with a Moses on each. These may make more sense, however, when seen in context and not taken in isolation. The more comprehensible assertions are the following. God creates unceasingly, and so he is everywhere equally present. When someone recites the Qur'ān, it is God who is heard speaking. God has a will (*mashī'a*) which is uncreated, whereas his particular volitions (*irādāt*) are created. His volitions concerning the faults of the creatures foresee these as in them (*bi-him*) but not as coming from them (*min-hum*). On the Day of Judgement God will show himself to all creatures, jinn, men, angels and animals, in a form appropriate to each, so that each will acknowledge his significance. God has a *sirr*, 'secret nature', and the same is true of prophets, scholars and indeed of everyone; and for the believer mystical union consists in becoming aware of the divine 'I' in himself to the extent to which it has been given him from all eternity; God's *sirr* is *sirr ar-rubūbiyya*, 'the secret of sovereignty'. The human soul continues to exist in the period between death and the Last Day.

The Sālimites were not far from conservative and traditional orthodoxy, but they allowed themselves some freedom in their theological speculations on the basis of their mystical experiences. It was this freedom which both roused opposition and gave them influence.

NOTES

1. Ḥanbalism: H. Laoust, art. Ḥanābila in *EI*[2], and also 'Le hanbalisme sous le califat de Bagdad', *Revue des Études Islamiques*, xxvii (1959), 67-128.
2. Al-Ajurrī (Abū-Bakr Muḥammad ibn-al-Ḥusayn): *GAL*, i.173; *GAS*, i.194.
3. Ibn-Sam'ūn (Abū-l-Ḥusayn Muḥammad): *GALS*, i.360; *GAS*, i.667.
4. Ibn-Baṭṭa: *GALS*, i.311; *GAS*, i.514f.; H. Laoust, *La Profession de foi d'Ibn Baṭṭa*, Damascus 1958, edition and translation; review of this by Louis Gardet, 'L'importance historique du Ḥanbalisme d'après un livre recent', *Arabica*, vi.225-32.
5. Qādiriyya: English version in Adam Mez, *The Renaissance of Islam*, Eng. tr. by S. Khuda Bakhsh and D. S. Margoliouth, Patna 1937, 207-9; cf. Makdisi, *Ibn 'Aqīl* (n.14/9), 299-310, with French version, 304-8; also Laoust, *Profession*, Introd., xcii-xcix.
6. Ibn-Ḥamīd (Abū-'Abd-Allāh al-Ḥasan al-Warrāq): *GALS*, i.311; *GAS*, i.515; Makdisi, op. cit., 227-30.
7. Abū-Ya'lā: *GALS*, i.686; Makdisi, op. cit., 232-6; Daniel Gimaret, 'Théories de l'acte humain dans l'école ḥanbalite', *Bulletin d'études orientales* (Institut français de Damas), xxix (1977), 157-78, esp. 161-5.
8. Abū-Ja'far: *GALS*, i.687; Makdisi, op. cit., 240-8. 337-40, 350-66, 426-39.
9. Ibn-'Aqīl (Abū-l-Wafā' 'Alī aẓ-Ẓafarī): *GAL*, i.502; *GALS*, i.687; George Makdisi, *Ibn 'Aqīl et la resurgence de l'Islam traditionaliste au XIe siècle*, Damascus 1963; also *EI*[2], art. Ibn 'Akīl (Abū 'l-Wafā'); also ed. *The Notebooks of Ibn 'Aqīl, Kitāb al-funūn*, 2 vols., Beirut n.d. (? 1970, 1971).
10. Ibn-Hubayra: *GALS*, i.687f.; *EI*[2], art. Ibn Hubayra (G. Makdisi).
11. 'Abd-al-Qādir al-Jīlānī: *EI*[2], art. 'Abd al-Ḳādir al-Djīlānī (W. Braune).

12. Ibn-al-Jawzī (Abū-l-Faraj ʿAbd-ar-Raḥmān ibn-Abī-l-Ḥasan): *GAL*, i.659-66; *GALS*, i.914-20; *EI*², art. Ibn al-Djawzī (ʿAbd al-Raḥmān) (Laoust).
13. *EI*², arts. Ibn Manda (F. Rosenthal); (al-)Anṣārī al-Harawī (S. de Beaurecueil).
14. Abū-l-Faraj ash-Shīrāzī: Makdisi, *Ibn ʿAqīl*, 239.
15. Ibn-Qudāma: *GAL*, i.502-4; *GALS*, i.688f.; Makdisi, ed. and translator, *Ibn Qudāma's Censure of Speculative Theology* (Gibb Memorial Series), London 1962; also *EI*², art. Ibn Ḳudāma.
16. Al-Ḥakīm as-Samarqandī (Abū-l-Qāsim Isḥāq): *GALS*, i.295; *GAS*, i.606; English translation of *As-Sawād al-aʿẓam* in an unpublished PhD thesis by Farouq ʿOmar ʿAbdallah al-ʿOmar, Edinburgh 1974.
17. Abū-l-Layth (Naṣr ibn-Muḥammad): *GAL*, i.210f.; *GALS*, i.374f.; *EI*², art. Abu 'l-Layth al-Samarqandī (J. Schacht).
18. Al-Pazdawī (Abū-l-Yusr Muḥammad ibn-Muḥammad ibn-al-Ḥusayn): not in *GAL*,; his *K. uṣūl ad-dīn*, ed. Hans Peter Linss, Cairo 1963.
19. Abū-Ḥafṣ an-Nasafī (ʿUmar ibn-Muḥammad): *GAL*, i.548-50; *GALS*, i.758-62; *EIS*, art. (al-)Nasafī II (A. J. Wensinck).
20. Abū-Muʿīn an-Nasafī (Maymūn ibn-Muḥammad): *GAL*, i.547; *GALS*, i.757; Eng. tr. of creed in A. Jeffery, *A Reader on Islam*, The Hague 1962, 375-456; *EIS*, art. (al-)Nasafī I (A. J. Wensinck).
21. Al-Ūshī (Sirāj-ad-dīn ʿAlī ibn-ʿUthmān): *GAL*, i.552f.; *GALS*, i.764f.
22. Ibn-ʿAbbād (Abū-l-Qāsim Ismāʿīl aṣ-Ṣāḥib aṭ-Ṭāliqānī): *GAL*, i. 136f.; *GALS*, i.198f.; *EI*², art. Ibn ʿAbbād (Cahen; Pellat).
23. ʿAbd-al-Jabbār (ibn-Aḥmad al-Qāḍī): *GALS*, i.343f.; *GAS*, i.624-6; *EI*², art. ʿAbd al-Djabbār b. Aḥmad (S. M. Stern); G. C. Anawati, R. Caspar, M. el-Khodeiri, 'une somme inédite de théologie muʿtazilite: Le Moghni du Qāḍī ʿAbd al-Jabbār', *Mélanges de l'Institut Dominicain des Études Orientales* (Cairo), iv (1957), 281-316; George F. Hourani, *Islamic Rationalism: the Ethics of ʿAbd al-Jabbār*, Oxford 1971; Michael Schwarz, 'The Qāḍī ʿAdb-al-Ǧabbār's Refutation of the Ašʿarite doctrine of "acquisition" (*kasb*)', *Israel Oriental Studies*, vi (1976), 229-63.
24. Abū-l-Ḥusayn al-Baṣrī (Muḥammad ibn-ʿAlī): *GAL*, i.600; *GALS*, i.829; *GAS*, i.627.
25. Abū-Rashīd: *GALS*, i.344; *GAS*, i.626; Max Horten, *Die Philosophie des Abu Raschid*, Bonn 1910.
26. Az-Zamakhsharī (Abū-l-Qāsim Maḥmūd): *GAL*, i.344-50; *GALS*, i.507-13; *EIS*, art. (al-)Zamakhsharī (C. Brockelmann); Ignaz Goldziher, *Die Richtungen der islamischen Koranauslegung*, Leiden 1920, 117-77.
27. A later Muʿtazilite was ʿAbd-al-Ḥamīd ibn-Abī-l-Ḥadīd: *GAL*, i.335f.; *GALS*, i.497; *Encyclopaedia Iranica*, art. by Madelung.
28. Karrāmites: *EI*², art. Karrāmiyya (C. E. Bosworth); Massignon, *Essai*², 255-72.
29. Sālimites: Ignaz Goldziher, 'Die dogmatische Partei der Sālimijja', *Zeitschrift der deutschen morgenländischen Gesellschaft*, lxi (1907), 73-80 (also in *Gesammelte Schriften*, Hildesheim 1970, v. 76-83); Louis Massignon, *Passion*² (B/E), i.631 and ii.140f. (Eng. tr., i.582 and ii.130f.), corrects some statements in *Passion*¹, i.301 and *EI*¹, art. Sālimīya (by himself); cf. his *Essai*², 294-300.
30. Abū-Ṭālib al-Makkī: *GAL*, i.217; *GALS*, i.359f.; *EI*², art. Abū Ṭālib al-Makkī (L. Massignon).
31. Ibn-Barrajān: *GAL*, i.559; *EI*², art. Ibn Barradjān (A. Faure).

CHAPTER FIFTEEN

THEOLOGY AND PHILOSOPHY IN THE ISLAMIC WEST

The Islamic West is a convenient term to designate Islamic Spain and North Africa, which are referred to in Arabic as the Maghrib or 'West'. Nearly the whole of Spain was conquered by the Arabs in the early eighth century and became a province of the Umayyad caliphate. Shortly after the overthrow of the Umayyads by the ʿAbbāsids in 750 a young Umayyad prince, who had managed to escape from the ʿAbbāsids, became independent ruler of the province of al-Andalus or Spain. The Umayyads maintained their rule in Spain until 1031. From then until 1090 over a dozen petty dynasties, the *reyes de taifas*, each controlled a small territory. From the middle of the eleventh to the middle of the thirteenth century north-west Africa was dominated in succession by two great Islamic empires ruled by Berber dynasties, the Almoravids and the Almohads (in Arabic al-Murābiṭūn and al-Muwaḥḥidūn). Both began as movements of religious revival or reform among young men, then later gained political power. The Almoravid empire at its greatest extent stretched from Senegal to Algiers, and from 1090 included nearly all Islamic Spain, which had asked the Almoravids for help against the Christian Reconquista. Between 1120 and 1150 the Almohads conquered most of this empire and even extended it to include Tunisia. As the Almohads in turn declined the Christians recovered Spain apart from the small sultanate of Granada, which maintained itself until 1492. The Almohad dynasty came to an end in Africa in 1269.

The culture of the Islamic West was continuous with that of the heartlands in many important respects. The relationship is not unlike that of the culture of Australia, Canada and the earlier America to British culture. It was usually possible for Muslim scholars to travel from the Maghrib to the eastern intellectual centres, at least as far as Baghdad, and many did so. A few scholars came from the east and settled in Spain. Contributions were made in Spain to the advancement of Islamic humanistic and religious studies. In its greatest periods Moorish culture is reputed to have had a brilliance comparable to that of Baghdad, but one wonders how much of this brilliance was outward and materialistic. Was there genuine spiritual vitality, or was the Islamic religion merely the framework of a largely secular way of life? Was there any attempt to adapt the general forms of Islamic culture to the special situation of the Spanish Muslims? Until these and similar questions have been more fully investigated, no more than a preliminary orientation can be given of the place of theology and philosophy in the intellectual life of the Islamic West.

The one outstanding theologian of Islamic Spain was Ibn-Ḥazm (*c.*993–1064), europeanized as Abenhazam.[1] His family is thought to have been an old Christian Spanish one which had adopted Islam. His father rose to the position of vizier in Cordova, but this involved him in the troubles following a breakdown of government in 1008, and he met his death in 1012. The young Ibn-Ḥazm suffered in the confusion of these years, but that did not prevent him taking up an administrative career, and becoming vizier to two or even three of the powerless and short-lived Umayyad rulers of the next decades. He had several spells in prison. After the disappearance of the last Umayyad in 1031 he went into semi-retirement and devoted himself to intellectual work. He was a many-sided scholar and wrote books in many different fields, his best-known one being *Ṭawq al-ḥamāma*, 'The Ring of the Dove', which is about love and lovers, and has been translated into at least five European languages. This was his first prose work, written about 1022, and, though the genre was already established in Arabic literature, Ibn-Ḥazm managed to show some originality.

His studies in Cordova had of course included jurisprudence, but he was dissatisfied with the Mālikite school dominant in al-Andalus and, after following the Shāfiʿites for a time, eventually found his spiritual home in the Ẓāhirite school. This is a minor school which has died out. The name is derived from its principle that the statements of the Qur'ān and the Ḥadīth are to be taken in their literal or outward sense (*ẓāhir*) and not in an inward or esoteric sense (*bāṭin*). While previous Ẓāhirites had applied the principle only to legal matters, and had held various views in theology, Ibn-Ḥazm attempted to apply it also in points of dogma, and so to bring law and theology together in a single intellectual structure. Indeed his coherent methodology also included grammar, as was shown by Roger Arnaldez' careful and detailed study.

Ibn-Ḥazm was very conscious of the way in which an individual's subjective motivations may cause his statements and interpretations to deviate from strict truth. He was trying to present a view of human life based solely on the objective divine revelation, the *ẓāhir*, and excluding everything subjective. This was the coherent elaboration of a religious intuition with deep roots in the Muslim soul—the intuition which finds expression in the traditional view that the Qur'ān was in no way influenced by Muḥammad's personality but was brought to him from outside himself (from God) by an angel. There is something of the same objectivity in the act which is the climax of Muslim worship, the act of *sujūd* or touching the ground with the forehead in the formal prayers, in total submission of one's humanity to the omnipotence of God. It is therefore not surprising that Ibn-Ḥazm had considerable influence in the Islamic West, even though he had no followers. His theological views were not taken up by other Ẓāhirites, but something of his outlook is to be found in later writers of the region, even when their general position is very different from his. His views in detail were not unlike those of the Ḥanbalites. Like them he attacked *qiyās*, 'argument from analogy', and insisted that the choice of the ground of comparison on which the analogy was based was necessarily subjective. There is a short statement of his doctrinal beliefs in the chapter on *tawḥīd*, 'the unity (of God)', in his legal work *Kitāb al-Muḥallā*.

His most important theological work is not a comprehensive treatise like those of the Ash'arites, but takes the form of a 'critical history of religious ideas'. The short title is *Kitāb al-fiṣal*. He seems to have conceived it primarily as a dogmatic work, but it is in part a heresiography, describing the views of the Islamic sects briefly and then giving in full the reasons for rejecting these views. It also deals with other religions, notably Christianity, in the same way. This last feature, which led the Spanish Islamist Miguel Asin Palacios to speak of Ibn-Ḥazm as 'the first historian of religious ideas', is perhaps due to the conditions of inter-religious contact in Spain. He was particularly bitter in his attacks on the Ash'arites and their doctrine of the divine attributes, for he regarded their use of 'analogical' reasoning in respect of this topic as a subjective element. He seemed to treat them more harshly than he did the Mu'tazilites. He himself aimed at avoiding both anthropomorphism and metaphorical interpretation, and in this he came close to the Ḥanbalite conception of *balkafiyya*, 'amodality'; in discussing various items in the descriptions of heaven and hell he said 'we believe in them, but do not know *how (kayfa)* they are'.

Of less importance, but still of some interest is Abū-Bakr ibn-al-'Arabī (1076–1148).[2] He set out from Seville in 1092 on a journey to the east with his father. He studied in Damascus and Baghdad, made the pilgrimage to Mecca in November/December 1096, returned to Baghdad, and then went with his father to study Ḥadīth in Cairo and Alexandria. On his father's death in 1099 he returned to Seville, where he was held in high esteem, perhaps chiefly for his knowledge of Ḥadīth. He attended lectures by al-Ghazālī, probably between 1093 and 1095 before he abandoned his professorship; but he also recorded having seen him again in Baghdad in May/June 1097. It is only recently that scholars have become aware of his views on Kalām through realizing that he and not Muḥyī-d-dīn ibn-al-ʿArabī was the author of *ʿAwāṣim al-qawāṣim,* a work which roughly follows the Ashʿarite school and includes a vigorous attack on Ibn-Ḥazm. For a time Abū-Bakr ibn-al-ʿArabī was chief *qāḍī* of Seville, but after Seville was taken over by the Almohads in 1145 he was removed to Marrakesh and imprisoned for a time, but died on a journey to Fez.

The theology of Ibn-Tūmart (*c.*1080–*c.*1130)[3] would hardly be worthy of mention had it not become the official theology of the Almohad empire. He was born in North Africa of Berber stock and about 1106 or 1107 studied in Cordova for a year. Then he went east to Alexandria, Mecca and Baghdad. There are stories of his meeting with al-Ghazālī, but these are almost certainly apocryphal, since after July 1106 al-Ghazālī was in Nishapur or Ṭūs and there is no suggestion that Ibn-Tūmart went further east than Baghdad. He did, however, come under Ashʿarite influence and his interest in philosophy may have owed something to the books of al-Ghazālī. While in Spain he probably became familiar with the ideas of Ibn-Ḥazm. He is often spoken of as having spread Ashʿarite views in the West, but he was not a consistent Ashʿarite, being apparently chiefly concerned to attack anthropomorphism. His conception of God depends more on philosophy than on revelation, since by emphasizing *tawḥīd,* 'unity' —the noun corresponding to the participle *muwaḥḥidūn,* Almohads —he ascribed to God a bare abstract unity. It is curious that in this point he seems to agree with Ibn-Ḥazm in rejecting the Ashʿarite view of the divine attributes.

His visit to the East is said to have inspired him with a plan for the reform of the West, so that he began preaching in the boat in which he made the return journey (about 1116 or 1117). He had to move from centre to centre, however, since by temperament he was prone to stir up opposition. Eventually he found supporters among the Berbers of the Maṣmūda and other tribes. About 1121 he publicly claimed to be the Mahdī, the expected 'guided one', who as a kind of Messiah would set everything right. Though he gained many adherents, his movement had little political or military success against the Almoravids up to the time of his death (about 1130). In 1132, however, ʿAbd-al-Muʾmin, a man with great administrative and military gifts, who had met Ibn-Tūmart in Bougie (in eastern Algeria) on the way back from the East and had become a follower, took control of the Almohad movement. By 1147 he had destroyed the Almoravid power in North Africa and then extended his sway over Islamic Spain, where he even recovered some territory from the Christians.

A potent factor in the replacement of the Almoravids by the

Almohads was doubtless the hostility of some Berber tribes for those other Berber tribes that supported the Almoravids; but the religious teaching of Ibn-Tūmart gave a focus to this hostility, even though his own primary interest was in religious reform. Though the idea of the Mahdī has close associations with Shīʿism, it was also popular with Sunnites from an early date. In the Almohad movement, however, its ready acceptance and its importance depended on the innate need of the Berbers for a divinely inspired or otherwise superhuman leader—a need witnessed to by the popular cults of Marabouts or holy men. It is interesting, too, that Ibn-Tūmart had composed books of instruction for his followers in the Berber language and had also used it in the call to prayer. The Almoravids he denounced as anthropomorphists, and spoke of fighting against them as *jihād*, 'holy war'.

While the Almohad movement did not itself contribute much to the general course of Islamic thought, it provided a tolerant environment for the great flowering of philosophy linked with the names of Ibn-Ṭufayl and Averroes. There had previously been one or two distinguished exponents of philosophy in Spain. It was said to have been introduced by Abenmasarra (Ibn-Masarra) (883–931), the son of an immigrant from the East, who combined Muʿtazilite views with ideas from Empedocles and the pseudo-Empedocles.[4] An ascetic and mystic, he had many pupils, but because of the opposition of the jurists could teach only in an isolated hermitage. After him the next philosopher of note was Avempace (Ibn-Bājja) (d. 1138).[5] Although he was vizier to the Almoravid governor of Saragossa, his philosophy was an ethical protest against the materialistic outlook and the worldliness of the upper classes of the day. The individual who has seen the folly and the wrongness of the prevailing attitude must keep himself aloof from it, at least in his thinking, by withdrawing into an intellectual isolation. In accordance with this viewpoint he called his chief work *The Rule of the Solitary*. Although the main underlying motive was probably this moral one, the conclusions are worked out in terms of a very thorough analysis of the human mind and human thinking, and this analysis has been of great interest and value to subsequent philosophers.

A young admirer of Avempace, though, despite the statements of some biographers, not an actual pupil, was Ibn-Ṭufayl (*c.* 1105–85), known in medieval times as Abubacer from his *kunya*, 'father-name', Abū-Bakr.[6] Born in the small town of Guadix north-east of Granada, he served in various administrative posts and finally became court-physician and vizier of the Almohad prince Abū-Yaʿqūb Yūsuf (1163–84). His chief work is the romance of *Ḥayy ibn-Yaqẓān* ('Alive son of Awake'), perhaps the most charming of all philosophical works in Arabic, and reminiscent in some ways of Plato.

The story of Ḥayy is that of a baby cast adrift in a box (or produced by spontaneous generation), who is brought up by a gazelle on an uninhabited island, and who, by the use of his reason, works out a complete philosophical religion for himself, which is crowned by the experience of mystical ecstasy. Eventually there comes to Ḥayy's island a young man called Asāl from a neighbouring island who has been brought up in the traditional religion but is inclined to metaphorical interpretation and to esoteric and spiritual meanings, and who now wants to devote himself entirely in solitude to the worship of God. When he and Ḥayy meet, they find that his spiritualized form of the traditional religion and Ḥayy's philosophical religion are really the same. Asāl tells Ḥayy of the island he has come from, where a friend of his Salāmān is ruler, who follows the literal meaning (*ẓāhir*) and avoids metaphorical interpretation. They go to the inhabited island and Ḥayy tries to instruct the ordinary people in his philosophical religion, but gives up in despair when he finds that their intellects are incapable of understanding it. In the end Ḥayy and Asāl return to the uninhabited island to spend their days in worship.

This is obviously a defence of the position of philosophy in the life of the Almohad state. Ḥayy stands for pure philosophy, Asāl for philosophical theology—possibly for that of Ibn-Tūmart—and Salāmān for the religion of the ordinary people and probably also of the Mālikite jurists. What is interesting here is the abandonment of the claim of the earlier philosophers like al-Fārābī that philosophy was necessary for the proper ordering of the state. For Ibn-Ṭufayl philosophy is seen to be incapable of directing the lives of the inhabitants of the state. It can lead a few selected individuals to the highest felicity, but to reach this they must retire from active life. In other words the *summum bonum* of the philosopher has become mystical ecstasy.

It is interesting to compare this attitude of Ibn-Ṭufayl with that of his younger friend Averroes or Ibn-Rushd (1126–98).[7] The latter came of a family of jurists, his grandfather being specially well known. He himself also received a legal training, and spent much of his life as judge in Seville and Cordova. He was well versed in the Greek sciences and for a short time (in 1182) followed his friend Ibn-Ṭufayl as physician at the Almohad court. The story is told in detail of how he was first introduced by Ibn-Ṭufayl to the Almohad prince Abū-Yaʿqūb Yūsuf possibly in 1153 (before he came to the throne). The prince asked him whether the philosophers considered the heavens created-in-time or eternal, but out of fear he excused himself and denied his study of philosophy. The prince then turned to the older man and spoke of the views of Plato, Aristotle and other philosophers and of the refutation of them by the theologians; and thereupon Averroes took courage and spoke to him freely, and retained his friendship and support until the prince's death in 1084. His fears were not entirely groundless, for the next sovereign, when the war against the Christian Spaniards was going badly for him and he needed the support of the jurists, had to take mild repressive measures against Averroes, though he subsequently found him a position in his court in Marrakesh.

At the centre alike of the life and of the thought of Averroes is the conviction that philosophy and revelation are both true. He reconciled the two in his life, since he was a judge (rising to be chief qāḍī of Cordova) and a writer on Mālikite law as well as a philosopher. He also gave considerable attention to the intellectual reconciling of the two in his philosophical works. Specially important is the essay known as *Faṣl al-Maqāl*; the full title may be rendered 'the decisive treatise, determining the nature of the connection (or harmony) between religion and philosophy'; but in English, following the hint of the latest translator, we might perhaps call it *The Harmony of Religion and Philosophy*. In this essay Averroes bases the discussion on the principles that philosophy is true and that the revealed scriptures are true, and that there cannot therefore be any disharmony between them. Most of the essay then consists in showing how apparent contradictions are to be removed. Philosophy is in general true and unalterable, though there may have been mistakes and misunderstandings in points of detail; and so the work of reconciliation has to be effected chiefly through finding harmonious interpretations of the scriptures.

The closing section of his book *The Inconsistency of the Inconsistency* has a succinct expression of his views on the relation of philosophy and religion. He does not believe that the philosopher should withdraw from active life or eschew popular religion, but that he 'should choose the best religion of his period'; it is assumed that this is 'the one in which he has been brought up', in short, Islam (though this is not explicitly stated). Because of the importance of religion for the life of the state the philosopher must accept its formulations and explain them. A religion of pure reason Averroes thinks inferior to the revealed religions when philosophically understood. All this shows that he has a full understanding of the place of religion in society and polity, and also in the early training even of the philosopher. He also saw that the class of religious intellectuals would only fulfil their functions adequately when they remained in contact with the ordinary people. He seems further to have held that part of this function was to criticize contemporary society, and he does this very acutely in the course of his commentary on the *Republic* of Plato.

What has just been said is an indication of the place of Averroes in the development of Islamic thought in Spain, but does not touch on his importance in the general history of philosophy. His greatness here rests first and foremost on his work as a commentator of Aristotle. He had a profound knowledge of Aristotelian thought, and in the commentaries he wrote on many of the works he was able to remove some of the Neoplatonic interpretations which had hitherto been current in Arabic. His superlative merits were recognized by the Christian and Jewish scholars then in Spain, and his commentaries were translated into Hebrew and Latin. This was the first main introduction of Aristotle to Europe, and was the seed which led to the flowering of medieval philosophy in Thomism, even if that was in part a reaction to the distortion of Averroes' teaching by the Latin Averroists into the theory of the 'double truth'.

Another major philosophical work was *The Inconsistency of the Inconsistency* in which he set out to refute what al-Ghazālī had said about philosophy in *The Inconsistency of the Philosophers.* This book, which is now available in an excellent English translation, is a masterly exposition of Averroes' faith in the capacity of reason to attain to a knowledge of the inner secrets of the world. Yet in some respects it was a failure. Averroes had no influence in the Islamic world comparable to his influence in Europe. This was not simply due to the collapse of Islamic civilization in Spain shortly after his death, for his *Inconsistency* at least was known in the East. More important was probably his failure to convince the main body of scholarly opinion in Spain and North Africa that there was a place for philosophy alongside their rather unphilosophical theology. Moreover, though he had written against al-Ghazālī, he had never had to deal with any prominent Ashʿarites in the flesh; thus his arguments would be unlikely to convince any Ashʿarites, and yet they were the people in the East most sympathetic to philosophy.

By the end of the twelfth century the Almohad hold on Spain was loosening, and by about 1225 they had abandoned it. Despite this political crisis and the Christian advance academic studies continued. An influential thinker was Muḥyī-d-dīn ibn-al-ʿArabī (1165–1240), who was primarily a ṣūfī but was also interested in theological questions.[8] The speculative scheme which he developed shows pantheistic tendencies, and, though sometimes called a 'philosophy', is better described as a theosophy. He was born in Murcia, and studied in Seville and other cities of Islamic Spain and North Africa until 1202 when he went on pilgrimage to Mecca. Thereafter he remained in the East, chiefly in Konya and Damascus. He has often been called 'Ibn-ʿArabī' by Western scholars to distinguish him from Abū-Bakr ibn-al-ʿArabī, but it appears that 'Ibn-al-ʿArabī' is the correct form.

A man who, though also a mystic, had a better claim to the title of philosopher was Ibn-Sabʿīn (*c.*1217–*c.*1270).[9] He spent most of his life in Spain or North Africa, constantly involved in quarrels and subjected to persecution, but attracting devoted followers mostly from among the humbler people. Some attention has been paid to the *Answers to Sicilian Questions* attributed to him; these were questions which the emperor Frederick II of Hohenstaufen had asked the Almohad sultan of the day to answer. Ibn-Sab'īn is reported to have died in Mecca by opening his veins as Stoics had done.

The consummation of the intellectual efforts of the Islamic West came with Ibn-Khaldūn, but he belongs to a later chapter.

NOTES

1. *GAL*, i.505f.; *GALS*, i.692-7; *EI*², art. Ibn Ḥazm (Arnaldez); I. Goldziher, *Die Ẓâhiriten, ihr Lehrsystem und ihre Geschichte*, Leipzig 1884, esp. 116-70 (Eng. tr. by W. Behn, Leiden 1971, 109-71); I. Friedlaender, 'Zur Komposition von Ibn Ḥazm's Milal wa 'n-Nihal', *Orientalische Studien Th. Nöldeke gewidmet* . . ., Giessen 1906, i.267-77; M. Asin Palacios, *Abenházam de Córdoba y su historia de las ideas religiosas*, Madrid 1927; Roger Arnaldez, *Grammaire et théologie chez Ibn Ḥazm de Cordoue, essai sur la structure et les conditions de la pensée musulmane*, Paris 1956; do., 'Controverses théologiques chez Ibn Ḥazm de Cordoue et Ghazali', *Mardis de Dar al-Salam*, Paris 1956, 207-48; do., 'La profession de foi d'Ibn Ḥazm', Congreso de arabistos y islamistos, Cordoba, 1962, *Actas*, 137-61; A. J. Arberry (tr.), *The Ring of the Dove*, London 1953.
2. Abū-Bakr ibn-al-'Arabī: *GAL*, i.525; *GALS*, i.632f.; *EI*², art. Ibn al-'Arabī (Abū Bakr . . .) (J. Robson); 'Ammār Ṭālibī (Talbi), *Arā' Abī-Bakr ibn-al-'Arabī al-kalāmiyya*, Algiers n.d.
3. Ibn-Tūmart: *GAL*, i.506f.; *GALS*, i.697; *EI*², art. Ibn Tūmart (J. F. P. Hopkins); I. Goldziher, 'Materialien zur Kenntnis der Almohadenbewegung', *Zeitschrift der deutschen morgenländischen Gesellschaft*, xli (1887), 30-140 (and in *Gesammelte Schriften* ii, Hildesheim 1968, 191-301), and also the introduction to Luciani (ed.), *Le Livre de Moḥammed ibn Toumert*, Algiers 1903; R. Brunschwig, 'Sur la Doctrine du Mahdi Ibn Tūmart', *Ignace Goldziher Memorial Volume*, ed. S. Löwinger, ii.1-13.
4. Abenmasarra: *GALS*, i.378f.; *EI*², art. Ibn Masarra (Arnaldez); M. Asin Palacios, *Abenmasarra y su escuela*, Madrid 1914, and Eng. tr. by E. H. Douglas and H. W. Yoder, *The Mystical Philosophy of Ibn Masarra and his followers*, Leiden 1978.
5. Avempace: *GAL*, i.601; *EI*², art. Ibn Badjdja (D. M. Dunlop); Georges Zainaty, *La morale d'Avempace*, Paris 1979.
6. Ibn-Ṭufayl: *GAL*, i.602f.; *GALS*, i.831f.; *EI*², art. Ibn Ṭufayl (Carra de Vaux); Eng. translations of *Ḥayy ibn-Yaqẓān*: (1) *The Improvement of Human Reason*, by S. Ockley, London 1708; revised by A. S. Fulton, London 1929; (2) *The Awakening of the Soul*, by P. Brönnle, London 1904.
7. Averroes: *GAL*, i.604-6; *GALS*, i.833-7; *EI*², art. Ibn Rushd (Arnaldez); Simon van den Bergh (tr.), *Averroes' Tahafut al-Tahafut (The Incoherence of the Incoherence)*, two vols., London 1954; G. F. Hourani (tr.), *Ibn Rushd (Averroes) on the Harmony of Religion and Philosophy*, London 1962, a translation of *Faṣl al-maqāl*; do., 'Averroes on Good and Evil', *Studia Islamica*, xvi (1962), 13-40; L. Gauthier, *La théorie d'Ibn Roschd sur les rapports de la religion et de la philosophie*, Paris 1909; Roger Arnaldez, 'La pensée religieuse d'Averroès', in *Studia Islamica*, vii, viii, ix (1957-9).

8. Muḥyī-d-dīn ibn-al-ʿArabī: *GAL*, i.571-82; *GALS*, i.790-802; *EI*², art. Ibn al-ʿArabī, Muḥyi ʾl-Dīn (A. Ateş); A. E. Affifi, *The Mystical Philosophy of Muḥyiʾddīn Ibnul-ʿArabī*, Cambridge 1939; H. Corbin, *L'imagination creatrice dans le soufisme d'Ibn ʿArabī*, Paris 1958, and Eng. tr. by R. Manheim, Princeton 1969.
9. Ibn-Sabʿīn: *GAL*, i.611; *GALS*, i.844; *EI*², art. Ibn Sabʿīn (A. Faure).

Chapter Sixteen

THE ELABORATION OF SHĪʿITE THEOLOGY

While among the Sunnites the Ashʿarite, Ḥanbalite and other schools of theology were developing in the ways described, something similar was taking place in each of the three main branches of Shīʿism.

(a) *the Imāmites*

After the organization of Imāmism in the years following the death of the Eleventh Imam in 874, and especially after the proclamation of the greater occultation about 940, leadership in the sect fell more and more to its scholars. In the early tenth century al-Kulīnī (d.939) had begun to lay the foundations of Imāmite law. The systematic elaboration of Imāmite belief, however, was the work of a number of scholars through the next century or so.[1] The most important were:

(1) ash-Shaykh aṣ-Ṣadūq, also known as Ibn-Bābawayh (or -Bābūya) al-Qummī (d.991), son of the shaykh of the Imāmites in Qumm, who spent some time in Baghdad and finally settled in Rayy, which was then under the vizier aṣ-Ṣāḥib ibn-ʿAbbād;[2]

(2) ash-Shaykh al-Mufīd (947–1022), who was latterly the head of the Imāmite school of Baghdad and somewhat critical of Ibn-Bābawayh;[3]

(3) ash-Sharīf al-Murtaḍā ʿAlam al-hudā (967–1044), a descendant of the Seventh Imam and *naqīb*, 'dean', of the ʿAlids, who had studied under ash-Shaykh al-Mufīd and succeeded him as head of the school in Baghdad, though he had also studied under non-Shīʿite teachers, including the Qāḍī ʿAbd-al-Jabbār the Muʿtazilite, and had come to hold views closer to Muʿtazilism than those of al-Mufīd;[4]

(4) ash-Shaykh aṭ-Ṭūsī, also known as Shaykh aṭ-Ṭāʾifa (995–1067), who came from Ṭūs and studied under the two previous scholars, then after the expulsion of the Buwayhids from Baghdad in 1055 went to Najaf, the Shīʿite shrine in Iraq;[5]

(5) al-Faḍl aṭ-Ṭabarsī (d.1153 or 1157), who was reckoned the leading theologian of his time, but is chiefly remembered for his great Qurʾān-commentary.[6]

The beliefs of the Imāmites, apart from those about the imamate, are similar to those of the Sunnites except in minor details. As Ignaz Goldziher emphasized, even the Sunna or example of the Prophet was of great importance among the Imāmites. At the same time, however, they considered that most of the Companions of the Prophet admired by the Sunnites (and first transmitters of their Ḥadīth) were unreliable, since they had rejected Muḥammad's designation of ʿAlī to succeed him as imam. They therefore made their own collections of Ḥadīth, and these normally had the name of one of the Imams or a respected Shīʿite scholar in the chain of transmitters (*isnād*).

Eventually what are known as 'the Four Books' came to be regarded as canonical. These are: *al-Kāfī fī ʿilm ad-dīn,* 'the Sufficiency for the Science of Religion', by al-Kulīnī; *Man lā yaḥduru-hu l-faqīh,* 'He who has no lawyer present', by Ibn-Bābawayh; *Tahdhīb al-aḥkām,* 'the Correction of Judgements', by ash-Shaykh aṭ-Ṭūsī; and also by him *al-Istibṣār fī-mā ikhtalafa fī-hi l-akhbār,* 'Examination of the Differences in Ḥadīth'. Many of the Ḥadīths of the Imāmites are similar to those of the Sunnites, and consequently many of their religious practices are similar. Detailed laws, too, are derived from the same principles of jurisprudence, namely, Qur'ān, Sunna (=Ḥadīth), consensus (*ijmāʿ*) and analogy (*qiyās*); but consensus has to be linked with the views of the Imams. More scope is given to analogical reasoning by the Imāmites, since the leading jurists at any time are held to have the right of *ijtihād,* that is, the right of applying the basic principles in a fresh way to a contemporary problem without slavishly following precedent. A jurist with this right is a *mujtahid.*

The earliest full statement of doctrinal belief is the *Risāla* or 'Epistle' on Imāmite beliefs composed by Ibn-Bābawayh. The structure of this *Risāla* is not unlike that of Sunnite creeds, and it may be divided into five sections: God and his attributes (pp.25–48 of the English translation); eschatology (48–82); revelation and the Qur'ān (82–9); the imāmate (89–116); miscellaneous methodological questions (116–28). In the first section God's oneness is insisted on, and the distinction between essential and active attributes (*ṣifāt adh-dhāt, — al-fiʿl*) is accepted, though the latter are said to be *muḥdath,* 'originating or appearing in time'; the reason for this last point is that, for example, God cannot be Provider (*rāziq*) until there is a creature for which he makes provision (*rizq*). The anthropomorphic terms applied to God are interpreted metaphorically. Thus in the verse 'everything is perishing except his (God's) face' (28.88) he interprets 'face' (*wajh*) as 'religion'. In the second section the common Muslim eschatological beliefs are accepted, but again some of them are interpreted metaphorically. The chief point to notice in the third section is that God is spoken of as creator of the Qur'ān as well as its utterer or speaker. As has already been seen, if the Qur'ān is created, it is not necessarily the expression of God's being, and may therefore be modified by an inspired Imam.

In Ibn-Bābawayh's creed the author's views come close to those of the Mu'tazilites at certain points; and one of the interesting features of the development of Imāmite theology is its increasing acceptance of Mu'tazilite conceptions and principles. In Ibn-Bābawayh's case, however, though some of his views corresponded to those of the Mu'tazilites, his method was closer to that of the Ḥanbalites and he disapproved of Kalām. Ash-Shaykh al-Mufīd, on the other hand, criticized Ibn-Bābawayh on various points, including his rejection of Kalām, and considered that he himself was a *mutakallim*. He held, however, that Imāmites like himself differed from the Mu'tazilites in two ways: first, they considered that the use of reason in theology required a basis in Qur'ān and Ḥadīth, whereas the Mu'tazilites trusted in reason alone; and secondly, they believed in the imamate of 'Alī from the time of the Prophet's death, whereas the Mu'tazilites accepted the doctrine of the 'intermediate position' (p.52 above). Ash-Sharīf al-Murtaḍā was even closer to the Mu'tazilites, for he abandoned the first of these differences and held that the truths of religion were to be established by reason alone. It is interesting that, where al-Mufīd had thought that the Mu'tazilite school of Baghdad was close to Imāmism, al-Murtaḍā preferred the school of Basra.

From this time onwards there have been two contrary tendencies in Imāmism, one making use of reason and engaging in Kalām and the other mostly restricting itself to Qur'ān and Ḥadīth and criticizing the use of reason. The opposition between these tendencies becomes prominent in the Safavid period.

(b) *the Ismā'īlites*[7]

Ismā'īlite theology was first elaborated under the Fāṭimid dynasty which established itself in Egypt in 969 and maintained itself there until 1171. There were, of course, others who held the main Ismā'īlite beliefs. Among these, for example, were a body of men known as the Qarmaṭians (Qarāmiṭa, Carmathians), who about 894 had established a semi-independent principality at Bahrein on the east cost of Arabia, which flourished at least until the end of the eleventh century. The relations of the Qarmaṭians with the Fāṭimids are obscure; sometimes they fought against them, but at other times they acknowledged suzerainty, as when in 951 in obedience to the Fāṭimid caliph they returned to the Ka'ba the Black Stone which they had carried off twenty years earlier. Fāṭimid missionaries and propagandists (sing. *dā'ī*) were sent throughout the provinces which acknowledged the 'Abbāsids, and gained the adhesion of many groups of discontented men in various localities. Since the Fāṭimids claimed to be the rightful rulers of the whole Islamic world, their propaganda constituted an underground revolutionary movement.

The long reign of the caliph al-Mustanṣir (1036–94) was a time of great prosperity for the Fāṭimids, even though by that date they had lost the North African provinces where there had been few conversions to Ismāʿīlism (as indeed was also the case in Egypt). On the death of al-Mustanṣir, however, a serious split occurred in the Ismāʿīlite movement. The vizier al-Afḍal ibn-Badr al-Jamālī, who was the real ruler in Egypt, managed to have the designated heir, Nizār, replaced by a younger son, al-Mustaʿlī, whom he supposed would be more amenable to himself. The Persian and Syrian Ismāʿīlites, who had begun to despair of the Fāṭimids ever invading ʿAbbāsid domains, took advantage of this happening to break their connection with the Fāṭimids by declaring themselves followers of Nizār. Nizār himself, after being defeated and imprisoned in Alexandria, disappeared, probably murdered; but the leader in Asia, Ḥasan-i Ṣabbāḥ, claimed that Nizār was only in hiding and that he was in touch with him. Indeed as late as 1164 the successor of Ḥasan-i Ṣabbāḥ claimed he had received two letters from the Imam in hiding.

A further schism took place among the Mustaʿlians on the death of the caliph al-Āmir in 1130. His infant son aṭ-Ṭayyib mysteriously disappeared, and after some fighting his cousin ʿAbd-al-Majīd became caliph with the throne-name of al-Ḥāfiẓ. Most of the Mustaʿlians in Egypt and Syria became Ḥāfiẓites (or Majīdites), but after the fall of the Fāṭimids they suffered some persecution and by 1250 had almost ceased to exist as a community. The Ṭayyibites, on the other hand, who had always been less numerous than the Ḥāfiẓites in Egypt and Syria, had almost died out there by 1250 but were flourishing in the Yemen and, as they still are, in India.

In 1090 before the death of al-Mustanṣir the Ismāʿīlites of Persia under the leadership of Ḥasan-i Ṣabbāḥ had gone into open revolt against the Sunnite Seljūq regime in Baghdad and had seized the mountain fortress of Alamut. In the following years they seized other fortresses and towns. Part of their policy was to carry out conspicuous political murders, such as that of the Seljūq vizier Niẓām-al-mulk in 1092. It is from this practice that the word 'assassin' has come; it apparently represents an Arabic word, probably *ḥashshāshīn* or *ḥasīshiyyīn,* meaning 'users of the drug ḥashīsh', but it is not certainly known why they were so called. The Crusaders in Syria had many picturesque tales about them and their leader, whom they called 'the old man of the mountain' (*shaykh al-jabal*). After 1094 most of the Syrian Ismāʿīlites had become Nizārites and acknowledged the lordship of Ḥasan-i Ṣabbāḥ. The fortunes of the Nizārites varied from time to time and from region to region, but the descendants of Ḥasan-i Ṣabbāḥ maintained themselves as Lords of Alamut until the fortress was captured by the Mongols in 1256, and even then the Nizārites were not exterminated.

From this simplified account of Ismāʿīlism up to 1250 something will have been gathered of the character of the movement. Some Sunnite writers tried to explain it as a resurgence of the old pre-Islamic religions; and the earlier European scholars tended to see in it a Persian national or racial movement. The latter suggestion is clearly wrong, since many non-Persians were Ismāʿīlites, while the Persian ruling classes mostly became Sunnites. Recent scholarly opinion has therefore come to regard Ismāʿīlism as essentially a series of revolutionary movements among labourers, artisans and other depressed classes. Dissatisfaction with the existing state of affairs probably led to a temper of revolt in many centres. It was in part the genius for organization of some of the Ismāʿīlite leaders which enabled them to produce a semblance of unity out of numerous disparate groups scattered over a wide area, and to create at certain periods a revolutionary underground movement with a not-too-definite doctrinal basis. A central point was obedience to one's superiors within the movement, together with the belief that the commands from one's superiors ultimately came from the Imam himself and were infallible. Great emphasis was placed on the missionary or propagandist effort of the movement, its *daʿwa*, and the focus of its organization was the *dāʿī*, missionary or propagandist. The *dāʿī* in an area, as an official representative of the Imam, often had considerable power. Thus for a time Ḥasan-i Ṣabbāḥ was the *dāʿī* in charge of the whole Fāṭimid *daʿwa* in Persia.

There are accounts which suggest that Ismāʿīlite propaganda was carefully graded. At the lowest level what was said was adapted to the position of ordinary people and the religious beliefs they had previously held. After they had progressed to a higher level they were apparently taught that truth in the positive religions is always relative, and that whatever truth they have is taken up into Ismāʿīlism. Doubtless something like this took place in some regions at certain periods, but it is difficult to say to what extent this was the normal procedure. Certainly in dealing with Muslims they made much use of the distinction between the external (*ẓāhir*) and the internal (*bāṭin*). They claimed that the Qurʾān, besides its external or obvious meaning, had an internal, hidden or esoteric meaning, and that this inner meaning could be learnt only from the Imam or his agent (such as a *dāʿī*). Because of this point in their teaching they are sometimes called Bāṭinites. They also spoke of what was given by the Imam or his agents as *taʿlīm*, literally 'teaching' but with the connotation of 'authoritative instruction'; and thus they may be called Taʿlīmites, as in the *Munqidh* of al-Ghazālī.

The distinctive belief of the Ismāʿīlites was their doctrine of the imamate. They are sometimes known as Sabʿiyya, 'Seveners', in contrast to the Imāmiyya, who are Ithnāʿashariyya, 'Twelvers'; but the chief difference between the two is not in the number of Imams. The formal difference, of course, is that, while they agree in acknowledging Jaʿfar aṣ-Ṣādiq as the Sixth Imam, the Imāmites hold that the Seventh was his son Mūsā and the Ismāʿīlites say it was another son Ismāʿīl. The more fundamental difference, however, is that, where the Imāmites are content to have an Imam in complete occultation, the Ismāʿīlites tend to look for an Imam who is active in the world in the present. Admittedly the Ismāʿīlites have at times acknowledged a hidden Imam, when that was temporarily advantageous; but on each occasion the hidden Imam before long gave place to an actual present Imam. Thus at Alamut Ḥasan-i Ṣabbāḥ (d.1124) appointed one of his generals to succeed him as *dāʿī*, and this man was followed by a son and grandson. The latter, Ḥasan II (known as Ḥasan ʿalā dhikri-hi s-salām), who reigned from 1162 to 1166, claimed openly the title of caliph and not-so-openly that of Imam. The son who succeeded him and the later Ismāʿīlite rulers of Alamut were all regarded as Imams and lineal descendants of Nizār. Something similar happened in several other cases. Because of its conception of the Imam the Ismāʿīlite movement became fissiparous, and besides the schisms already mentioned several others took place later.

Something can be learnt about other aspects of Ismāʿīlite belief from several credal statements which have been preserved.[8] One is found in the first chapter of *Daʿāʾim al-islām*, 'the Pillars of Islam', the fundamental work on Ismāʿīlite jurisprudence, composed under the Fāṭimids by the Qāḍī an-Nuʿmān (d.974). The basic creed contains only nine simple clauses, of which the first two repeat in a slightly enlarged form the two clauses of the Shahāda, 'there is no deity but God; Muḥammad is the Messenger of God'; four deal with eschatology, and the remainder with the authority of prophets and Imams. The same author has also a book entitled *Asās at-taʾwīl*, 'the Foundations of (authoritative) Interpretation', in which he explains the inner or esoteric meaning of a large number of Qurʾānic verses, which he arranges according to six of the seven eras recognized by previous Ismāʿīlites; each era is inaugurated by a *nāṭiq*, 'enunciating (prophet)', namely, Adam, Noah, Abraham, Moses, Jesus and Muḥammad, while the *nāṭiq* of the seventh era is the Mahdī.

A summary in English of a much fuller creed was published in 1936 by W. Ivanow under the title of *A Creed of the Fatimids*. The author, who died in 1215, was the fifth Ṭayyibite *dāʿī muṭlaq*, 'absolute *dāʿī*', in the Yemen. The book comprises one hundred articles of belief, and Ivanow reckoned that a printed edition would occupy about 300 pages. Some of the articles deal with religious practice rather than doctrine, and the arrangement is haphazard. Nearly a score of articles deal with belief in God, but are largely negative: he is not a body nor a substance nor matter nor form; he has no names, no attributes, no limits and is not in space and time. There are articles on prophethood and the imamate, as might be expected, but the treatment of eschatology is abstract; that is, while the reality of eternal reward or punishment is asserted, the more picturesque beliefs derived from the Qur'ān or the Ḥadīth are passed over in silence. The Ismā'īlites would not deny these, of course, but would interpret them symbolically. The work is essentially a positive presentation of Ismā'īlism and there is no explicit argument against other sects, but the author has so worded his assertions that Sunnite and other non-Ismā'īlite doctrines are clearly denied.

This work and similar ones illustrate a further feature of Ismā'īlism. Although the authors may be described as philosophically minded and seem to have been familiar with some of the features of Sunnite and Imāmite Kalām, they cannot have entered into overt discussion with these disciplines and they did not develop a philosophical theology of their own. This was doubtless because Ismā'īlites hold that, since human reason has limitations and cannot reach the fullness of truth, this can only be received from the Prophet or one of the Imams. What we do find among Ismā'īlite writings, however, are elaborate semi-philosophical gnostic cosmologies. Among the writers of these are Abū-Ya'qūb as-Sijzī (d. after 971?); Ḥamīd-ad-dīn al-Kirmānī (d.*c.* 1021); Ibrāhīm al-Ḥāmidī (d. 1162); and the Persian-writing poet Nāṣir-i Khusraw (d.*c.* 1080). These works are not theological in the usual sense, and, though they are sometimes called 'philosophy', this is not the normal rational discipline but one dependent on the esoteric knowledge of the Imams. Since they are well outside the main currents of Islamic thought, they are left aside here.

As already noted, the Ikhwān aṣ-Ṣafā', though a distinct group, had some connection with Ismā'īlism about which there is little agreement. Out of Ismā'īlism there also developed two small groups, the Druzes and the Nuṣayrites ('Alawites, Alouites), which are now virtually independent religions.

(c) *the Zaydites*[9]

By the tenth century Zaydism seems to have been restricted to two small states under Zaydite rule. One of these was in regions to the south of the Caspian Sea and existed from about 870 to 1126. The other, established in the Yemen before 900, has managed to survive into the present century in one form or another under the Zaydite Imams of Sanaa. Even to speak of 'states' here is perhaps to give a false impression, and 'communities' might be a better word. Sometimes a son succeeded his father, but at other times there seems to have been a kind of interregnum for several years. The Zaydite principle was that any suitably qualified descendant of al-Ḥasan or al-Ḥusayn, who publicly put himself forward as Imam, was to be accepted and followed. There seem to have been cases, however, where a man was accepted as Imam without being actual ruler of any district. Altogether the history of these Zaydite communities is so complex that it is difficult to make generalizations.

What is clear, however, is that there was extensive intellectual activity among the Zaydites, and a relatively large number of books has been preserved. One of the qualifications for the Imamate was religious learning, and among the Zaydite authors are many Imams. Some of the intellectual activity was directed to the elaboration of Zaydite jurisprudence, which is not considered here, but there were scholars in most of the religious disciplines, and some attained distinction.[10] In an account of Zaydite theology, however, the most interesting point is the relation to Muʿtazilism. This is a problem as early as the caliphate of al-Ma'mūn, but the character of the problem changes after the establishment of the Zaydite states. The Imam al-Qāsim ibn-Ibrāhīm (d.860) was deeply influenced by Muʿtazilite doctrines, but a little later the northern leader al-Uṭrūsh vigorously criticized the Muʿtazilites. Towards the end of the tenth century, again, some Zaydite scholars were closely associated with the Muʿtazilite school in Rayy under the patronage of the Ṣāḥib Ibn-ʿAbbād and some even studied under the Qāḍī ʿAbd-al-Jabbār. Such was the Imam al-Mu'ayyad (944–1020) and some of his followers. Indeed certain Zaydites identified themselves completely with the Muʿtazilites, at least in theology; for example, the Imam an-Nāṭiq bi-l-ḥaqq Abū-Ṭālib (951–1053) and Mānekdīm (Abū-l-Ḥusayn Aḥmad) (d. 1034).

The men named so far are all from the northern Zaydite community at the Caspian Sea. Sometimes their Imams were recognized as Imams by the community in the Yemen and sometimes not; and the same was true of the Imams in the Yemen. Besides the recognized Imams there were men who claimed the imamate but gained no more than local recognition. Though some of the earlier Imams in the Yemen have left books, the more important works came with the flourishing of intellectual studies there under the imamate of al-Mutawakkil-ʿalā-llāh, who ruled from 1137 to 1170. He wanted to unite all the Zaydites—the 'state' in the north had ceased to exist in 1126—and wrote a book in which he acknowledged the northern Imams and also tried to smooth out the slight differences between the northerners and the Yemenites. His efforts were strongly supported by the Qāḍī Jaʿfar (d.1177). These were followed by several scholars of the family of ar-Raṣṣāṣ. The tasks confronting such scholars included the defence of Zaydism not merely against heretical groups within (the Ḥusaynites, who expected a 'hidden Imam' to return as Mahdī, and the Muṭarrifites, who adopted a nature-philosophy and various strange views), but also against the Bāṭinites or Ismāʿīlites who were now established in the Yemen. The father and brother of the Qāḍī Jaʿfar had actually been Ismāʿīlite intellectuals.

The Muʿtazilite theological doctrines on which the Zaydite scholars differed from one another and from the Muʿtazilites proper were mostly slight. Some Zaydites were closer to the Muʿtazilite school of Baghdad, others to that of Basra. One hair-splitting difference of which much was made was with regard to God's creative will. Despite their acceptance of much Muʿtazilite theology the Zaydites thought of themselves as having a separate identity from the Muʿtazilites. Sometimes they expressed this by saying that they themselves restricted the imamate to the descendants of al-Ḥasan and al-Ḥusayn, whereas the Muʿtazilites held it to be open to any qualified man of the tribe of Quraysh. What is here alleged to be the Muʿtazilite view may be connected with the question of the recognition of the caliphate of Abū-Bakr and ʿUmar. The early Zaydites had recognized them and spoke of this as 'the imamate of the inferior', since ʿAlī was superior (*afḍal*); but some later Zaydites did not recognize the two. It is conceivable, too, that recognition of the ʿAbbāsids was also involved, since local Zaydite leaders, unlike the Fāṭimids, did not claim to be rightful rulers of the whole Islamic world. The essential focus of Zaydite identity was, of course, the recognition of the Imams.

In all this it appears that Muʿtazilite theology in its Zaydite version has suffered a transformation of function. It has ceased to be an attempt to deal with the intellectual problems facing all Muslims, and instead has become the basis of identity, in part, of a small community which wants to maintain its separateness from the large community around it.

NOTES

1. Imāmism: *EI*², art. Ithnāʿashariyya (S. H. Nasr); ʿAllāmah Sayyid M. H. Ṭabāṭabāʾī, *Shīʿite Islam,* ed. and tr. from Persian by S. H. Nasr, London 1975; Donaldson, *The Shīʿite Religion* (n.3/1); Centre d'Études Supérieures Specialisé d'Histoire des Religions de Strasbourg, *Le Shīʿisme Imāmite,* Paris 1970 (papers given at a colloquium), esp. W. Madelung, 'Imāmism and Muʿtazilite Theology', pp.13-30; Goldziher, *Vorlesungen*² (B/E), 226-40.
2. Ibn-Bābawayh: *GAL,* i.200; *GALS,* i.321; *GAS,* i.544-9; *EI*², art. Ibn-Bābawayh(i) (A. A. A. Fyzee); Asaf A. A. Fyzee, *A Shīʿite Creed,* London 1942, translation of a *Risāla* on doctrine.
3. Ash-Shaykh al-Mufīd: *GAL,* i.201; *GALS,* i.322; *GAS,* i.549-51; Martin J. McDermott, *The Theology of Al-Shaikh al-Mufīd,* Beirut 1978; I. K. A. Howard (tr.) *Kitāb al irshād* (The book of guidance into the lives of the Twelve Imams), London 1981; D. Sourdel, 'L'imamisme vu par le cheikh al-Mufīd', *Revue des Études Islamiques,* xl (1972), 217-96.

4. Ash-Sharīf al-Murtaḍā: *GAL*, i.510-2; *GALS*, i.704-6.
5. Ash-Shaykh aṭ-Ṭūsī: *GAL*, i.512f.; *GALS*, i.706f.
6. Aṭ-Ṭabarsī: *GAL*, i.513f.; *GALS*, i.708f.
7. Ismāʿīlism: *EI*², art. Ismāʿīliyya (Madelung), excellent; also arts. Alamūt, Ḥasan-i Ṣabbāḥ (M. G. S. Hodgson); al-Afḍal b. Badr al-Djamālī (G. Wiet); al-Afḍal Kutayfūt, al-Āmir (S. M. Stern); Ḥashīshiyya (B. Lewis); Ḳarmaṭī (Madelung); B. Lewis, *The Origins of Ismāʿīlism*, Cambridge 1940; do., *The Assassins*, London 1967; W. Ivanow, *Ismaili Tradition concerning the Rise of the Fatimids*, London 1942; do., *A Creed of the Fatimids*, Bombay 1936, translation of *Tāj al-ʿaqāʾid*; do., *Brief Survey of the Evolution of Ismailism*, Leiden 1952; M. G. S. Hodgson, *The Order of Assassins*, The Hague 1955. Corbin, *Histoire de la philosophie islamique* (B/D), 110-51.
8. Ismāʿīlite writers: *GAS*, i.571-83; *GALS*, i.714-6.
9. Zaydism: *EI*¹, art. Zaidīya (R. Strothmann); Wilferd Madelung, *Der Imām al-Qāsim ibn Ibrāhīm und die Glaubenslehre der Zaiditen*, Berlin 1965.
10. Zaydite writers: *GAS*, i.552-71; *GAL*, i.507-10; *GALS*, i.697-704.

Part Four

THE LATER ISLAMIC MIDDLE AGES, 1250–1850

Chapter Seventeen

THE STAGNATION OF PHILOSOPHICAL THEOLOGY

The European historian is horrified at the thought that the Middle Ages might be regarded as lasting until the nineteenth century, but the idea is appropriate in an Islamic context. Little had changed there for three or four hundred years, and it was only in the nineteenth century that the intellectual and cultural reactions to the impact of Europe and the West came to be of primary importance. Otherwise it is difficult to characterize the period. It may be called a period of darkness or of stagnation, but this fails to do justice to some aspects of its life, as will become apparent in what follows.

In the earlier part of the period, until about 1500, there was a strong state in Egypt under the Mamlūks, and this usually controlled Syria as well. In the East the Mongols continued to rule Transoxiana, and under Timur-Lenk (Tamerlane) spread westwards once more, occupying Persia and temporarily invading Iraq, Syria and Anatolia. Between Egypt-Syria and Transoxiana various lesser dynasties maintained peace over smaller or larger areas. With the liquidation of the ʿAbbāsid caliphate in 1258 Baghdad had become a provincial city—Iraq was a province of Persia—but something of its old cultural life continued until the invasions of Timur when it was practically destroyed. By this time, however, centres of Islamic learning had developed in Persia, Central Asia, Afghanistan and India. Thus the vast political upheavals produced less dislocation in intellectual life and social structure than might have been expected. There were indeed great changes, but surprisingly much managed to survive the storm.

The pattern of the four centuries from 1450 or 1500 to 1850 is much simpler. Three empires developed. That of the Ottoman Turks, with its capital at Constantinople (Istanbul) from 1453, eventually spread its rule over Syria and Egypt, much of Iraq and the Arabian peninsula, and most of North Africa—and indeed also for a time over large regions of Europe. By 1800 its power was in decline, but it continued in existence until after the First World War. Persia was united by the Safavid dynasty founded by Shah Ismāʿīl (1501–24), and sometimes had parts of Iraq added to it. It has continued a single state, though with several changes of rulers. The third empire was that of the Moguls in India, whose real founder was Akbar (1556–1605). It was shorter-lived than the other two empires, and was declining before other Indian states by about 1700, and then receding as the British East India Company advanced, until it was extinguished in 1857. These empires gave a certain stability to the Islamic world.

During the period from 1250 to 1850 Islam was also spreading in lands which had never been included in the caliphates of Damascus, Baghdad or Istanbul. Communities of Muslims were gradually forming in East and West Africa, in Malaya and Indonesia, and in other peripheral areas. Colleges were founded—in Timbuctoo and Kano, for example—for the study of Islamic jurisprudence and theology, and a slow islamization of the local cultures began. Before this process of islamization was complete, however, these lands began to feel the impact of Europe, and the Islamic Middle Ages were at an end.

With the appearance of many new centres of Islamic learning the volume of theological thought probably increased, but its quality is usually held to have declined, especially in the field of Kalam. Little originality was shown, and the chief effort of theologians went into the production of commentaries, super-commentaries and glosses on earlier works. Thus for the short creed of Najm-ad-dīn an-Nasafī (mentioned above) about a dozen commentaries are listed, about thirty glosses (on the commentary by at-Taftāzānī), and about twenty super-glosses on one of these. Most such works were in Arabic, which remained the language of scholarship throughout the Islamic world (as Latin was for long in western Europe); but an Islamic religious literature was also springing up in Turkish, Persian, Urdu and other languages. A few original works were still composed, mainly in the form of creeds of varying length, probably designed as a basis for commentaries. The writing of commentaries may have been encouraged by the fact that lectures normally consisted of comments on texts.

The lack of originality and the general rigidity and conservatism in theology accompanied a low level of cultural achievement in other respects, and many scholars, both Muslim and Western, have suggested reasons. One view is that the cause is to be looked for in the Mongol invasions and the devastation they occasioned. This may help to explain the relative decline of Baghdad, for example; but Egypt, on the other hand, was never invaded by the Mongols, so that they cannot be the sole cause. Another suggestion is Ottoman domination, and this tends to find favour with writers of Arab nationality. For the Arabic-speaking regions which came under the Ottomans there may be some truth in this; but even in these regions it is doubtful if it can be the whole truth since cultural decline is found also in lands which were never under Ottoman sway. The further suggestion that the seeds of decay were present in the Islamic religion from the beginning seems to be an expression of anti-Islamic prejudice and not worthy of serious consideration. It is best to leave the problem unsolved, realizing that mysterious changes of various kinds occur in the case of most religions.

Theological rigidity, of course, is not to be condemned outright, since it may often have a social function. The Christian creeds attained a degree of fixity after some five centuries of Christianity, and there may be a subtle reason for the appearance of a comparable fixity in Islam after the elapse of about the same time. A distinction can be made, however, between the formulation of a definitive creed and the theological discussion of articles of belief. A fixed creed helps to give stability to a religious community; and in the disturbed circumstances of the Islamic world for some of the centuries in question rigidity in theology may have helped to stabilize the social structure and even to compensate for the loss of political unity. It is possible, too, that to the Western scholar the rigidity appears to be greater than it really is, since it is easy for him, bored with the repetition of nearly identical arguments whose point he does not appreciate, to transform his own boredom into a characteristic of the material.

The dependence of the ulema on governments or rulers should also be taken into consideration. The Inquisition begun under the caliph al-Ma'mūn had made it clear that the class of ulema was under the power of the government. It was not the brave endurance of Aḥmad ibn-Ḥanbal that brought the Inquisition to an end, but reasons of state unconnected with the attitude and conduct of the ulema. Advancement in the scholarly career was in the hand of governments, and most scholars were too worldly to give up the prospect of a good salary for the sake of religious principle. There were exceptions, such as al-Ghazālī and Ibn-Taymiyya, but the general attitude towards the rulers was one of subservience. On the other hand, there was a large field within which the ulema resisted the encroachments of the rulers. Rigidity strengthened the hands of individuals who were prepared to hold out against pressure to 'bend' the rules in the interests of the government, and prevented a betrayal of the rights of the ulema in general by a weak individual who had succumbed to governmental inducements. The rigid intellectual structure reduced individual discretion and made it possible to refuse illegal requests from those in authority; but, if in this way it had a positive function, in other circumstances it had disadvantages. This is notably so in adapting jurisprudence and theology to the contemporary world.

Also relevant is another feature of the outlook of the ulema, which may be called 'the discouragement of contemporary argument'.

There is a deep-seated Arab dislike of paying attention to what one considers false. Rather than study false views in order the better to refute them, the Arab prefers to pass them over in silence. When al-Muḥāsibī wrote a *Refutation of the Muʿtazilites,* his master Aḥmad ibn-Ḥanbal objected to his giving a full statement of their views before refuting them, on the ground that someone might read the statement of Muʿtazilite views and not the refutation. In most of the theological works mentioned in the previous pages opposing views are stated very briefly. In the later writers, too, there are no discussions of the views of contemporary Muʿtazilite writers, for example, but only of those of the 'classical' period. In the first ʿAbbāsid century caliphs and viziers arranged theological debates in their salons, and Niẓām-al-mulk may have done the same, at least for scholars of certain groups; but al-Ghazālī was apparently unable to have live arguments with philosophers. Perhaps one did not argue against contemporary opponents, since this would have helped to spread their false views. It may also be that the Ḥadīth about the seventy-three sects prevented contemporaries from being regarded as a new sect, since the seventy-two heretical sects had already been described by the heresiographers. Whatever the reason for it, this avoidance of arguments with contemporary heretics and deviants must have helped to make theology 'academic' in the bad sense and so contributed to its stagnation.

It must also be asked whether during the centuries being considered the ulema were tending to become cut off from the common people. In the thirteenth century dervish orders began to make their appearance, and many ordinary men came to find their spiritual needs more fully met by the *dhikr* or worship of the orders than by the official *ṣalāt,* 'prayers', presided over by the ulema. Before it can be asserted, however, that this led to a cleavage, there are many questions to be answered. In practice did the worship of the orders replace the *ṣalāt,* or did it complement it? Had the Ḥanbalite theologians a closer relation to the common people than the philosophical theologians? The latter, whether calling themselves Ashʿarites or not, seem by their interest in philosophy and their rational arguments to have been largely cut off from the springs of spiritual life. Yet the philosophical theologians, despite this weakness, deserve much of the credit for an important positive achievement of the ulema as a whole, namely, the preservation of a framework of outward conduct and intellectual dogma within which it was possible for Muslims to live lives of moral uprightness and true religious devotion.

Since little attention has so far been paid by scholars, either Muslim or Western, to the history of theology during the six centuries after 1250, and since there is a vast amount of material, mostly still in manuscript, it is impracticable in a survey such as the present to give an adequate account of the various trends. In lieu of such an account brief notes are offered on the best-known theologians.

(1) Al-Bayḍāwī was born at Bayḍā near Shiraz, occupied the position of *qāḍī* in various places, including briefly in Shiraz, and finally lived in retirement in Tabriz. His death probably occurred in 1308 or 1316, though earlier dates are mentioned. He had a reputation for piety and asceticism, but his outstanding gift was his ability to select what was best in the works of previous scholars and to summarize it acceptably. His greatest work was his commentary on the Qur'ān which is still regarded as authoritative. It was based mainly on that of az-Zamakhsharī, but amended that author's Mu'tazilite interpretations. Al-Bayḍāwī also wrote books in various other religious disciplines, including a comprehensive statement of his views on Kalām. In this he follows roughly the order of topics in the *Muḥaṣṣal* of Fakhr-ad-dīn ar-Rāzī, but is somewhat more philosophical.[1]

(2) Ḥāfiẓ-ad-dīn Abū-l-Barakāt an-Nasafī (d.1301 or 1310) was born in Bukhara and apparently studied there under a teacher who died in 1244. He himself became a teacher, mainly of jurisprudence according to the Ḥanafite school, in Kirman in southern Iran. He is said to have died on his way back from a visit to Baghdad (which at this period had recovered from the first Mongol invasion). His legal works were widely used and much commented on. Among his lesser writings is *Al-'Umda fī uṣūl ad-dīn*, 'The Pillar of the Creed', together with his own commentary on it. Its doctrines are similar to those of the creed of Najm-ad-dīn an-Nasafī, but it is about four times the length. It is noteworthy, however, in it that it says less about epistemology than the shorter creed, perhaps because the author felt that philosophical discussions were out of place in a creed.[2]

(3) Al-Ījī, with the honorific title of 'Aḍud-ad-dīn (*c.*1281–1355) was educated in Shiraz under the pupil of a pupil of al-Bayḍāwī. This gives some evidence for the continuity of Shāfi'ite and Ash'arite teaching in Shiraz. Most of his life is said to have been spent as a *qāḍī* in the recently-built capital of the Īl-Khān dynasty, Sultaniyya; but in his later years he was again in the neighbourhood of Shiraz and is spoken of as *qāḍī* there. As an important man he was involved in the troubled and confused politics of the period, and is said to have died in prison in 1355 in his native Īj, east of Shiraz. In theology he is known chiefly for two works. One is the short creed known as the *'Aḍudiyya*, which has no philosophical articles. The other is the *Mawāqif*, a comprehensive work designed as a systematic handbook for use in lecturing. It is arranged in roughly the same way as the *Muḥaṣṣal* of ar-Rāzī but devotes more space to the philosophical preliminaries—two-thirds as against a half.[3]

(4) Aṭ-Ṭaftāzānī (1322–1389 or 1390) was born in Khorasan and is said to have been a pupil of al-Ījī. He is heard of at Herat and also at

one of the minor Mongol courts. When this whole region came under Timur-Lenk, aṭ-Ṭaftāzānī was stationed for a time at Sarakhs in the centre of Khorasan, and then moved to the court at Samarqand. He is the author of a theological treatise not unlike the *Mawāqif* of al-Ījī, but he is best known for his commentary on the creed of Najm-ad-dīn an-Nasafī, which for centuries was one of the chief textbooks of theology. Although the creed is Māturīdite, aṭ-Ṭaftāzānī is usually said to have been an Ash'arite, but the point is by no means certain. His choice of a text could be due to the fact that he was teaching in a region where Māturīdite views were dominant. He expresses himself carefully, but there are a number of points where it is clear that he disagreed with the text he was commenting on.[4]

(5) Ibn-Khaldūn (1332–1406) was born and educated in Tunis. His family claimed Arab descent and had moved from Spain in the early thirteenth century before Seville fell to the Christians. The men had occupied high government posts or had beeen engaged in scholarship. Between the ages of 20 and 46 Ibn-Khaldūn himself was mainly involved in governmental administration in Fez, Tunis, Granada and other places, though he also found time to study and write. In 1378 he went to Egypt and was sometimes a professor, sometimes a *qāḍī*. Though he suffered much from the disturbed political conditions of the time, he managed to compose a history of the world in many volumes. His fame rests chiefly on the *muqaddima*, 'Introduction', to this history, which itself occupies three large volumes in translation and is a highly original investigation in the fields of philosophy, of history and of sociology. The *Muqaddima* contains a perceptive chapter on the development of philosophical theology in Islam; and after this it is not surprising to find that his competence in Ash'arite theology was such that as a young man he wrote a book in the field. This book is essentially a summary of the *Muḥaṣṣal* of ar-Rāzī. In jurisprudence he was a Mālikite.[5]

(6) Al-Jurjānī, known as as-Sayyid ash-Sharīf (1340–1413), was born near the south-east corner of the Caspian Sea, and studied in Herat, in Kirmān (in southern Iran) and in Egypt, besides visiting Constantinople. About 1377 he obtained a professorship at Shiraz through his friend aṭ-Ṭaftāzānī. After the conquest of Shiraz he went to Timur-Lenk's court at Samarqand, and in a celebrated debate showed himself superior to aṭ-Ṭaftāzānī, at least according to the majority view. Returning to Shiraz after Timur's death in 1405, he produced many works in many fields of study. Theologically most important was his commentary on the *Mawāqif* of al-Ījī, where his interest in theological questions was given full scope.[6]

(7) As-Sanūsī (d. 1486 or 1490 aged 63) was born at Tlemsen in the west of Algeria, and spent most of his life there. Among his teachers was at least one who had studied and taught in Granada, and

who abandoned it as the prospects for the Muslims there became gloomy. He was a ṣūfī and had such a reputation for piety and asceticism that some regarded him as the 'renewer' (*mujaddid*) of Islam for the tenth Islamic century (which began in 1494). In jurisprudence he is a Mālikite, and in theology is reckoned an Ash'arite, though he was also very interested in philosophy. He wrote several works on Kalām, but more attention has been paid to his short creed, the Sanūsiyya. This has been popular with Muslims in North and West Africa, and has been translated into French and German. It is much more philosophical than the 'Aḍudiyya, and begins, for example, by asserting that every believer must know twenty attributes necessary in respect of God and twenty attributes impossible for him. Since among the twenty attributes necessary for God are seven 'attributes of forms' which have to be distinguished from seven very similar 'attributes pertaining to forms', it is clear that the average believer is expected to be a philosopher! It is strange that one who was both pious and widely respected should have laid so much emphasis on abstract philosophy.[7]

(8) Ad-Dawānī (or ad-Dawwānī), with the honorific name of Jalāl-ad-dīn, and also called aṣ-Ṣiddīqī as claiming descent from the first caliph Abū-Bakr aṣ-Ṣiddīq (1427–1502), came from a district some 80 km west of Shiraz. He later completed his studies in Shiraz and became a professor and *qāḍī* there. Just before his death a political upheaval caused him to flee from Shiraz towards his native district. He produced a vast number of books, chiefly in the fields of ṣūfism, philosophy and theology. His best-known work, written in Persian and commonly called *Akhlāq-i Jalālī*, was translated into English in the early nineteenth century under the title of 'The Practical Philosophy of the Muhammadan People'. This was an adaptation of *Akhlāq-i Nāṣirī* by the Imāmite Naṣīr-ad-dīn aṭ-Ṭūsī, a work dealing with ethics, economics and politics, and brought the ideas expressed there more into accord with the outlook of Sunnite Islam. In particular ad-Dawānī insisted that the titles 'caliph' and 'imam' could properly be given only to a righteous ruler who governed in accordance with the Sharī'a. In theology ad-Dawānī was an Ash'arite and wrote commentaries on the 'Aḍudiyya and on al-Jurjānī's commentary on the *Mawāqif* of al-Ījī, thus continuing what might be called the school of Shiraz. The statement of Brockelmann that he was an Imāmite must be mistaken; it is at variance with what is found in his works, since in his commentary on the 'Aḍudiyya, for example, he accepts without criticism the article on the imamate of Abū-Bakr.[8]

(9) Birgevi or Birgili (1522–73) was a Turkish scholar from south-west Anatolia. He completed his education in Istanbul, and eventually taught in a college in the little town of Birgi in the province of Smyrna. He stood boldly for the strict and faithful observance of the Sharī'a, and considered, for example, that it was wrong to teach

the Qur'ān for money. His unswerving rectitude and the popularity of his preaching gained him a numerous following among the common people, but some leading scholars of the time were bitterly opposed to him. Many works of his in Arabic have been preserved, including textbooks and pamphlets on points of conduct. His best-known work is a Turkish creed or statement of the principles of religion, which has achieved a wide circulation and has had many commentaries written on it. Because of this creed (and because his legal school was Ḥanafite) he is included here, although his outlook was closer to the Ḥanbalites than to the philosophical theologians.[9]

(10) Al-Laqānī (Ibrāhīm Burhān-ad-dīn) was a professor at the university of al-Azhar in Cairo, and belonged to the Mālikite legal school. He is remembered for a creed in verse called *Al-Jawhara*, which has been the basis of some well-known commentaries, and is similar in form to the short creed of as-Sanūsī. He died in 1631 on his return from the pilgrimage to Mecca, and was succeeded as professor by his son ʿAbd-as-Salām al-Laqānī (d.1668), who wrote a commentary on *Al-Jawhara*.[10]

(11) As-Siyālkūtī (ʿAbd-al-Ḥakīm) (d.1657) was an adviser at the court of the Mogul emperor Shah-Jehan (*regnabat* 1628–58). He wrote commentaries and glosses on some of the theological works regularly studied in Iran and Egypt, such as aṭ-Ṭaftāzānī's commentary on the creed of an-Nasafī. His writings were so highly thought of that they themselves came to be used as textbooks.[11]

(12) Al-Faḍālī (or -Fuḍālī or -Faḍḍālī) was an Egyptian from the Delta and a professor at al-Azhar in Cairo, who died in 1821. He wrote an exposition of Islamic belief of medium length with the short title *Kifāyat al-ʿawāmm*, 'The Sufficiency of the Common People'. Of its fifty articles forty-one deal with attributes necessary, impossible and possible in respect of God, and nine in respect of prophets. It is similar in content to the Sanūsiyya but much longer. The author expects the ordinary Muslim to know the fifty articles and a general proof for each.[12]

(13) Al-Bājūrī or -Bayjūrī (1783–1860), from the Egyptian province of Menouf, became a professor at the Azhar and latterly rector (*shaykh al-azhar*). Like al-Faḍālī, who was one of his teachers, he was a Shāfiʿite in law. He was reckoned outstanding in his day, but his work consisted mainly of commentaries and glosses, including commentaries on the Sanūsiyya and on the *Kifāyat al-ʿawāmm* of his teacher, and a gloss of a commentary on the *Jawhara* of al-Laqānī.[13]

These notes on individual theologians are far from being an adequate history of the theology of the period, but they give a provisional indication of certain trends.[14] The study of Kalām clearly retained its 'international' character, but one or two centres, such as Shiraz and Cairo, were specially important, at least at certain periods.

After 1258 scholars still travelled, though less extensively, it would seem, than before that date; but the chief books were widely known throughout the Islamic world, even to some extent among Shīʿites. Most of the men named here seem to have regarded themselves as Ashʿarites, but after the fifteenth century philosophy invaded even some of the short credal statements. The only Māturīdite is Ḥāfiẓ-ad-dīn an-Nasafī (2), and it is difficult to know what happened to the Māturīdite school after him. It presumably continued to exist in association with Ḥanafite jurisprudence, which was the official school of the Ottoman empire. In his creed al-Faḍālī mentions the Māturīdite view that one of the attributes of God was *takwīn*, 'making to exist'. Māturīdite theologians probably contented themselves with writing commentaries and glosses, and produced no fresh theological work of any significance.

NOTES

1. Al-Bayḍāwī: *GAL*, i.530-4; *GALS*, i.738-43; *EI*², art. (al-)Bayḍāwī (J. Robson); J. van Ess, 'Das Todesdatum des Baiḍāwī', *Die Welt des Orients*, ix (1978), 261-70; A. F. L. Beeston, *Baiḍāwī's Commentary on Sūrah 12 of the Qur'ān*, Oxford 1963, translation and notes, with facsimile of text.
2. Ḥāfiẓ-ad-dīn an-Nasafī: *GAL*, ii.250-3; *GALS*, ii.263-8; *EIS*, art. (al-)Nasafī (3) (W. Heffening).
3. Al-Īdjī: *GAL*, ii.267-71; *GALS*, ii.287-93; *EI*², art. (al-)Īdjī (J. van Ess); J. van Ess, *Die Erkenntnislehre des ʿAḍudaddīn al-Īcī*, Wiesbaden 1966, translation of first part of *Mawāqif*; do., 'Neue Materialien zur Biographie des ʿAḍudaddīn al-Īgī', *Die Welt des Orients*, ix (1978), 270-83.
4. Aṭ-Ṭaftāzānī: *GAL*, ii.278-80; *GALS*, ii.301-4; E. E. Elder, *A Commentary on the Creed of Islam*, New York, 1950, translation of the commentary on the creed of an-Nasafī.
5. Ibn-Khaldūn: *GAL*, ii.314-17; *GALS*, ii.343-4; *EI*², art. Ibn Khaldūn (M. Talbi); Franz Rosenthal, *Ibn Khaldūn: The Muqaddimah*, 3 vols., London 1958, Eng. translation, with account of Kalām, iii.34-55, partly continued 55-75.
6. Al-Jurjānī: *GAL*, ii.280f.; *GALS*, ii.305f.; *EI*², art. (al-)Djurdjānī (ʿAlī b. Muḥammad) (A. S. Tritton).
7. As-Sanūsī: *GAL*, ii.323-6; *GALS*, ii.352-6; *EIS*, art. (al-)Sanūsī (Abū ʿAbd-Allāh) (M. Ben Cheneb).
8. Ad-Dawānī: *GAL*, ii.281-4; *GALS*, ii.306-9; *EI*², art. (al-)Dawānī (Ann K. S. Lambton); W. F. Thompson (tr.), *The Practical Philosophy of the Mohammedan People*, London 1839.
9. Birgevi: *GAL*, ii.583-6; *GALS*, ii.654-8; *EI*², art. Birgewi (K. Kufrevi).
10. Al-Laqānī: *GAL*, ii.412f.; *GALS*, ii.436f.
11. As-Siyālkūtī: *GAL*, ii.550; *GALS*, ii.613.
12. Al-Faḍālī: *GAL*, ii.641; *GALS*, ii.744; *EI*², art. (al-)Faḍālī (J. Schacht); translation of *Kifāya* in Macdonald, *Development* (B/E).
13. Al-Bājūrī: *GAL*, ii.639; *GALS*, ii.741; *EI*², art. (al-)Bādjūrī (Th. W. Juynboll).
14. Period in general: R. Brunschvig, G. von Grunebaum (eds.), *Classicisme et déclin culturel dans l'histoire de l'Islam*, Paris 1957, esp. L. Gardet, 'De quelle manière s'est ankylosée la pensée religieuse de l'Islam?', 93-108.

Chapter Eighteen

THE VITALITY OF THE HANBALITES

There had been vigour, even if tinged with fanaticism, among the Ḥanbalites of Baghdad in the eleventh century. Up till then Baghdad seems to have been their main centre, although, as noted above, there were Ḥanbalites in other places such as Ispahan and Herat. Before 1100 there were Ḥanbalite schools in Jerusalem and Damascus, but Jerusalem was captured by the Crusaders in 1099, and the jurists there fled to Damascus. The group in Damascus was further strengthened by other refugees from the troubled eastern and central provinces, such as the family of the Banū-Qudāma, one of whose members, Muwaffaq-ad-dīn ibn-Qudāma (d.1223), has already been mentioned. This family arrived in 1156. Fully a century later in 1269 another scholarly family came from Ḥarrān, bringing with it a boy of about five who was to become the greatest Ḥanbalite after Aḥmad ibn-Ḥanbal himself.

This was Ibn-Taymiyya (more fully, Taqī-d-dīn Aḥmad ibn-Taymiyya) who was born in January 1263 and died in September 1328.[1] It was through him that Henri Laoust approached the study of Ḥanbalism, and thus he stands in brilliant light compared with the obscurity surrounding the Ash'arites of the same period. What follows is based on the conclusions of Laoust.

The career of Ibn-Taymiyya is best understood when his primary problem is seen to be the same as that of al-Ghazālī, namely, the corruption of the ulema or religious scholars. As a class they were nearly all mainly interested in their own promotion in their academic or judicial career; and, since promotion was in the hands of the rulers, they were subservient to these. Ibn-Taymiyya, following in the tradition of Ibn-Ḥanbal, stood up for what he believed to be right, regardless of the suffering it might bring upon him personally. As a result of his intellectual brilliance he is said to have been qualified to give formal legal opinions at the age of seventeen; and in 1284 at the age of twenty-one he succeeded his father as leading professor at the Sukkariyya *madrasa.* This was followed by other teaching positions. In

1293 he publicly took an intransigent view of the case of a Christian who had insulted the Prophet, and he was imprisoned for a time. Then about 1298 in response to a request from the people of Hama for instruction on the attributes of God and their relation to his essence, he drew up a statement of his dogmatic position, known as *Al-Ḥamawiyya al-kubrā,* 'The Large (Creed) of Hama'. In this he expressed forceful criticisms of Kalām and of Ashʿarism. Some of his many enemies, annoyed at his attacks on Ashʿarism and astrology, and jealous of his good relationship with the governor of Damascus, accused him, on the basis of the Ḥamawiyya, of holding the heresy of anthropomorphism. They even got a crier to parade the city proclaiming that Ibn-Taymiyya was a heretic, and the governor had to intervene to preserve order. The jurists, asked to examine the creed carefully, reported that there was nothing objectionable in it, and the incident was closed.

Since about 1260 Syria had been ruled by the Mamlūks who had succeeded the Ayyūbids in Egypt about 1250 and had Cairo as their main capital. They were not a dynasty but a ruling élite of highly-trained former slaves, which perpetuated itself by importing further slaves mainly from South Russia and the Caucasus and giving them the same advanced training in military and civil administration. One of their innovations in both provinces was to give an official organization to the four legal schools or 'rites', the Shāfiʿite, Ḥanafite, Mālikite and Ḥanbalite. Each Muslim has to belong to one of them and have his legal affairs (such as inheritance) judged according to its principles. For each of the rites, in both Cairo and Damascus, the Mamlūks created a chief *qāḍī,* and the order of precedence was as given, following the numbers attached to each. The Shāfiʿites resented this, since previously only they had had a chief *qāḍī,* and there was friction between the four groups of jurists. This was the framework of the career of Ibn-Taymiyya.

In the years after 1299 he took a share in the public life of Damascus, was a member of diplomatic missions, and joined an expedition against revolted Nuṣayrite heretics. After the conquest of the Nuṣayrites he was consulted by the Mamlūk sultan on their treatment. About the end of 1305, however, he once again found himself in trouble. He publicly attacked the ṣūfī order of the Aḥmadiyya (Rifāʿiyya) for engaging in various practices contrary to the Sharīʿa; but the head of the Aḥmadiyya order was on friendly terms with influential persons in Cairo, and early in 1306 Ibn-Taymiyya was summoned thither. After a short trial of dubious validity he was imprisoned, and kept in prison until September 1307. On his release he was not allowed to return to Syria, so he set up as a professor and gave lectures; but his attacks on the pantheism of many ṣūfīs soon brought him into prison again, first in Cairo and later in Alexandria, since in the latter his freedom to receive visits was less dangerous. A change of government led to his release in March 1310, but he spent nearly three more years in Cairo before returning to Damascus.

The remainder of his life was spent in Damascus where he was generally held in honour and respect and had many pupils and other followers. On the whole he was less implicated than previously in public incidents, but an attack on the cult of saints led to his imprisonment in the citadel in July 1326, together with some persecution of his followers, and he was kept a prisoner, under increasingly rigorous conditions, until his death in September 1328.

Laoust conceives the thought of Ibn-Taymiyya as culminating in a 'political sociology', but one based on a theological position; and he sees the central point of this theology as a development of the old Islamic idea of the absolute dissimilarity of God and man. From this Ibn-Taymiyya concluded that it is impossible to attain knowledge of God by rational methods, whether those of philosophy or of Kalām, and also impossible to attain the ṣūfī aim of union with God. He was no mere obscurantist, however, for he had made a careful study of the main Arabic philosophers, as well as of theologians like al-Ghazālī and Fakhr-ad-dīn ar-Rāzī. His criticisms of the philosophers are acute and well founded, notably in *Radd ʿalā l-manṭiqiyyīn,* 'Refutation of the Logicians'. To ar-Rāzī he was strongly opposed, because he regarded him as bringing many foreign elements into theology from philosophy and other sources; but in the general direction of his thought he was influenced by ar-Rāzī, even if only by way of reaction. From al-Ghazālī, to whom he was more sympathetic, he seems to have learned much.

His attitude to ṣūfism is complex. He rejects everything resembling 'union with God' as the highest aim for human life. Absorption into the One, or even contemplation of the highest Good, he felt to be at variance with the Sharīʿa. For him the supreme end was the worship or service (*ʿibāda*) of God—the relation of slave (*ʿabd*) to master—and the basis of this was the observance of the prescriptions of the Sharīʿa. On the other hand, in his own make-up there was something of the ṣūfī; and from the standpoint of his conception of *ʿibāda* he proceeded to give a new meaning to many of the distinctive terms of the ṣūfīs, such as fear of God, confidence in him, humility, love for him. He even saw in the perfect fulfilment of the Sharīʿa a kind of 'annihilation' (*fanā'*), equivalent to that of which the ṣūfīs spoke. This emphasis on observing the Sharīʿa was doubtless one of the factors behind an important work, *Minhāj as-sunna an-nabawiyya,* in which he criticized the Imāmite theologian al-ʿAllāma al-Ḥillī (p.150 below); his use of the methods of Kalām and acceptance of Muʿtazilite theses, as well as his theory of the imamate, were anathema to Ibn-Taymiyya.

Ibn-Taymiyya's attacks on saint-worship were linked with his insistence on adhering to the original forms of Islam, just as his attacks on philosophical conceptions were linked with his rejection of foreign elements. All this grew out of a realization that the concrete, 'poetical' or 'symbolic' language of the Qur'ān kept men closer to the deep springs of religious vitality than the abstractions of philosophical thinking. From an early period of his life he must have had spiritual experiences of sufficient profundity to give him confidence to adopt an independent and critical attitude towards his teachers and textbooks. In the simple, but by no means naive, acceptance of Islamic dogma in its Qur'anic formulation he had found, in a form suited to his own needs, the source of real life and power; and the acceptance of this material was followed by constant meditation on it and by the effort to bring his conduct into accord with his beliefs.

Something of this outlook and attitude Ibn-Taymiyya managed to convey to his followers, though none was outstanding and none shared his independence of mind. Nevertheless he profoundly altered the course of theological thought in Islam, and his influence is still pregnant for the future. He had the advantage of living at a period when Cairo, as capital of the relatively stable Mamlūk state, was becoming one of the cultural foci of Islam in place of Baghdad, and when Damascus, as second Mamlūk capital, was also rising in importance. The reputation of Ibn-Taymiyya and the number of his disciples thus ensured that Ḥanbalism was well represented in the new phase of Islamic thought brought about by the change of location from Baghdad. Ḥanbalism here gained a base—or should we say a beach-head?—from which it was able to influence later centuries.

The names are known of many Ḥanbalites who were the immediate pupils of Ibn-Taymiyya, as well as of others, scattered through the following centuries, who admired him and were to some extent influenced by him; and these were found not only in Damascus and Cairo but in several other centres. Most were primarily jurists. The only one who may be regarded as having made some contribution to theology was Ibn-Qayyim-al-Jawziyya (1292–1350).[2] His name means 'the son of the *qayyim* (warden?) of the Jawziyya (college)', and the only permissible shortening is to 'Ibn-al-Qayyim'. He became a close disciple of Ibn-Taymiyya in 1313 after the master's return from Egypt, and was thought sufficiently important to be imprisoned in the citadel in 1326 at the same time as Ibn-Taymiyya, though separately from him. He was not released until 1328 after the master's death. From 1342 until his own death he taught in the Ṣadriyya *madrasa*. He had absorbed all Ibn-Taymiyya's views and propagated them as a kind of literary executor, but he was more strongly attracted to ṣūfism, and is sometimes thought to have altered his master's later works not only in language but also in sentiment. Undoubtedly, however, both by transmitting the works of Ibn-Taymiyya and by publicizing the ideas in his own works in a faultless style, he did much to spread and perpetuate their influence.

The vitality imparted to Ḥanbalism by Ibn-Taymiyya is generally held to have led to the appearance in the eighteenth century of the Wahhābite movement.[3] The theological founder of this movement, Muḥammad ibn-ʿAbd-al-Wahhāb (1703–92), came, like many other theologians, from a family which had already produced many scholars. This particular family had held posts in various small towns in Nejd (Central Arabia). After preliminary studies in the oasis of al-ʿUyayna under his father and in Mecca, he spent some time in Medina as a student, and then travelled in quest of knowledge to Basra, Baghdad, Hamadhan, Ispahan, Damascus and Cairo. It was apparently at Medina that he first became aware of the importance and the relevance, from the point of view of his own interests, of the thought of Ibn-Taymiyya. From an early age he had seen the decadence of popular religion in Arabia and the need for a thoroughgoing reform. His first attempts at reform, after his return to Arabia, met with opposition, but in 1744 he was able to make an agreement with the emir (belonging to the family of Suʿūd) of the small town of Darʿiyya. Following on this agreement, and in part because of it, the dynasty of Suʿūd prospered enormously, and in the opening years of the nineteenth century, when they were already rulers of much of Arabia, also occupied Mecca and Medina. The occupation of the holy cities, however, by a dynasty professing Wahhābite doctrines, disturbed many Sunnites, and on the instructions of the Ottoman sultan an Egyptian army invaded Arabia (1813–18) and put an end to the Suʿūdite principality for the time being. Through the dynasty's vicissitudes of fortune up to the establishment of the kingdom of Saudi (Suʿūdī) Arabia in 1930 the association with Wahhābism remained, and the present kingdom is essentially a Wahhābite state.

The theology of the Wahhābites is characterized by Laoust as not so much an elaboration of the ideas of Ibn-Taymiyya but rather 'a new edition of Ḥanbalite doctrines and of the prudent agnosticism of the traditional faith'. Its clearest dependence on Ibn-Taymiyya is in its attack on the cult of the saints and in its general insistence on a return to the purity of original Islam. For the most part it is concerned largely with externals, like much of Islamic religious thought. It shows no interest in the methodology of Ibn-Taymiyya, which he devised in order to escape from the rigidity of the scholastic methods and to make possible an adaptation of Islamic truth to contemporary conditions.

Beyond the world of the Arabs Wahhābism influenced certain

Indian Muslims in the early nineteenth century. The so-called Wahhābites of India are associated with an armed movement under Sayyid Aḥmad (1786–1831) against the Sikhs and the British. In its origins the movement was due to internal Indian causes, but in 1823 Sayyid Aḥmad came under Wahhābite influence while on the pilgrimage to Mecca, and thereafter insisted on a reform and purification of Islam in accordance with Wahhābite ideas. Something of the Wahhābite spirit has been retained in the important theological seminary at Deoband, but, in contrast to Ibn-Taymiyya, it is very rigidly conservative.

The upsurge of vitality in Ḥanbalism in the person of Ibn-Taymiyya continues to the present time. His insistence on maintaining or returning to the purity of original Islam points out to the Islamic thinkers of today, whether professional theologians or not, the surest way of finding a solution to their problems. Some have in fact become great admirers of Ibn-Taymiyya and in particular of his methodology.

This is a convenient point at which to mention briefly the development of theology prior to 1850 in the Indian subcontinent and in the peripheral regions of the Islamic world. Although this theology is not Ḥanbalite, it is relatively close to Ḥanbalism.

The Indian subcontinent is the area beyond the heartlands where Islam is most deeply rooted. From the eleventh century onwards the names are known of Muslim scholars living in India, but in general they were dependent on the central stream of Islamic scholarship and made no original contributions. The outstanding figure up to 1850 was Shāh Walī-Allāh of Delhi (1703–62), roughly a contemporary of Muḥammad ibn-ʿAbd-al-Wahhāb, who studied in the Hijaz under a number of distinguished teachers.[4] His outlook is described as 'fundamentalist' in that he kept close to Qur'ān and Ḥadīth, but he was alive to the intellectual needs of the India of his time and adapted his teaching to meet these needs. By his writings, which were in Arabic, he has influenced Islamic thought in India to the present time; and his influence has been perpetuated by his establishment of a tradition of religious scholarship, centred in a school in Delhi. The leader of the Indian Wahhābites, Sayyid Aḥmad, was a disciple of Shāh Walī-Allāh's son, who succeeded him as head of the school. There has so far been no study in depth of the thought of Shāh Walī-Allāh in the social and political context of his times, and among the few scholars who have written briefly about him there are differences in the interpretation and assessment of his achievement.

West Africa—in particular the Sudan in the wider sense, which is all the steppe country between the Sahara desert and the equatorial forest along the coast—was another region where Islam and Islamic scholarship took root at an early period. In the eighteenth and nineteenth centuries religious movements of a special type developed here and led to states of the form known as 'theocracies', in which political leadership derived from the religious revival. The most important of these was the sultanate of Sokoto, which grew out of the religious revival initiated by Usuman dan-Fodio ('Uthmān ibn-Fūdī) (1754–1817).[5] The basis of these movements was a special theological emphasis, which was expressed in the oral teaching, poetry or writings of the founder. A large number of books and pamphlets by Usuman dan-Fodio are still extant, and even more by his disciples and followers. Such works cover law and ritual as well as theology, and the latter is relatively simple and unlikely to have much attraction for the more sophisticated Muslims of the heartlands. When further study of this material has been undertaken, it will probably be found to deserve a place in a general history of Islamic theology.

NOTES

1. Ibn-Taymiyya: *GAL*, ii.125-7; *GALS*, ii.119-26; *EI*², art. Ibn-Taymiyya (Laoust); Henri Laoust, *Essai sur les doctrines sociales et politiques de Taḳī-d-dīn Aḥmad b. Taimīya*, Cairo 1939; do., 'La biographie d'Ibn-Taymiyya d'après Ibn Kathīr', *Bulletin d'études orientales*, ix (1943), 115-62; do., 'Le ḥanbalisme sous les Mamlūks Baḥriyya', *Revue des Études Islamiques*, xxviii (1960), 1-71; do., in Welch and Cachia (eds.), *Islam* (n.11/4), 'L'influence d'Ibn-Taymiyya', 15-33, with brief notices of later Ḥanbalites; Cl. Wein, *Die islamische Glaubenslehre ('Aqīda) des Ibn Taimīya*, Bonn 1973, with translation of the Wāsiṭiyya creed.
2. Ibn-Qayyim-al-Jawziyya: *GAL*, ii.127-9; *GALS*, ii.126-8; *EI*², art. Ibn Ḳayyim al-Djawziyya (Laoust).
3. Wahhābism: *GAL*, ii.512; *GALS*, ii.530-2; *EI*¹, art. Wahhābīya (D. S. Margoliouth); Laoust, *Essai* (n.18/1), 506-40.
4. Shāh Walī-Allāh: *GAL*, ii.550; *GALS*, ii.614f.; Aziz Ahmad, *Studies in Islamic Culture in the Indian Environment*, Oxford 1964, 201-17; Wilfred C. Smith, *Islam in Modern History*, Princeton 1957, 44-7.
5. Usuman dan-Fodio: *GAL*, ii.656; *GALS*, ii.894; Murray Last, *The Sokoto Caliphate*, London 1967, 237-54.

Chapter Nineteen

THE TRANSFORMATION OF SHĪ'ISM

In the period between 1250 and 1850 the two main forms of Shī'ism, the Imāmite and the Ismā'īlite, underwent a complete transformation. Their main dogmatic position remained the same, but there was a great change in their function in the life of the Islamic community as a whole. The Zaydite community in the Yemen maintained itself, although its imamate was under a cloud from the end of the thirteenth century until the end of the sixteenth. It continued to produce some literature, but nothing, it would seem, of theological significance.

(a) *The Imāmites*

Until the year 1501 the Imāmites were simply a theological party intermingled with the Sunnites in a single community of Muslims. There were towns where the Imāmites were dominant, and others where they were hardly represented at all; but on the whole it is correct to say that the Imāmites and the Sunnites were living side by side. Some of their theologians were in the main stream of Islamic thought, certainly being influenced by it and perhaps to some extent influencing it; like the Sunnites they were producing short creeds and lengthy commentaries, and introducing much philosophy into theology. In 1501, however, Shāh Ismā'īl, who was already ruler of much of Iran, made Imāmism the official religion of his kingdom. The result was that Iran became almost wholly Imāmite, while, though Imāmites continued to live elsewhere, notably in Iraq, they were probably fewer in numbers and less dispersed.

The most notable Imāmite thinker of the thirteenth century was Naṣīr-ad-dīn aṭ-Ṭūsī (1201–74).[1] He has also some connections with Ismā'īlism, since prior to 1256 he was for a number of years an official in the service of the Ismā'īlite ruler of Qūhistān (a region of eastern Persia to the south of Khurasan), and then subsequently resided in the Ismā'īlite 'capital', the fortress of Alamut; but his relation to the Ismā'īlites is not clear. He may have had some sympathy with their views; on the other hand, Alamut in the year before its destruction had the reputation of cultivating 'a broad Islamic outlook'. He is accused, however, of advising the Ismāʿīlite leader to surrender Alamut in 1256; and the surrender led to the execution of the leader and the massacre of his followers. Yet this, like the story of his advising Hulagu, the Mongol general, to put the ʿAbbāsid caliph to death in 1258, may be a libel of his opponents. What is certain is that before 1258 he had gained the favour of Hulagu, and that for the rest of his life he held various high appointments in the Mongol administration. This may have been due in part to his skill as an astrologer, since the Mongols seem to have consulted him about auspicious dates for important occasions.

Naṣīr-ad-dīn aṭ-Ṭūsī was more a philosopher than a theologian. Indeed he was well versed in all the Greek sciences, especially mathematics and astronomy. His philosophy was not the pure philosophy of Avicenna, but was ostensibly a preliminary to theology. He lived in much the same world of thought as Fakhr-ad-dīn ar-Rāzī (d. 1209), on whose *Muḥaṣṣal* he composed a commentary, largely positive and expository, but where necessary showing his disagreements. This and other of his works were freely studied by philosophically-minded Sunnites; as noted above, his Persian ethical work *Akhlāq-i Nāṣirī* was revised and adapted for Sunnites by ad-Dawānī.

In the period up to 1500 the only other important Imāmite theologian was a pupil of Naṣīr-ad-dīn called Ibn-al-Muṭahhar al-Ḥillī, mostly known as ʿAllāma-i Ḥillī (1250–1325).[2] Ḥilla, a town some 110 km south of Baghdad, was an important Imāmite centre for centuries, and produced many noted scholars. The ʿAllāma was not much interested in the more philosophical aspects of theology, though he made use of some philosophical concepts. A short creed of his has been translated into English, along with a fifteenth-century commentary, under the title *Al-Bābu 'l-hādī ʿashar,* 'the eleventh chapter'. This is still regarded by many Imāmites as one of their standard texts, as is also his commentary on Naṣīr-ad-dīn's *Tajrīd al-ʿaqāʾid,* 'the Summary of the Doctrines'. A less well-known work of his, *Minhāj al-karāma,* found its way into the hands of Ibn-Taymiyya and influenced him considerably. It is primarily a defence of the Imāmite theory of the imamate, but it also contains a critique of Sunnite jurisprudence; and to both these matters Ibn-Taymiyya made a vigorous response in his *Minhāj as-sunna.*

About half a century later a different type of Shīʿite theologian was represented by Sayyid Ḥaydar al-Āmulī, who was born in 1320 in Āmul near the Caspian Sea, who made the pilgrimage to Mecca about 1350, who lived at least until 1385 in various cities of Iran and Iraq, but whose date of death is unknown.[3] The distinctive character of the thought of al-Āmulī arises from the fact that he was attracted to ṣūfism, especially as expounded in the writings of Muḥyī-d-dīn ibn-al-ʿArabī, on at least one of whose books he wrote a commentary. A recent student of his work has concluded that his philosophico-theological method is one of pious ṣūfistic meditation rather than of pure speculation.

With the crowning of Shāh Ismāʿīl in Tabriz in 1501, steps were taken to make Imāmism the official religion of his realm. He soon completed the conquest of Iran, and with the impetus derived from his political successes Imāmism eventually became not merely the state religion, but in effect the only tolerated religion. In 1501, however, Imāmism was by no means the dominant religion; in Tabriz, for example, two-thirds of the population are said to have been Sunnites; and religious teachers for law and theology were apparently scarce in Iran, though some existed elsewhere in Imāmite centres such as Ḥilla (Iraq), Bahrein and Mount ʿĀmila (Lebanon). The problem of how Iran became almost wholly Shīʿite and how Imāmite law and theology were elaborated is now realized to be a complex one, but scholars have begun to devote attention to it and in due course matters should become clearer.

One of the main differences between Imāmite (or Jaʿfarite) jurisprudence and that of the Sunnites is that among Imāmites duly qualified jurists give decisions that are based directly (that is, by their own arguments) on the general principles contained in Qurʾān and Ḥadīth, whereas among the Sunnites by the sixteenth century (apart from some Ḥanbalites) it was held that even the most learned jurist had to base his decisions on those of earlier jurists. The giving of independent decisions was known as *ijtihād*, and the person qualified to do so was a *mujtahid*. The main Sunnite position came to be expressed (but perhaps not until the nineteenth century) by saying that 'the gate of *ijtihād* is closed'. The Imāmite belief in the continuing right of *ijtihād* presumably helped in the adaptation of the existing legal system to the needs of the new state; but in the last century the Imāmites have not been noticeably more successful than Sunnites in adapting their rules to modern conditions.

The questions of *ijtihād* led to a split within Imāmism which came to be of serious proportions in the seventeenth century, though there are traces of it earlier. Muḥammad Amīn al-Astarābādhī (d. 1624) is regarded as the leader of the attack on the *mujtahids* and the believers in *ijtihād*, and the founder of the subdivision of the Imāmites known as the Akhbārites.[4] Their distinctive view was that legal opinions should not be derived from general principles (*uṣūl*) by analogical or other reasoning, but should be based on *akhbār*, 'accounts', of the Imams; and by this they meant primarily Ḥadīth (of the Prophet) where an Imam was one in the chain of authorities, though other sayings of the Imams were also included. The holders of the more usual Imāmite views were known as Uṣūlites and Mujtahidites. After a century and a half of activity the Akhbārites dwindled away and disappeared almost completely.

A noteworthy feature of sixteenth- and seventeenth-century Iran was an outburst of intellectual activity in the fields of theology and philosophy. This did not attract much interest outside Imāmite circles, but in recent years Henry Corbin tried to bring it to the attention of Western scholars.

One of the earliest theologians of this type was Bahā'-ad-dīn al-'Āmilī (1546–1622), mostly known in Iran as Shaykh-i-Bahā'ī.[5] The name al-'Āmilī indicates that he came from Mount 'Āmila in Syria; and his father was one of the Imāmite scholars who had to flee from Syria because the Sunnite Ottoman regime regarded all Imāmites as a 'third column' acting on behalf of the Safavids. Among his teachers in Iran was one who had been a pupil of ad-Dawānī. He was a prolific writer on many subjects in both Arabic and Persian, and was noted for works not only in jurisprudence and theology but also in astronomy and mathematics, as well as for a literary anthology.

Mīr Dāmād, more fully Mīr Muḥammad Bāqir b. Muḥammad-i-Dāmād (d.1630), was born in Astarābādh, studied in Meshhed, and spent most of his life in Ispahan, where al-'Āmilī was also active.[6] Like the latter he wrote in Arabic in many fields, including logic and metaphysics, and he also wrote poetry in Persian.

A pupil of these two scholars and son-in-law of the latter was Ṣadr-ad-dīn Muḥammad ibn-Ibrāhīm ash-Shīrāzī (d.1640), mostly known as Mullā Ṣadrā.[7] Born in Shiraz, he went to study in Ispahan, then withdrew to the neighbourhood of Qumm to live in seclusion. He devoted his writings chiefly to philosophy and for this reason incurred vehement criticism from the theologians. He is said to have seen Mīr Dāmād in a dream and complained that, though their views were similar, he alone was attacked as an infidel, and then to have received the explanation that he wrote plainly for all to understand, whereas his teacher had written in such a way that only the philosophers could understand, not the theologians. The efforts of Max Horten early this century to interest Western scholars in his philosophy did not have much success. The reason may be that the theosophical aspect of Mullā Ṣadrā's thought was felt to make it other than philosophy in the strict sense. It was in fact considerably influenced by the theosophy of Suhrawardī Maqtūl (d.1191), which he spoke of as *ḥikmat al-ishrāq*, 'the philosophy of illumination'. Another similar influence was that of Muḥyī-d-dīn ibn-al-'Arabī (d. 1240), but further study is required to determine the relative importance of these two influences.

The mystical element found in Mullā Ṣadrā is present to an even greater extent in the writings of Mullā Muḥsin-i-Fayḍ al-Kāshī or al-Kāshānī (d.1679).[8] Though a pupil and son-in-law of Mullā Ṣadrā, he showed much less interest in philosophy than in mysticism. In contrast to him another pupil and son-in-law followed rather the philosophical side of Mullā Ṣadrā. This was al-Lāhijī (Mullā ʿAbd-ar-Razzāq), the date of whose death varies between 1640 and 1670.[9] A work of his commenting on *Tajrīd al-ʿaqāʾid* of Naṣīr-ad-dīn aṭ-Ṭūsī was studied by Max Horten.

This period of the flowering of theosophical philosophy came to an end about this point. It is usually held, however, that about two centuries later the tradition of Mullā Ṣadrā was revived by another thinker, Ḥajjī Mullā Hādī as-Sabzawārī (1797–1878).[10] In a recent scholarly edition of one of his works Toyohiko Izutsu contributes a long introduction in English on 'The Fundamental Structure of Sabzawari's Metaphysics'.

The thought of Mullā Ṣadrā was also influential in a slightly different direction, namely, in the development of Shaykhism. This was the movement founded by Shaykh Aḥmad al-Aḥsāʾī (1753–1826), an Arab from al-Aḥsāʾ who spent most of his life in Iraq and Iran.[11] He was widely respected as a religious thinker, but towards the end of his life was criticized by the Imāmite *mujtahids* and excommunicated, apparently because he was alleged to believe in a purely spiritual and incorporeal resurrection. He attached great importance to the Imams in his metaphysics, regarding them as hypostases of the supreme Being. In the end Shaykhism became very different from the philosphy of Mullā Ṣadrā and contributed to the emergence of Bābism and Bahāʾism, which developed into separate religions.

The most interesting aspect of Imāmite thought in recent centuries is undoubtedly the philosophical movement round Mullā Ṣadrā, but it is difficult to make an objective assessment of it. Iranian scholars, supported by enthusiasts like Henry Corbin, have tried to convince the world of the importance of the Iranian national contribution to world philosophy; but the world has not yet been convinced, and has seen the Iranian achievement not as philosophy and metaphysics in an Aristotelian sense but as a kind of late-classical *sapientia* or 'theosophy' comparable to that of Proclus and Iamblichus. This has deterred general philosophers from studying it. In the future, however, if, as is not impossible, the concepts of incarnation and christology come to attract the attention of general philosophers, they will find useful parallels and resemblances in the imamology of the Imāmite 'philosophers'.

(b) *the Ismāʿīlites*

The transformation of Ismāʿīlism may be dealt with more briefly.[12] The fall of Alamut to the Mongols in 1256 was followed by massacres, but many Ismāʿīlites survived and the son of the last imam was preserved safely in hiding. The subsequent history is complex and is adequately known in general outline, but it is political rather than theological, and so need not be described in detail here. The division, already mentioned, which took place in 1094, into Nizārites and Musta'lians has persisted, and each group has become further subdivided, though some of the subdivisions are now of slight importance, and there have also been amalgamations. The Musta'lians disappeared from Egypt and came to have their main base first in the Yemen and then in Gujerat. The Nizārites, though maintaining themselves in Syria and Iran, eventually also came to be strongest in India (where Ismā'īlite propaganda had begun in the ninth century). The main body of the Nizārites is now the community which has as its head the Aga Khan. Theological writing has mostly been the work of the Imams, and some idea may be gained of its quality and content from a short Persian treatise, composed by a son of the 47th Imam who died prematurely in 1885, which was published with an English translation by W. Ivanow.

The most interesting thing about the Nizārites is the transformation of their community. Their Ismā'īlism, which was at one time the revolutionary faith of rebellious mountaineers, has become the binding force of a closely knit and prosperous community of merchants and men in other urban or industrial occupations. Under the leadership of recent Imams they have given other Muslims an example of how Islamic faith may be adapted to the modern world and may lead to effective action in it.

NOTES

1. Naṣīr-ad-dīn aṭ-Ṭūsī; *GAL*, i.670-6; *GALS*, i.924-33; these give only Arabic works, but he also wrote in Persian.
2. 'Allāma-i Ḥillī: *GAL*, ii.211f.; *GALS*, ii.206-9; *EI*², art. Ḥillī (1) (S. H. M. Jafri); H. Laoust, 'La critique du sunnisme dans la doctrine d'al-Ḥillī', *Revue des Études Islamiques*, xxxiv (1966), 35-60; *Al-Bābu'l-ḥādī 'ashar*, tr. W. McE. Miller, London 1928.
3. Ḥaydar al-Āmulī: *GAL*, ii.213; *GALS*, ii.209; Peter Antes, *Zur Theologie der Schi'a: Eine Untersuchung des Ǧāmi' al-asrār wa-manba' al-anwār von Sayyid Ḥaidar Āmolī*, Freiburg 1971, with further bibliography.
4. Al-Astarābādhī: *GALS*, ii.577, 590; *EI*², Supp., art. Akhbāriyya (W. Madelung).
5. Al-'Āmilī: *GAL*, ii.546; *GALS*, ii.595-7; *EI*², art. (al-)'Āmilī.
6. Mīr Dāmād: *GALS*, ii.579f.; *EI*², art. Dāmād (A. S. Bazmee Ansari).
7. Mullā Ṣadrā: *GAL*, ii.544; *GALS*, ii.588f.; M. Horten, *Die Gottesbeweis bei Schirazī*, Bonn 1912, and *Das philosophische System von Schirazī*, Strassburg 1913; Edward G. Browne, *A Literary History of Persia*, vol.iv, Cambridge 1924, 408, 429-32 (with further material relevant to this chapter, pp.353-411, 415-37).
8. Al-Kāshī: *GAL*, ii.543; *GALS*, ii.584f.; Browne, op.cit., 432-5.
9. Al-Lāhijī: *GALS*, ii.590; M. Horten, 'Die philosophischen und theologischen Ansichten von Lahigi (um 1670)', *Der Islam*, iii (1912), 91-131.

10. As-Sabzawārī: *GALS*, ii.832f.; M. Mohaghegh, T. Izutsu (eds.), *Sharḥ-i Manẓūma*, Teheran 1970.

11. Al-Aḥsā'ī: *GALS*, ii.844; *EI*², art. (al-)Aḥsā'ī (A. Bausani); *EI*¹, *EIS*, art. Shaikhī (Cl. Huart); cf. Corbin, 'Imāmologie et philosophie' in *Le Shīʿisme imāmite* (n.16/1), 143-74.

12. Ismāʿīlism in recent times: *EI*², arts. Agha Khān (H. A. R. Gibb), Bohorās (A. A. A. Fyzee), Ismāʿīliyya (Madelung), Khōdja (Madelung); Shihabu 'd-dīn Shah al-Husayni, *True Meaning of Religion*, ed. and tr. W. Ivanow, Bombay 1933.

Part Five

THE MODERN PERIOD

CHAPTER TWENTY

THE THEOLOGICAL RESPONSE TO THE IMPACT OF THE WEST

The aim of this chapter is to indicate the various intellectual aspects of the Islamic response to the impact of Europe and more generally of the West.[1] No attempt will be made, however, to describe all this in detail, since that has been done for the period up to about 1965 by Kenneth Cragg in the volume *Counsels in Contemporary Islam* in the present series. What will be attempted is to give a general picture of the lines along which Muslim intellectuals are trying to meet the challenge presented to them by the West. In all this there is little theology in an academic sense, and virtually no philosophy.

In so far as modern European culture is an expression of the Greek spirit, the impact of Europe on the Islamic world might be called 'the third wave of Hellenism'. Such a term, however, would obscure important differences between the present situation and those referred to as the first two waves. In the previous cases the impact was mainly intellectual, though the bearers of the alien intellectual culture were mixed with the Muslim inhabitants of the caliphate. The present impact of Europe, on the other hand, has been much more than intellectual. It began with commercial dealings in the easterly regions of the Islamic world after the discovery of the route to India by Vasco da Gama in 1498. Commerce eventually led to political interference and then to political domination. With the expedition of Napoleon to Egypt in 1798 the Ottoman and Persian empires began to feel the full impact of Europe; and commercial and political penetration were soon supported by financial operations. It is hardly too much to say that when the new educated classes in the various Islamic countries came to an awareness of their position in the modern world, their countries were already inextricably entangled in the web of international finance. Extended visits to Europe by students, translations of European books, and the showing of American and European films meant that traditional Islamic culture could not avoid confrontation with an alien social structure and way of life.

Another difference was that there was now an element of discontinuity in the intellectual sphere. The Greek philosophical ideas and methods which came in with al-Ghazālī in the 'second wave' were a further instalment of what had been brought in by the first enthusiasts for Hellenism. The achievement of theologians like the Muʿtazilites and then the Ashʿarites had been to express Islamic doctrine in terms of the most advanced intellectual culture of the times. By the nineteenth century, however, in the Sunnite Islamic world there was no cultivation of philosophy except by the theologians. There was no 'secular' philosophical thinking, and no contact between Islamic theology and any other living tradition of thought, religious or secular. Meanwhile there had appeared in Europe a complete new universe of philosophical discourse. The achievement of medieval Christian scholasticism, especially Thomism, might be regarded as comparable to that of the Ashʿarites and other philosophical theologians of Islam; but when the scholastics tried to erect barriers against the new currents of creative intellectual activity, these were swept away, and the mind of European man came to be dominated by the modern philosophical outlook, formed on the one hand by the Continental philosophers from Descartes to Kant and Hegel and on the other by the British empiricists. If Islamic theology was to come to terms with this pluriform modern 'secular' philosophy, it could only be by radical changes of attitude.

The problems raised by the impact of Europe on the Islamic world may be considered here under three heads. First, much of the Islamic world had become politically or economically dependent on Europe and the West, so that political and economic independence was a primary aim for many Muslims. Secondly, contacts with the West and the acceptance of the products of Western technology had led to many subtle changes in Islamic society, while many Muslims were being attracted by the secular forms of thought in the West, including its science. Thirdly, some of the attitudes found among Western colonialists had given many Muslims a feeling of inferiority. In the Muslim response to the total impact of the West political factors were prominent, but these will only be incidentally described here, and attention will be focused on the intellectual factors.

Already before 1850 there were signs among the traditional Islamic religious scholars of a conservative withdrawal into their own ivory tower and an unwillingness to learn from foreigners and non-Muslims. As Muslim rulers, such as Muḥammad ʿAlī in Egypt in the early nineteenth century, realized their military inferiority to the Europeans, they decided that it was necessary to have an army on the European model, and that for this their officers must have some education of a European type. They also realized that, because of the attitude of the religious scholars, they could not achieve this within the existing educational institutions, and so they imported European teachers and set up new institutions. From such beginnings there developed in many Islamic countries a complete system of Western education, stretching by the early twentieth century from primary schools to universities. Meanwhile the religious leaders showed no interest in the new education, and alongside the new system allowed the old to continue without even a change of curriculum, with its Qur'ān-schools in the villages and its traditional-type universities like al-Azhar in Cairo.

One result of having two educational systems functioning side by side was to create two different classes of intellectuals—the old-fashioned religious intellectuals or ulema and the new Western-educated intellectuals. Another result was a great loss of power and influence by the ulema as an ever-increasing proportion of young people attended the Western-type institutions. Up to about 1850 in the Ottoman empire the religious institution, which was hierarchically organized under its head, the Shaykh al-Islam, had complete control of all higher education and all administration of justice and the formulation of new legal rules; but its conservatism in education lost it most of its power in that sphere, as Western-type institutions superseded the traditional ones; and a similar conservatism in the legal sphere led the sultans to make extensive use of supplementary legal codes and, to administer these, new types of lawcourt in which traditionally trained lawyers were not qualified to serve. Something similar happened in most Islamic countries.

In India the British authorities introduced Western-type education, partly in order to provide junior personnel for the administration, but, while the Hindus made the most of the opportunities, the Muslims kept suspiciously aloof. This led to a deterioration in the general position of the Muslims compared with that of the Hindus, and that was one of the factors leading to the—largely Muslim—Indian Mutiny of 1857. The Muslims, in even greater gloom after their defeat, were roused from their pessimism and inactivity by Sayyid (Syed) Ahmad Khan, among others. He persuaded them to accept Western education for their children and to co-operate with the British, and his efforts led to the foundation of a college, which eventually became the University of Aligarh, in which the new type of education was combined with adherence to Islamic doctrine. One of his associates was Ameer Ali, whose book *The Spirit of Islam* has had a wide and continuing influence. The writer's aim was to show that Islam had all the values of nineteenth-century European liberalism, thus trying to improve the perception of Islam by the rest of the world and also helping Muslims to get rid of their sense of inferiority.

By the twentieth century most Muslims wanted independence and not co-operation with the colonialists, but acceptance of Western ideas and ideals (outside the sphere of religion) has been characteristic of many 'secular' Muslim intellectuals and statesmen. Leading statesmen in particular, who have frequent contacts with Western colleagues, come to think in similar terms to the latter, and make use of Western political ideas to guide their political activities. Some have been attracted even to aspects of fascism and Marxism. They have mostly resisted the demands of the ulema for further implementation of the Sharīʿa, but in the religious sphere they have adhered to Islamic doctrine, even though some may have found it difficult to combine this with their general westernized outlook.

In the long struggle for independence some groups brought in an Islamic element, and argued that for its full expression Islam required statehood. Thus Islam was made both a reason for independence and also a programme for an independent state. Such was the attitude of the Muslim Brotherhood (Al-Ikhwān al-Muslimūn) in Egypt and, with some variants, that of Mawdoodi and the Jamāʿat-i-Islāmī in India. Both these movements, however, had a programme going beyond the mere return to original Islam and envisaging some reforming measures, though on an Islamic basis (that is, in accordance with the Sharīʿa).

These two movements may be regarded as premonitions of the Islamic resurgence or revival which has been a feature of the last decade or two. They doubtless contributed something to the resurgence, though they are somewhat aloof from its most recent manifestations. The basic reason for the resurgence is the rapid social change experienced by all Islamic societies, and the feeling of anxiety resulting from this change. The change has come about partly through the spread of Western ideas, and partly through the acceptance by Muslims of the products of Western technology—Western forms of transport, Western military weaponry, Western food, Western dress, Western entertainment, and so on. The acceptance of such things in vast quantities inevitably disrupts the social structure, for some groups lose their livelihood while others prosper. In some cases people feel they are ceasing to be Muslims and are becoming Westerners, and indeed some want to be exactly like Westerners at least in respect of the material side of life. So the demand for a return to the original Islam of the Prophet and the earliest Muslims is accompanied by special emphasis on the things which signify the distinctive Muslim identity—no alcohol, no usury and the veil for women. Insistence on these makes Muslims obviously different from Westerners. It is often suggested that such a return to the original Islam, if carried out, will solve all the problems of the world at the present time, but such evidence as there is seems to show that this is romantic and unrealistic. The main thrust of the resurgence is the reassertion of Muslim identity, and it is seldom associated with serious attempts to deal

with contemporary social problems.

In most countries the ulema or religious scholars are in sympathy with the resurgence; they themselves feel the same anxiety, and in addition are aware of their own loss of power and influence. They try to persuade the statesmen—in Pakistan, for example—that all legislation should go before a committee of ulema to decide whether it is in accordance with the Sharī'a; but the statesmen resist such proposals since they realize that the ulema have no detailed knowledge of the working of a modern state. Clearly, if all legislation must be declared to be in accordance with the Sharī'a, then the ulema, as the only accredited interpreters of the Sharī'a, will have regained much of their lost power. This, of course, is what has happened in Iran, but, because of differences in the situation, it is unlikely that the ulema in Sunnite countries will be able to repeat the success of their Iranian brothers.

Iran became an extreme example of westernization because of the great wealth derived from oil and the driving force of the Pahlevi Shahs. The changes had been so rapid and so extensive, however, that there were many groups of discontented persons ready to listen to a vigorous and persuasive leader. That leader appeared in the Imam Khomeini, and in 1979 the Shah fled and the Islamic Republic of Iran was established. It has to be remembered, however, that in Iran the corps of ulema or religious institution was in a specially strong position because Imāmite Shī'ism was the official religion. This meant that in theory the mullahs (as the ulema were usually called in Iran) were the representatives of the hidden Imam and in a sense above the Shah. For at least two centuries they had been endeavouring to increase their power and, when there was a favourable opportunity, had supported the ordinary people against oppressive rulers. Moreover they had managed to achieve some financial independence of the state, because they received certain religious taxes directly from the people and their careers were not controlled by the Shah. At the moment of writing (Spring 1983) it is impossible to say what the final outcome will be of this resurgence of Iranian Islam. It has achieved much, but many of the leaders have virtually no experience of life outside an Islamic enclave.

In all the events of the last century academic theology has played only a slight part. The intellectual debates of previous centuries were largely irrelevant to contemporary problems. Basic Islamic dogma, of course, has continued to be prominent, and there has been a strong reaffirmation of those aspects at least with a bearing on social and political action. By way of exception there were two important attempts to present a defence of Islamic doctrine in terms of modern Western thought. The earlier of these was *Risālat at-tawḥīd* by the Egyptian Muḥammad 'Abduh (1849–1905), first published in 1897.[2]

It is a reasoned apologetic for the main Islamic doctrines, addresse[d to] Western-educated men, both Muslims and others. The author mai[n]tains, however, that reason has only a restricted competence in th[e] field of theology and that acceptance of revelation must be central. In this way many problems are left aside. In itself this was a notable beginning but it was not followed up.

Very different was *The Reconstruction of Religious Thought in Islam* by Mohammad Iqbal (1876–1938), based on lectures first delivered in 1928 and published in 1934.[3] Where the Egyptian had written in terms of a fairly general form of modern thought, Iqbal was under the spell of recent and contemporary thinkers such as Bergson, Nietzsche and even Freud. Kenneth Cragg speaks of this book as 'a Muslim's ventures in religious speculation' and 'the most ambitious and inventive adaptation of dogma attempted by a Muslim'. Iqbal's forceful personality and the expression of it in his poems helped to rouse Muslims to political and social activity, but the time was not ripe for further theological speculation.

Mention must also be made of *The Tarjumān al-Qur'ān* of Mawlana Abul Kalam Azad (1888–1958), the first part of which appeared in Urdu in 1930 though he had been working on it for at least a dozen years previously.[4] Though this work is primarily a commentary on the Qur'ān, it contains long theological discussions, especially in the first volume which is devoted to Sura 1 (al-Fātiḥa). An interesting point is his attitude to other religions. He was one of the Muslim leaders opposed to a separate Pakistan and ready to live in a state in which Muslims and Hindus both participated on a footing of equality, and so it is not surprising to find that he holds that all religions are true in their primary form, though their adherents have often deviated from this form. True belief about God and the universe is found in the Qur'ān, but only when traditional interpretations are left aside and the Qur'ān is allowed to speak for itself. The Mawlana leaves many questions unanswered and some not even raised, but to those who live in a world where there is a meeting of religions he has shown a way of handling the problems this creates.

When the last decade or two are considered it is seen that many younger Western-educated Muslim intellectuals have been and are working at the expression of Islamic faith and practice in terms appropriate to the modern world with its many intellectual, cultural, social and political problems. This effort takes many forms. Some are chiefly interested in political activity and social reform. Others are concerned to apply contemporary literary and philological criticism to the study of the Qur'ān, and historical criticism to the study of early Islamic history. Many think it important to engage in dialogue with Christians, because they realize that there is a sense in which all believers in God are engaged in a common struggle against material-

ism, atheistic humanism and other anti-religious forces. So far no one thinker has stood out above the rest, but this liberalizing movement is making progress, even if slowly. It has, of course, to contend with the dead-weight of the religious establishment, which has gained much popular support as a result of the resurgence. The liberalizing movement, on the other hand, includes not merely thinkers and writers, but also active statesmen and others in positions of power, so that its future prospects are good. It would not be surprising if before the end of the century some important new names had come to the fore in the field of Islamic theology.

NOTES

1. *General accounts*: H. A. R. Gibb, *Modern Trends in Islam*, Chicago 1947; Wilfred Cantwell Smith, *Modern Islam in India*, London 1946, etc.; do., *Islam in Modern History*, Princeton 1957; Kenneth Cragg, *Counsels in Contemporary Islam*, Edinburgh 1965, with an extensive bibliography; G. E. von Grunebaum, *Modern Islam: The Search for Cultural Identity*, Berkeley 1962.
2. Muḥammad ʿAbduh: Charles C. Adams, *Islam and Modernism in Egypt*, London 1933, a study of Muḥammad ʿAbduh and his followers: Ishaq Musa'ad and Kenneth Cragg, *The Theology of Unity*, London 1965, translation of *Risālat at-tawḥīd*.
3. Iqbal: Iqbal, *The Reconstruction of Religious Thought in Islam*, London 1934; Annemarie Schimmel, *Gabriel's Wing*, Leiden 1963, with full bibliography to 1963 of the vast literature about Iqbal; do., EI^2, art. Iḳbāl; Cragg, *Counsels* (n.1), 48-66.
4. Abul Kalam Azad: *The Tarjumān al-Qur'ān*, tr. Syed Abdul Latif, London 1965 (vol.1), 1967 (vol.2); EI^2, Supp., art. Āzād, Abu 'l-Kalām (A. Guimbretière); Cragg, *Counsels*, 125-39.

GENERAL BIBLIOGRAPHY

(A) Works of Reference

CARL BROCKELMANN, *Geschichte der arabischen Literatur,* two vols., second edition, Leiden 1943, 1949; also three *Supplementbände,* Leiden 1937–42.

FUAT SEZGIN, *Geschichte des arabischen Schrifttums,* vol. 1 (Islamic disciplines, including theology, until about 1050 AD), Leiden 1967; philosophy is promised for vol. 13.

GEORG GRAF, *Geschichte der christlichen arabischen Literatur,* Vatican 1944–53, five vols.; has full articles on the separate authors, who include Christian philosophers and writers of theological polemics against Islam.

J.D. PEARSON, *Index Islamicus, 1906–55,* Cambridge 1958; an exhaustive list of articles on Islamic subjects in learned journals and composite volumes; the sections relevant to philosophy and theology are: II; IV,a,b. The work has been continued to date by a series of supplements.

Revue des études islamiques (Paris); the second half of each annual volume, entitled *Abstracta,* has lists of printed books and articles, sometimes with short descriptions, but the coverage of articles is not so full as Pearson's *Index Islamicus.*

The Encyclopaedia of Islām: first edition, four vols. and supplement, Leiden 1913–42; second edition, Leiden (and London) 1961 continuing, has now reached L. Articles on religion from the first edition, often with some revision, were reprinted in a separate volume in German and English editions: *Handwörterbuch des Islam,* 1941; *A Shorter Encyclopaedia of Islam,* 1953. Many of the articles are important, since they contain material not otherwise accessible in European languages; but some of the older ones in the first edition are now unsatisfactory.

(B) Heresiographical Works

AL-ASHʿARĪ, *Maqālāt al-Islāmiyyīn,* 2 vols. (continuous paging), ed. H. Ritter, Istanbul 1929–30.

AL-BAGHDĀDĪ, *Al-farq bayn al-firaq,* ed. M. Badr, Cairo 1910. Translations: *Moslem Schisms and Sects,* Part I, by Kate C. Seelye, New York 1920, withdrawn because of errors but reprinted 1970; do., Part II, by A.S. Halkin, Tel Aviv 1935.

ASH-SHAHRASTĀNĪ, *Kitāb al-milal wa-n-niḥal,* ed. W. Cureton, London 1846; also 3 vols., Cairo 1948. Translations: by Th. Haarbrücker as *Religionsparteien und Philosophenschulen,* 2 vols., Halle 1850–1; by A.K. Kazi and J.G. Flynn (only the sections dealing with Islamic sects) in the periodical *Abr-Nahrain*, beginning with 'the Muʿtazalites' in vol.8 (1969), 36–68.

AN-NAWBAKHTĪ, *Kitāb firaq ash-shīʿa*, ed. H. Ritter, Leipzig 1931.

(C) Older Works on Philosophy

SALOMON MUNK, *Mélanges de philosophie juive et arabe*, Paris 1859; has still some value.

TJITJE DE BOER, *The History of Philosophy in Islam*, English translation by E. R. Jones, London 1903.

DE LACY O'LEARY, *Arabic Thought and its Place in History*, London 1922; best on the transmission of Greek thought into Arabic and then into Latin, but now dated.

GOFFREDO QUADRI, *La filosofia degli arabi nel suo fiore*, 2 vols., Florence 1939; French translation by R. Huret, Paris 1947; unduly emphasizes Averroes.

P. J. DEMENASCE, *Arabische Philosophie*, Berne 1948; a bibliography of European books and articles.

ALFRED GUILLAUME, 'Philosophy and Theology', in *The Legacy of Islam*, ed. by Sir Thomas Arnold and A. Guillaume, Oxford 1931, 239–83; chiefly concerned with the influence of Islamic thought on Europe and its transmission through Spain.

(D) Recent Works on Philosophy

HENRY CORBIN, *Histoire de la philosophie islamique*, vol. 1 (all published), Paris 1964; also deals with some theologians, but goes only to 1198.

M. M. SHARIF (ed.), *A History of Muslim Philosophy*, 2 vols., Wiesbaden 1963–6; very uneven.

RICHARD WALZER, 'Islamic Philosophy', in his *Greek into Arabic*, Oxford 1962, 1–28.

MAJID FAKHRY, *A History of Islamic Philosophy*, New York 1970.

DWIGHT M. DONALDSON, *Studies in Muslim Ethics*, London 1953; has chapters on the ethics of philosophers and theologians.

H. A. R. GIBB and R. WALZER, 'Akhlāḳ' (Ethics), *EI²*; good.

NICHOLAS RESCHER, *The Development of Arabic Logic*, Pittsburgh 1964.

(E) Older Works on Theology

ALFRED VON KREMER, *Geschichte der herrschenden Ideen des Islams*, Leipzig 1868; photomechanical reprint, Hildesheim 1961.

DUNCAN BLACK MACDONALD, *The Development of Muslim Theology, Jurisprudence and Constitutional Theory*, New York 1903; long influential but now outdated; has translations of several creeds.

IGNAZ GOLDZIHER, *Vorlesungen über den Islam*, second

edition, Heidelberg 1925; translated into English.

ARENT JAN WENSINCK, *The Muslim Creed,* Cambridge 1932; a study based mainly on Ḥadīth and on three Ḥanafite creeds.

LOUIS MASSIGNON, *La passion . . . d'al-Hallaj, martyr mystique de l'Islam,* first edition, 2 vols., Paris 1922; second edition, 4 vols., Paris 1975; English translation of the second edition by Herbert Mason, Princeton 1982. Chapter 12 (pp.535–771/iii.61–234) deals with the dogmatic theology of al-Ḥallāj, comparing him with other thinkers, and giving a wide conspectus of Islamic theological thought.

LOUIS MASSIGNON, *Essai sur les origines du lexique technique de la mystique musulmane,* second edition, Paris 1954; has notices of individual mystics up to about 950 with some account of their theological views.

(F) Recent Works on Theology

LOUIS GARDET and M. M. ANAWATI, *Introduction à la théologie musulmane,* Paris 1948; a lengthy work dealing chiefly with Ashʿarite Kalām (rational theology) in the period after 950, its general structure and its relation to Christian theology.

LOUIS GARDET, *Dieu et la destinée de l'homme,* Paris 1967; a full account of the way in which the writers in the field of Kalām treat various problems about the relations of God and man.

MORRIS L. SEALE, *Muslim Theology,* London 1964; largely concerned with tracing Christian influences; has a translation of a short tract by Ibn-Ḥanbal.

HENRI LAOUST, *Les schismes dans l'Islam: introduction à une étude de la religion musulmane,* Paris 1965; detailed study of theology in its political setting.

W. MONTGOMERY WATT, *The Formative Period of Islamic Thought,* Edinburgh 1973; the German translation mentioned on p.vii is contained in: Watt and M. Marmura, *Der Islam II* (Die Religionen der Menschheit, Band 25,2), Stuttgart 1985; this has also a section on Islamic theology, 950–1850 and a section (by Michael Marmura) on Islamic philosophy up to Averroes.

DANIEL GIMARET, *Théories de l'acte humain en théologie musulmane,* Paris 1980; studies the theories found in Muʿtazilite, Ashʿarite and Māturīdite authors.

INDEX

The Arabic article *al-*, with its variants such as *an-*, *ash-*, etc., is ignored in the alphabetical arrangement, except in the case of the word *Allāh*.